TREADING ON SERPENTS

A DAILY DEVOTIONAL FOR THOSE WHO ARE BULLIED, GANG STALKED, OR HARASSED

Suite 300 - 990 Fort St
Victoria, BC, V8V 3K2
Canada

www.friesenpress.com

Copyright © 2018 by Tina Plakinger
First Edition — 2018

All rights reserved.

No part of this publication may be reproduced in any form, or by any means, electronic or mechanical, including photocopying, recording, or any information browsing, storage, or retrieval system, without permission in writing from FriesenPress.

ISBN
978-1-5255-1145-5 (Hardcover)
978-1-5255-1146-2 (Paperback)
978-1-5255-1147-9 (eBook)

1. RELIGION, BIBLICAL MEDITATIONS

Distributed to the trade by The Ingram Book Company

Table of Contents

INTRODUCTION 1

JANUARY 1 21

FEBRUARY 1 55

MARCH 1 87

APRIL 1 121

MAY 1 157

JUNE 1 189

JULY 1 221

AUGUST 1 255

SEPTEMBER 1 289

OCTOBER 1 323

NOVEMBER 1 357

DECEMBER 1 393

PRAYER SECTION 427

PHOTOS 433

AUTHOR 443

(*Prettygirl* & *Mama*)
(*RIP—May 02, 2013*)

This book is dedicated to Mama and Prettygirl—two throwaway junkyard dogs that became my faithful and loyal bodyguards. They were not only my best friends, but more often, they were my *only* friends. Each day was an adventure, whether we were running or hiding—spinning in a nationwide underground network called gangstalking: a government form of social control—a sanctioned plan for legal harassment and murder by suicide.

Introduction

I was held captive in the South Bay area between the port of San Pedro and Long Beach, California. It was an industrialized region inundated with heavy equipment, hard hats, and local roughnecks. People referred to it as "hell's gateway": a place where various types of engineering, manufacturing, and production took place by day. At night, the murkiness of evil lingered over the harbor. A heavy fog concealed everything that slithered through it, making it an eerie place to be. Just like clockwork—right before the witching hour—a dreadful stench would rise to the element. It reeked something fierce. By five in the morning, it was always gone.

Bone yards, crane yards, scrap and salvage yards, garbage dumps, warehouses, and offshore drilling rigs went on for miles. Rumors had it that displaced women were sexually exploited there, and male transplants-- those who transferred from another place down to the junkyards, were used as bottom feeders. Each had similar stories of existing in an ensnared, almost spellbound, state of consciousness, in which they had become both unable and unwilling to leave. I, too, was held hostage within a radius of only a few miles. If I tried to leave, my vehicle would mysteriously shut down: the radiator would overheat, or I would run out of gas outside of what seemed to be an invisible perimeter. A mechanic told me that my gas tank had been sealed off to hold only two gallons of gas. The oppression switch on my life was flipped on—by whom, I was not sure.

Voyeurism took place daily under the blanket of industrial espionage. This was practiced almost two decades before spying would become the phenomenon it is today. This is when I first heard about microwave radiation. One guy would always point upward, as he rattled on about being nuked by the government. I thought they were just burnt-out dope fiends, running around and talking crazy. Now I beg to differ. They were probably prototypes used in the trials of directed-energy weapons (DEWs) and electromagnetic energy. They knew something more about those big, bright stars up in the sky (although they were not stars at all) called satellites.

I continued to live around warehouses, while I bounced from the grips of one street gang to another. I tried desperately to hang on to my possessions through what I thought was merely a paradigm shift; something I was going through since my husband's recent death. Whatever it was, I semi-convinced myself that it would not last long. I had my gym equipment stored at a nearby welding yard, where I checked on it daily. A shot-caller for the Nazi Low Riders had two dogs chained in the yard. They wore no collars, while each one had a heavy chain wrapped around its neck with a padlock. They did not have names and were referred to as Dog and Dog. They had no muscle tone, no shelter, and one would eat their feces to not have to lay in it.

Most nights I would sneak food and water under the front gates. The two canine sisters got to know me. I would pull up and honk my horn and, on those rare nights that they were unchained, they would come running to greet me. One time my loneliness was as heavy as the fog, so I pulled up next to the back fence where they were on their chains. The backside of the welding yard was located on a dead-end road with nothing nearby except a deserted pallet company. You could not see in or out due to a block-long canvas tarp that hung on the inside of the fence. I was sure the dogs knew it was me on the other side of that twelve-foot-high, chain-linked enclosure with circular barbed wire at the top. The back gate had a coal-rolled chain wrapped tightly around one pole and padlocked to the other. Even with a hacksaw or bolt cutter, I would not have been able to get through it. It felt good just knowing they were within twenty feet of me, for I did not feel so alone. One of them would bark incessantly whenever she was on high alert about something. She was known to bark for hours if a situation did not correct itself. I fell asleep to the rhythmic barking of the dog that would later become known as Prettygirl. Her bark gave me a sense of security that night, and I quickly relaxed and grew heavy-eyed. As I drifted off to sleep, a thick blanket of fog wrapped itself around my Jeep. It was as though God had me in the palm of His Hand as I slept like a baby on that desolate back road that led nowhere.

The level of hatred and disrespect that I received from strangers had simply dumbfounded me. It was possible that I had been put on gang turf to be punished for witnessing a racial crime a year earlier. I would often hear someone refer to the legal term, guilty by association, as they either walked by me or engaged in a nearby conversation. Nevertheless, God had His hand on me. Through all the hatred, He sent me love when the shot caller decided to cut the two dogs loose and throw them away. I sat on a pallet in the middle of the welding yard with one dog under each arm. I did not know how I was going to do it, because for the first time in my life, I was homeless. I did not know yet that I had been strategically disarmed over the past year to be in this situation. In time, I would come to learn many things. With both dogs embraced, I asked God for help because now there were three of us that were unwanted and homeless.

I am a firm believer that love comes along when you least expect it, to help heal those wounds far too long unattended. Love is by far more powerful than hate. It was our love for one another and God's love for us that kept us alive and together. We shared many close calls in our lives. I was in their hood now, and their purpose was to protect me. I would soon trade-in my Jeep Cherokee for a thirty-foot motor home, rent a spot at a forklift repair hanger, and try to keep all my possessions in nearby storage units until the storm passed. At least that was my plan.

I had never been in an RV. Although people considered them to be the upper class to homelessness, living in one quickly grew old, and it was not long before I began to resent it. I knew nothing about surviving without utilities like gas and electricity for central air and heat. I had no idea how to live without appliances, running water, and lights. In fact, I had never gone camping in my life; I did not even know how to grill. I had spent years traveling the globe and staying at 5-star hotels, while I taught health and fitness and signed autographs for fans. I had not touched drugs or alcohol in nineteen years, and I knew no one who did. I had never been to jail. For over a decade, I lived in a huge, modern, rent-controlled apartment with a balcony and underground gated parking in North Hollywood. Now, I was living in a motor home, hot-nosing for parking places to sleep at night without being disturbed. I could never stay parked for more than two nights in a row without getting a parking ticket, so we had to keep moving around within an eight-mile radius: *Have House, Will Travel*.

Mama and Prettygirl slept with me everywhere: in shipping yards, next to loading docks, at truck stops, in parking lots, under bridges, behind shopping centers, around parks, near railroad tracks, and alongside many roads that led nowhere. The worshipping of Satan frequently took place in nearby fields around a bonfire. I would plead the blood of Jesus over us, as I watched from inside my motor home. I often wondered why nobody was rescuing me. Where were the Feds? Certainly, they knew something was going on after I had paid a visit to their office, asking for help.

On the nights the Luciferians gathered, you could cut the air with a chainsaw. The fog would metamorphose into a peasouper, while it coexisted with that unseen fowl-smelling force that seemed to upsurge from the bowels of hell. Everything—including animals—would move through it in time-consuming action like it was another dimension. It was like watching a movie in slow motion. In all my travels around the world, this was by far the strangest thing I had ever seen or experienced. In the morning, there would be neatly packed cardboard boxes left in the fields near the smoldering fire site. The glass containers were once candles and had the image of Satan on them. I soon discovered that everything from the dark side—things you only heard about but had never seen—dwelled down there. It was an ugly place to be, and I wanted to go home. I wanted my life back.

My thoughts were getting more narrow-minded by the day. Life had become all about survival and trying to keep my stuff. I was constantly scouting out faucets where I could quickly wash my hair without getting caught and then let it air-dry under the California sun. Throughout the day, I would give much concern toward finding a hideaway place to park the motor home at night. Always hoping to avoid the police, I often found myself where no one would go in their right mind, even during daylight hours. All I wanted was to get a good night's sleep without being woken up, frisked, and taken to the police station for the sheer purpose of group entertainment.

Not to mention, I was always troubled that law enforcement might kill my dogs. I won't sugar-coat it: Mama and Prettygirl were a handful! They had lived on chains since they were born. The only way they could play was to stand on their hind legs with their front legs wrapped around each other, often drawing blood as they wrestled out their frustrations. Plus, I was becoming all too familiar with just how far the cops would go to harass me. There had already been an incident where one police officer came to my camper door with his gun drawn, and something like shooting my dogs would be easy for them to get away with. With one wrong move from either dog, a cop could say he was at risk of being attacked and get away with shooting them. The pressure was always on! I thank God that I was equipped to handle it. Being an IFBB World Champion Bodybuilder had turned out to be the best physical and mental development for what I was about to encounter in the creepy underworld of gangstalking.

My attempts to stay in touch with my parents had always been covertly intercepted and restricted. I believe that my dad knew where I was; he knew more about what was going on than I did. I am convinced that I was not murdered for the simple reasons: he was still alive and somewhat independently wealthy, and after he died, they would come after me for his money. Still, whenever I called him, the phone would either be busy or just keep ringing. I did, however, receive a couple letters from him, rousing me to get out of there.

At least once a month, a law enforcement officer would pull me over. I was routinely handcuffed and forced to sit in the back of his car, from where I would watch him tear apart my vehicle. Then, he would get back into the squad car to do some paperwork. After a few moments of silence, and without looking at me, he would nonchalantly tell me to call my mother, who was busy harassing the police department for answers, while filing reports on her missing daughter. She knew the gangs were on me and that I was not able to get out. She would routinely call the Los Angeles County morgue to make sure I wasn't there. It would be years before we put the pieces together that our calls were routinely interrupted, rerouted, and/or disconnected. My every move was now under the scrutiny and domination of both the police officers and street thugs.

My two dogs and I had become known as the "Traveling Trio". We went everywhere together, but were nowhere, if you get my drift. Despite it all, we had a lot of fun together, and I loved them dearly. There was never a dull moment. One morning, I was pulled over by two local cops while I was using someone's car to go shopping. I was told that the vehicle had violations and that I could either get out and walk away from it or go to jail. I had to carry 10 large cans of dog food along with other grocery items, while trying to finagle the two strong dogs by holding onto their halter harnesses. On foot, we quickly ducked into a nearby truck terminal to hide under a detached 18-wheeler semi-trailer. We were there all afternoon, until I learned it had been a hoax. Having to maneuver with the two dogs like that put everybody in danger. If they had gotten out of line, animal control would have taken them away from me. I always had to carefully plan our trips, considering they had no social skills, whatsoever. If they attacked a person or another animal, we would be on the lam again, running and hiding from what seemed to be everybody. Just a month earlier, we had to hide out when Prettygirl seriously injured a gangstalker, sending him to the hospital. The guy was yelling and waving his arms as he walked toward me, and she bit him in his upper thigh, barely avoiding his family jewels. Crackhead gangstalkers can be desperate for their next fix, as well as stupid.

Escaping fires seemed to be something else we did quite often, when thingamajigs would mysteriously burst into flames. All the fires and explosions were dangerously scary, but the worst time was when my truck blew up next to the fuel pumps at a busy gas station—while I was in it. I should have known something was brewing when the crew from West Coast Choppers approached me with an invitation to pull onto their private property for the night. We were always safer on private property than the public streets, so I jumped at the opportunity, just like they knew I would.

That night, a man who worked in one of the warehouses had an emergency and needed something from the store. I repeat: I should have known that something was up. I would only be gone less than ten minutes, so for the first and only time—ever—I went without Mama and Prettygirl, leaving them in the trailer on the private yard. I jumped into my SUV and hurried down the road to a large corner gas station, where I would also fill my gas tank. I was unaware that a hose clamp to the fuel filter had been loosened, causing gasoline to drip onto my new starter, which was just installed that morning. When I got back into my truck and turned the key, I heard a loud *poof* as it ignited underneath me like a propane grill. Frozen in position, with my right hand still on the key and my left gripping the steering wheel, I turned my head toward the storefront window and caught the reflection of my entire undercarriage engulfed in flames just inches below me. It was something you don't see every day—not even once in a lifetime.

The gas station attendant ran out with a fire extinguisher as I simultaneously jumped out of the truck. Police cars and fire trucks whipped in from all directions, like they were already waiting. Multiple sirens, huge flames, and flashing lights lit up the area for blocks. I remember not having any feelings as I watched the commotion from across the street, wondering if it was the Good Lord who prompted me to leave my dogs at home. After everyone had left and things died down, the gas station remained soaked with water. It had become so quiet that all I could hear were water drops. My truck sat, smoldering, on four melted tires. Thoughts bombarded my mind: *How was I going to pull my trailer? How would I get back to my dogs?* I was not brave enough to chance walking back home. Even if I ran the mile, I would still have to pass warehouses and vacant lots in the dark. I was probably traumatized, but I did not show it. I guess being the highly trained champion that I was, even in the violent aftermath of someone's repugnance for me, I wasn't going to let them see me sweat.

My mind raced with thoughts of getting back to my dogs, just when another unusual scene began to unfold. A guy wearing a cop uniform rolled up in an authentic cop car, but he was a counterfeit—someone poorly casted for the call. Maybe I had judged too many bodybuilding competitions, but I distinctively remember how unsymmetrical this guy was. His body parts simply didn't fit together. His oversized feet carried a small frame with narrow shoulders and no hips. His soft, boyish body did not correlate with his older masculine face, nor was anything proportionate to his unusually small hands. I wasn't sure if this person was male or female, and now I even contemplate that I might have been dealing with an alien-human hybrid. After all, this was a place where evil manifested itself differently each night, and no one really fully knows what lurks there. With no emotion or personality of any kind, he softly told me that I had one hour to remove what was left of my truck or I would face legal charges. He swiftly walked back to the police car and disappeared in the fog.

Other times, it would be police officers in helicopters. I must not forget to mention all the helicopters. Every day or so, they would swoop down on me and my dogs or obtrusively circle above us. One day a helicopter outrageously flew toward us, head-on, as we traveled into the San Fernando Valley on the 405Freeway. They harassed us at all hours of the day and night, until we were finally escorted right out of Los Angeles. After two years of this kind of constant chaos, it was time to pack up the dogs and roll. I did, however, manage to chuckle, as we successfully made our big escape out of California. Heading eastbound toward Arizona, I couldn't believe that I was finally leaving the West Coast with my two dogs, with nothing more than a stolen car that had less than a half-tank of gas. My dad wanted to fly me home, but I would not leave Mama and Prettygirl, so I had no choice but to find wheels.

A great deal of people had been in and out of my life those two years. It was like they came and went through a revolving door; as soon as one would leave, another one showed up. I was badly beaten up: my hair was chopped; my hands looked like those of a mechanic; my clothes were filthy; my boots looked like I had found them in a dumpster; and my famous smile—a trademark for being free-spirited—was now missing a tooth. The fact that I gave those creeps a good run for *my* money and was still alive to tell it was enough for me. It took them a long time of being unshakable to get all my stuff. And they indeed got it all: bank accounts, vehicles, heavyweight gym equipment, cameras and office equipment, rare antique furniture, high-quality tools, expensive jewelry, an awesome gun collection, and all my trophies and irreplaceable bodybuilding memorabilia. Despite it all, I fought through hell and high water to keep Mama and Prettygirl. It was only by the grace of God that the three of us were still together. Had it been a fair fight, I would have had a chance, but there was an army on me, including law enforcement. Gangstalking and harassment groups will keep draining you, even after there is nothing left to drain.

When we got into Cottonwood, Arizona, my parents quickly helped me to get out of the stolen car and to land yet another motor home. The dogs and I would have to endure a 3,000-mile road trip to Illinois. Things got serious real fast after I realized we were being followed by government-looking officials all the way. If we stopped somewhere for too long, a sheriff would show up to ask me about my travel plans. I guess we were being escorted.

We were at a gas station on the outskirts of Arizona, when a man wearing khakis and penny loafers showed up out of nowhere. He looked like one of the Beach Boys from the late 1960s, and he just seemed out of place. He was laughing as he stated, "Now, that's a girl's motor home!" Then *bam*, he was gone. I never saw him get into a car nor heard him drive away. I didn't know where he came from or where he went, but he surely hit a cord with me since he resembled the guys who followed me around in Woodland Hills—an upscale neighborhood where I used to live. There would always be one of these "types" in the aisle whenever I shopped. Whether I was in Home Depot, Fry's Electronics, or Tower Records—there they were. And they all looked the same. I do not know if they were rogue undercover detectives or if it was just one guy—someone who was assigned to me that would occasionally change his hair color and appearance. Why they would be interested in me, I had no idea. Even bodybuilding fans with fetishes did not stalk me like that. It was undeniably creepy, and it boggled my mind.

When the three of us arrived in Chicago, we met my mother at a gas station. I didn't even have a hairbrush to my name. Her once-successful daughter was now showing up with her tail between her legs. Little did I know, the nightmare was not over and the gangstalking had moved to yet another level. The nationwide hate group had new perpetrators, including my sister, and were anxiously awaiting my arrival.

After a much-needed rest, I geared up to look for answers at a well-known bookstore. I had never heard of the word "gangstalking", so I just browsed the self-help section, the Christian sector, and even True Crimes, looking for something remotely like the devil's cauldron from which I had just escaped. With nothing to be found, I left empty-handed. I believe it was then that God put a yearning in my heart to write this book—to fill a void where there was a desperate need. There had to be other people like myself, looking for answers and solutions. Although I had become a TI, I never heard of the term "targeted individual". I had much to learn.

Having to adapt to the freezing weather in Chicago was a drag. Looking for a place to rent in the dead of winter wasn't any fun and finding a landlord willing to take two junkyard dogs was nearly impossible. Even more difficult for me would be the process of transitioning back into mainstream living—indoors, with the convenience of running water and electricity. Though I had been fighting for my life in RVs and travel trailers for two years, I had become at home under the light of the moon and stars. I could not have that in Chicago, since the weather did not permit such a lifestyle. Living inside made me feel trapped and bored like I was missing something. With some effort, I managed to find a rental home on Chicago's south side, near my mom. Oddly enough, it was in an area loaded with police officers, retired firemen, and disabled folk, who were home all day and able to spy on my every move. I kept busy for the first five years, building fences and gates everywhere I rented. Each year I had to move on and would have to start all over again. They were using me to upgrade selected properties for the participating perpetrators.

A year before my girls were, sadly, diagnosed with breast cancer, they finally got their own yard on an acre of land in the State of Georgia. It had taken me ten years to get it for them, and if it were not for my father, it would never have happened. Mama and Prettygirl were buried on their own yard, just outside my bedroom window. I will say one more thing on their behalf: After they were gone for one year, there was another attempt at breaking my spirit, when I would be covertly drugged and despicably assaulted in my own home. The perp came in for the kill, using hidden electronics to broadcast the incident. That's right, the entire degrading episode was captured for the local community's entertainment. By eight o' clock the next morning, the employees at the local stores were freshly viewing it. While still heavily spaced-out, I searched for over-the-counter relief for what felt like a fire between my legs. As I stood in the checkout lines, the criticism and disgust toward me was preposterous. Nobody had ever treated me like that in my life. For someone who had just been sexually violated, I was being treated as though I had slaughtered the grandmother of a local Good Ole Boy. Oh, how I longed for my girls; God, how I missed them. Had Mama and Prettygirl been alive, the sexual assault would never have happened.

My message in laying this out is to give the reader a colorful perspective of how becoming lackluster about our life can turn into a dangerous thing. Walking around ungrateful and full of self-pity can open portholes and cracks for demonic activity. You see, after my husband, Christopher, died from multiple sclerosis in 1997, I opted to give up. In all honesty, I had started getting into trouble while he was on his way out. I had tossed my life to the wind, and it was the worst thing I could have done. I went on a sabotage spree that ended up rerouting my life to a place I would barely escape years later. I still pay for that stinking, self-pitying attitude that led me to make bad decisions twenty-some years ago. We cannot fly too low when we are grieving, or someone will shoot us down. Somewhere along the line, doing something I shouldn't have been doing, or being somewhere I had no business being, I managed to turn the tables on myself. Somebody had the power to take the issue to the streets. As the balls rolled, they got bigger, and I did what any person from my background would have done: I called the police department, took out restraining orders, and tried my best to stay safe. Little did I know that by trying to take care of myself, I was adding fuel to the fire. I was in a no-win situation. Being the highly achieved champion that I was, I did not know how to let go or walk away from anything. I just did not understand that concept. Consequently, I lost everything that meant anything to me.

I had entered an element of life I knew nothing about. Even while growing up, I was never involved in gangs, nor did I know anyone who was. I wasn't street smart and, certainly, not enticed to hurt people. The only fighting I knew was from back in the early 80s when I had to deal with gym wars. My then-husband, Bob Plakinger, was the Amateur Athletic Union (AAU) physique chairman for the State of Wisconsin. He also owned the biggest, hardcore weightlifting gym in the Midwest, founded on Milwaukee's south side. Before I came onto the scene, it was strictly a men's facility; that is how far back I go. Wedgewood Fitness Center was the place where champions trained, and pencil-necks strived to get big. It was *the* place to be, and it was my second home. The gym wars were full of hatred, violence, and envy, and they were real. I always had to be better than necessary to avoid any rumors of the competitions being fixed; which they never were.

The night of the 1980 Ms. Wisconsin bodybuilding championships was a turning point for me—a dress rehearsal in developing "staying power". When half of the theater audience cheered for me, at the same time, the other half tried to boo me off the stage. That night, I learned to never bow out for being envied or hated and to hang on and stand tall until the high winds died down. Not many people get to stand in front of hundreds of people and experience something like that. Never would I have thought that 23-years later, I would reach in my grab bag and use that experience as a survival tool on the mean streets of Los Angeles.

In 1982, after capturing the titles of the *AAU Ms. America* and *AAU American Pairs Championships*, a local competitor from the YWCA would use me as the focal point for a character-assassination smear campaign. It was a thorough plan to annihilate me and to destroy my future as a professional bodybuilder. It was done out of sheer jealousy. She and her cohorts set out to distribute smut, all the way up to the International Federation of Body Builders (IFBB), the professional ranks out of Montreal, Canada. These player-haters brought so much attention to me through their complaining that the professional committee sought me out. It was a blessing in disguise. Even back then I had God's favor in my life. He took something meant for evil and turned it around for my good. Only God can do that, and it is awesome when He does. One day, the IFBB liaison called me while I was at work in the Wedgewood Nutrition Center. I was so excited to get the call. It did not matter that they wanted to use me to set an example of what *not* to do in the amateur ranks of the sport. Women's bodybuilding was new. A few of us were cornerstones in setting standards and would become legends in the sport. For political reasons of being affiliated with the AAU and not the American Federation of Women's Bodybuilding (AFWB), I was put on a year suspension by the IFBB. After the year was up, they would invite me to compete in the upcoming Caesars World Cup in Las Vegas (where I won $10,000) and would star in the film *Pumping Iron II: The Women*. Even as some people tried to knock me down, I took the blows, got back up, and kept moving forward. The suspension was to my advantage in gaining ten pounds of muscle mass that year. I was becoming a seasoned warrior in more ways than I could have imagined.

My bodybuilding career steered me right when I was a teenager. As an adult, it made me a star. I shared my respectable character traits of morals, principles, and values with my fans. I have always carried these qualities deep in my soul, where I believe real magnetism gets developed. In that respect, I can say that I learned to fight, and I learned how to win. At least, it was a fair game, for the most part. I did not have training on becoming a targeted individual for gangstalking hate groups, nor in defending myself from perpetrators who wanted to devour me at soul level. Having my name put on a nationwide gangstalking and harassment list was way out of my league. However, from all those years of working on my soul, I surprisingly remained grounded when the big bad wolf came to blow my house down. I am grateful that when evil came knocking in the midnight hour, I had God's Hand on me. Only a fool builds his house on sand. I guess, during my bodybuilding career and the 19-years in twelve-step programs, I managed to build my house on a rock.

I could go on sharing spooky stories about the things that I saw at the junkyards. I could add a few more chapters discussing the deplorable events that gangstalkers and law enforcement officials have put me through since then, but I don't want to. I agree that for long-standing problems, we ought to kneel. Sometimes, to make it through another day, we need something to take hold of. As a retired World Champion bodybuilder, I still harbor those hopeful traits that keep me believing there are solutions to all problems. I know that we can fix certain body issues with proper weight training and supplements, and some long-term mental troubles can get straightened out with proper fitness and nutrition. It is "solution-finding". If you want bigger arms: superset dumbbell bicep curls with preacher bench cable curls and eat lots of protein. Boom.

Gangstalking is a whole other thing because this world does not govern it. Demons come up from the innards of hell to intervene supernaturally through perpetrators—those people who have given up their rights by selling their soul to the devil or by simply opening doors to the demonic realm through ruinous behavior like practicing witchcraft. The demons come and go while using the perps whenever they want; this explains the split personality we come to recognize in our dealings with them. This is authentic spiritual warfare between darkness and light: Heaven and hell. We are caught in the middle where the game gets played out. Because this battle is not ours, and it belongs to the Lord, our solution for survival is living life one day at a time. We must find coping techniques and strategies to acquire some level of peace of mind. These coping tactics become our spiritual warfare weapons, as we learn to fight offensively. I believe that we are living in the last hour before Jesus returns. We are up against a worldwide anti-Christ spirit that manifests itself in a variety of ritualistic systems besides gangstalking. Do not be afraid of these evil doers and take note: We were made for such a time as this.

Today, I am sixty years old. I am still around. Any normalcy of going to a gym was stolen from me years ago, as well as any dream of becoming a life coach. I have recently built an old-school jungle gym for my deck. Even though it was not from scratch, the assembly was monumental with hundreds of nuts and bolts. It all quickly came back to me, as I put it together, one piece at a time: cables, pulleys, stackable plates, and various stations. I think I could have done it blindfolded, but honestly, I needed readers to follow the instruction manual. It was finally assembled in 4 days, and I treated myself to a long overdue workout. While I was overjoyed with knowing muscle has memory, my brain quickly shifted into overdrive with racing thoughts from the past: *Had I not been authentic back in the day, I would never have put this together so swiftly, neither would I have slipped through the grips of those soul scalpers in hell's gateway, nor from those perpetrators who prowled the area to feed off new prey.* Although the sport of bodybuilding had developed character traits in me like tenacity, discipline, and endurance, it is only by the grace of God that I am alive today and working out with weights again.

In between sets, I further reminisced about my personal training business and the special people I was acquainted with through *Tina's Nonsense Training (TNT)*. On occasion, I still get asked about my six-foot trophy collection—those awards I won in the amateur ranks of bodybuilding. They, too, were stolen from my storage unit in Long Beach, California. As I continued to work out, I decided that my memories were mine and that I had won those trophies, not anyone else. No matter what they took, my memories belong to me. Granted, the rug was pulled out from under me when I was forty-three years old, but The Lord has been good to me. I have lived an extraordinary life—both then and now. I am proud of the fact that I am a *has-been* not a *wannabe*; I would not trade that for the world.

With that said, I wrote this book for people who are made to suffer a lifetime of punishment for making a spur-of-the-moment bad decision; for those who did nothing wrong, but were picked as opportunistic targets and used for practice; for the blinded souls who still think they are just magnets for attracting bad luck; for others who are made to pay for simply making someone jealous; and lastly, for anybody who became guilty by association by being in the wrong place at the wrong time. I have written this book to portray that suicide is not an option. Our life on Earth does not last forever, but rather it prepares us for life after death. I have integrated certain scriptures and prayers in my daily readings that have helped me: warrior prayers, cancellation prayers, and binding and loosing prayers—all gathered throughout the years from various preachers and teachers. I have included special quotes from movies, books, songs, and a one-liner by a famous, or not-so-famous, person. And finally, there is a prayer section in the back of the book, and most importantly, a prayer for salvation.

Treading on Serpents is like me. It is not perfect. It is eclectic. This book was not written for non-targeted individuals and would be much more beneficial to those in the grips of organized gang-stalking and harassment. Most of my writing style is from the perspective of us and we. I want other targets to know they are not alone. On the last day of each month, I illustrate a personal story in the first person, as I do on occasion throughout the book. Our hidden injuries, rarely seen by others, are the deeper wounds that can eventually take us out. It is unlikely that we even register the emotional abuse that we endure while in the daily whirlwind of being gang stalked.

I have added only a few photos in the back of the book to show that this can happen to anyone. Any type of life can be taken away in an instant. I pray that these words have supernatural healing power—physically, mentally, spiritually, and emotionally. Although our life is not forever, there is one requirement for our survival: to know Jesus, the Son of God. Having a relationship with Him is like getting directions to where we need to go. He is like our personal GPS, if you will. We cannot wrestle the gangstalking demons without Him. This book is a spiritual war plan and survival guide for Targeted Individuals of gangstalking and organized harassment.

The best part of this collection was written when Mama and Prettygirl journeyed with me in a fifteen-foot vintage travel trailer (without a driver's license). We typically lived off the grid, with a thousand eyes always watching us. It was truly one of the loneliest times, when I really had to rely on the Holy Spirit for guidance. With life's normal ups and downs, along with the chaos, destruction, and continual setbacks of gangstalking, it has taken seven computers and fifteen years to complete this book. The spiritual warfare that I have encountered, just trying to get it properly edited, laid out, and published, has been nothing short of slaying dragons. I had promised God, I would write it for those people whom He intended to read it. I had to cling to Jesus every step of the way. I am glad He knows who we are and sees what we go through, as it has been a long and unforgiving journey.

I would like to thank my mother for keeping me grounded with laughter; it is something she takes very seriously. I am also grateful for my four rescue dogs; they bring me daily comfort, joy, and multiple headaches.

January 1

There's something addicting about a secret.
—J. Edgar Hoover

We marvel at the size of these organizations and how many members swarm one person. The hate groups are a secret society, and unless you are a perpetrator or a targeted individual, you have never heard of them. We cannot believe our life turned out like this. It is like getting dropped into *The Twilight Zone*. Evil energy can be very cunning and powerful. We usually do not pay it any mind, until we are wallowing neck deep in it. A lot of us consider ourselves average. We grew up in average families. We learned right from wrong, landed jobs, married, had kids, bought the house, and built the white picket fence. We rolled with the punches that life threw our way. We felt compelled to keep the principles and values we learned as kids and secretly yearned to pass them on to our next generation. That sounds so simple. Nevertheless, life is not simple, nor easy. We constantly come up against hard lessons, and it seems we are always facing change. Life is hard enough without people making themselves out as vindicators. We do not learn about these end-times battles, filled with spiritual warfare, until we are on the job as a targeted individual. We may not know that we are here to take a stand for the kingdom of God. We may have gray hair before we ever find our way to the Bible. In Satan's desperate attempt to win souls, he uses gangstalking to orchestrate the art of suicide. The entire intent behind bullying and gangstalking is to cause the targeted individual to kill themselves; to sacrifice our self to Satan. How horrible. We must now view the Bible as an instruction book—a manual on how to win the war. This is where God has given us freedom of choice. Committing suicide is not the answer.

It may not be what I had expected, but I do have a life worth living.

January 2

I have sometimes been wildly, despairingly, acutely miserable... but through it all, I still know quite certainly that just to be alive is a grand thing.
—Agatha Christie

By forcing us to live a mere existence, the gangstalkers work collectively to minimize us. Their daily goal is to raise their status within the group, and they do this by hurting, destroying, and ruining people's lives. It is our job to keep from becoming empty and used up. They become more powerful if they destroy us, since they feed off our energy, leaving us depleted. The obsessed perps will go as far as to try taking on our looks, our actions, our hobbies, while they secretly and deeply lust for our soul. Their evil deeds supply their egos with a vast amount of venom that soon dissolves their insides. Yes. They self-destruct from the inside out. Not for one minute, do we need to envy them. We must keep moving along, because depletion can manifest itself into a very dangerous thing. Each day, we should do one beneficial thing for ourselves: brush our teeth; make an appointment; go to the market; wash our hair; do laundry; change the bed linens; or walk around. One personal accomplishment each day keeps us where life is—in motion. We cannot just lay down and become stagnant. We really cannot even slack off. We must stay sharp to avoid getting run over and left in the middle of the road.

God, you said You would be an enemy to my enemies and an adversary to my adversaries (Exodus 23:22).

January 3

Ain't nothing over, 'til it's over
—Rocky Balboa

Becoming stagnant is the breeding ground for living an apathetic life. Like many foreclosed homes that sit unoccupied, we, too, can become dangerously uncared-for. Houses left to sit and rot do just that: They sit and rot. Their emptiness causes problems. An unattended, abandoned home sticks out like a sore thumb. These structures were once thriving on the inside with daily life. They now look ragged and tattered, and the emptiness of them invites more than just a lonely and haunted appearance. Uninvited people and varmints take over. Pipes rust out. Fires happen. Some things, like buildings, are at their best when they are fully occupied, with water running through the pipes and the electricity turned on. Many Christians believe our body is the temple of God—that God lives in us, so we must care for our body because we have just one. Even prisoners on death row stay on a schedule. They wait years, by living one day at a time. They read, write, exercise, play cards, get haircuts, and so on. We can learn innovative ways to live by watching how others survive their fate. We must not let our pipes get rusty, nor leave our souls to become vacant.

Today, I will be attentive to my needs.

January 4

Emptiness will always invite some "thing" to occupy its space.

A demonic spirit will always look for a place to exist; searching, until it finds an emptiness that it can slip into and thrive. Some of us have been robbed of everything before landing on the Boulevard for the Homeless. We might have put the whole shebang into a storage unit, only to find it emptied out by a professional thievery ring that had the storage company on the books. When we find everything gone: tools, camera equipment, books we wrote, clothes we designed, our sewing machine, computer, artwork we painted, our father's baseball cards, our grandfather's WWII uniform, our mom's recipes, and everything that ever meant anything to us—we feel empty. The gangstalkers have two goals: to get our stuff and to erase us. We make it through the first few months, but years later, we can still miss our things. Our dogs are playing, and we think of capturing the moment on film, but we do not have our camera anymore. Our mind wanders off and we start wondering, *who has it? Does anyone use it? Has it been pawned?* There goes our mind again…off to the races. For us to survive with any quality of life, we must fill the void. Slowly, we must find things to do. Our spirit is broken, but not destroyed. We watch the news about people who have lost everything in floods and hurricanes. They tell us that they are grateful, because everyone in the family, including the pets, have survived. We hear them speak of how grateful they are to be alive, and that everything else can be replaced. Granted, losing everything to an Act of God is different from losing everything to gangstalkers. But the result is still the same: Everything is gone. It leaves a void—a hole so deep and dark, you can almost hear it. We cannot allow ourselves to take on that depth of darkness. We must find something that motivates us to keep moving forward, or we will surely suffer a slow and drawn-out death sentence.

Self-discipline is self-caring.

January 5

We would never be targeted individuals if we were not special.

Professional thievery and gangstalking rings consist of various ranks of people, but the geniuses behind them are the ones with the gifts. They can read people and will generally supervise the group's psychological profiling department. Some of us are targeted because we are extraordinary achievers with lots of toys and nice things. Empty out our lives at forty-five, and we suffer a mid-life crisis that most individuals wouldn't survive. It is an unsympathetic and merciless act of punishment to sentence a high-achiever to a lifestyle that lacks purpose. If there is a jealous person behind the gangstalking, this type of retaliation is calculating and made as personal as it gets. This off-shoot of gangstalking is known as Cause Stalking.[1] Having a personal vendetta makes erasing a targeted individual's life much more acceptable within the organization. Low-level perpetrators, as well as members of society, tend to believe every lie they are told, especially when it comes from somebody wearing a badge. Despite this vindictiveness, whenever we click into who we really are and to whom we belong, we grasp onto something that no thievery ring, jealous person, or scorned lover could ever take from us.

I am no one's victim. I am where I belong. I am grateful for the gifts and talents God blesses me with.

---

[1] Cause Stalking uses gangstalking tactics: harassment, break-ins, staged incidents, vandalism, and theft, but includes a personal hater and revenge package for further torment; available to anyone who has the connections and capital, including sex and illegal drugs, to finance it.

January 6

Walking in a target's shoes is not for the weak hearted.

Anything God gives us no enemy can take away. They will try, but to no avail. The things we can see will always change, so we turn our focus toward those things that are eternal and not subject to change. We learn an entirely new way of life, as we study God's Word. We are soldiers, and we must believe that we serve a loving God, who watches over us and protects us, as we do His work. God's Word is eternal, and it holds 7,000 promises that cover every situation we could possibly face. We live on another level now—a spiritual level, where the fight is really between God and Satan. We must serve one of them, and the one we serve is Jesus. If this were not our calling, we would be on the other side, serving Satan and partaking in his gangstalking and demolition of lives. We are not targets by accident. We are soldiers for The Lord, and we have been called to serve in this war. No longer do we settle for the dejected existence the world tells us we must have. We center our attention on God and those things that are eternal and do not change.

Father, thank you for giving me favor, that my enemies cannot triumph over me (Psalms 41:11).

January 7

Gangstalkers will fool the target into believing one thing, when it is really something else.

The more we study God's way, the clearer we see similarities between the trickery of Satan and the work of gangstalkers. Jesus was meek. He was not a pushover. He got angry and took care of business when He had to. He knew of the dangerous ways of the devil, and He took measures and precautions whenever it was necessary. Lying is a major tool that gangstalkers use for successfully hoodwinking people. They, like Satan, are known to throw a rock and hide the hand that threw it, making us think they did nothing wrong. Gangstalking thieves go to great lengths to get us, looking to the left, when they are on our right. Once we learn this, we can free ourselves up from some of the heavy confusion within the game. We do not need to be on a wild goose chase. If we stay grounded in the Word of God and wear our armor (Ephesians 6), we can war against the wiles of this evil by staying on top of it.

I bind and rebuke all wrath the devil directs against my life (Revelation 12:12).

January 8

When God called Abraham, He told him to leave his family, friends, and his home.

It had to be hard for Abraham to walk away from everything. Sometimes, God will remove people from our life, or He will take us away from one place and move us to another. There might be big plans for us that we cannot carry out in our current environment, or He does not want us to be around bad people or those who are mediocre in their goals. If we are going to serve God, He is going to deal with us. We may kick and scream all the way, without realizing He is doing the best thing for us. We must go through this process as He changes us little by little, so we can live glory to glory.

Lord, I give my will and my life over to your care today.

January 9

You don't want to sit like a mouse in the middle of a field.
—An anonymous gang member

We acknowledge being a targeted individual but shot callers[2] and gangsters do not own us. We belong to God, who calls and separates us, so He can divinely use us. Of course, there are days when we do not feel so special, and we learn to live by what we know and not by how we feel. We must learn to embrace these spiritual ways, because it is a tall order and a difficult calling to live life as a targeted individual. Satan knows this, and he sends his top soldiers to persecute us in countless ways. God knows these gangstalking torture tactics are excruciating to endure, but the turmoil we undergo will be turned around in His marvelous plan for our lives. We are separated and set aside for God's own personal use—for the higher good of humanity. It is not easy. It will not be pain-free. If we want to be happy, we need to let go and allow Him to prepare us.

Today, I will keep a connection to God. In return, I will receive serenity and a level of peace.

---

2 Shot caller: an individual in a gang who has a high status. This person "calls the shots", but he does not carry them out, as he has already done that role; hence, his elevated status. A shot caller in prison has everyone's lives in their hands. He/she has the final say over everything, including who gets whacked.

January 10

God will pull the plug on their plans.

Being gang stalked and hated brings us such misery and darkness that we cannot imagine how to help someone else. Some of us were once successful, based solely on our reputation through public opinion, but ruthless smear campaigns have ruined our good public standing and destroyed our lives. The spreading of lies has caused us to suffer the loss of many things: jobs, friends, money, stability, and sometimes, our will to live. God sent His Only Son, Jesus, to die on the cross, so we would have a good life. We should strive for it, even if it means caring less about what others think of us. This is semi-contradictory for those of us who once thrived in the entertainment business. Dying to self is all about the process of letting go. If we care that people think we are crazy, we certainly cannot come out of the woodwork and move forward. Our shared information on this covert form of murder can help others. Satan is slick in all his ways. He knows that most people do not want to go public because the art of gangstalking is so unbelievable. It sets us up to look nuts, so we get criticized and discounted. Still, God needs soldiers to do the footwork, so that He can get involved in the outcome. This is where we come in.

For I know the thoughts and plans that I have for you, says the Lord (Jeremiah 29:11).

January 11

And this ain't no place for the weary kind,
And this ain't no place to lose your mind
—from "Crazy Heart" by Ryan Bingham

Something good was designed by the National Security Agency (NSA) in America but may have landed in the wrong hands and is now torturing people. Coincidences may not be coincidences, but rather events regimented through Remote Neural Monitoring: Satellite Harassment. There are targeted individuals around the world who have fallen victim to Remote Neural Monitoring (RNM). Some are claiming to be like machines—controlled by mobile devices or the demonic people behind them. These electromagnetic waves are not good for our health, to say the least. As much as we would like to escape them, they can even permeate through the walls of our home. We might be victims of satellite psychotronic weaponry when we get sudden thoughts from left field about something we do not want to think about. When our thoughts are manipulated, we wage war to focus our attention on something good. We must read the Bible, pray, and be gentle with ourselves, as we fight to keep from losing our mind.

Today, I turn my will and my life over to the care of God because He understands exactly what is happening to me. He hears my cry and helps me.

January 12

It makes more sense to read the Bible and switch the word devil with gangstalkers.

It is common for regular folk to minimize our attacks. They say our problems are just circumstance—merely something naturally happening. This aloof response is also found commonly from a friend who is really a perp, which makes us feel very alone and with no one to talk to. Still, when we can distinguish a gangstalking attack from a natural occurrence, we are moving forward leaps and bounds. Once we learn their tactics, we are no longer an average target without a clue. There are T.I.s who mosey around in life, feeling beaten down by their efforts, never working it out. They think life is full of bad breaks; all the while, operatives are in the background, secretly dismantling their lives. Although, having knowledge about this underground activity does, in fact, raise our awareness and instincts, we tend to walk alone. The attacks we meet are demonic in nature, working through the vessels of gangstalkers, who want to destroy us. The thing about demonic attacks is that they are difficult to spot because they come to us camouflaged. When we belong to the Lord, he watches over us, knowing we are in a war with peculiar counterparts.

I live with dependence on God. Living in tough times amplifies my awareness of His presence. It is He who gives me strength.

January 13

The secret to vitality is sitting face to face with someone for 6-hours a day, not on Facebook.
—from *If You're Not in the Obit, Eat Breakfast*

We can be so lonely that we give people who have done us wrong too many chances, in hopes that they will turn around. All the while, there are nets being laid out for our entanglement. Wolves dressed in sheep's clothing are merely *plants*[3] who have been secretly placed in our lives. They are sometimes even charming. It is a tool they use to pry their way into our lives to cause us further mayhem. Even if we have had laughs together, we must shut them out because they are bad for us. Spiritually, we verbally cast them down in Jesus' name, and we bless and release them. We have faith that God will take care of everything else. This also includes weeding out two-faced friends and replacing them with either divine connections or no connection at all. We must have faith that God will meet all our needs.

Revive me, O Lord, and repair the desolation in my life (Ezra 9:9).

---

3 A plant is a person who has been secretly placed into a situation to report back to someone or execute an order. An example of a plant is an undercover FBI agent acting as a drug dealer. Verb—to plant a person, often with the implication of intending deceit.

January 14

As we dwell in the secret place, we watch God deal with those who curse us.

We tend to make swift transitions in our moods. We can be up one minute and down the next. Our reality can sometimes cause our disposition to change in a New York minute. We can go along thinking everything is okay, and then suddenly, face the ugly reality of being gang stalked, or we get zapped with beams of energy that unexpectedly change our attitude. There is nothing we can do about the fact: We face an army of haters, even while we are isolated. We know they are secretly working together to destroy us, yet we cannot seem to put together a proper line of defense. Some of us get verbally attacked in public by *Directed Conversation,* where two or more gangstalkers engage in a conversation near us and talk loudly about our private life. Certainly, we conclude, they must have a hearing device in our home. These things can be overwhelming, as we take apart the back of a television, looking for a bug. We try accepting the fact that we cannot change some things without driving ourselves nuts. In most cases, we learn to be quiet. We begin by not having personal conversations in our home. If we want to buy a product, we do it quickly and quietly. We do not talk about it for two weeks, giving them an opportunity to botch it up in some way. We notice these small behavioral changes begin to transition us out of their reach for brief periods of time. We begin to experience a few victories in areas that used to be hopeless. We could not even order a pair of prescription eye glasses without them mysteriously disappearing in the lab. After years of constant defeat, we find that having just a couple victories can empower us. Our journey of a thousand miles begins with our first step of silence.

My life is built on layers of small everyday accomplishments.

January 15

When a TI becomes brainwashed to cause his own destruction, he frees up the gangstalkers to work on others.

Sadly, over time, we wake up expecting something awful to happen. We do not plan anything nice anymore, because it never works out. We even stop setting personal goals. We just sit and wait for the other shoe to drop—*Not!* We inadvertently side with the enemy when we think like this. We help them in our own destruction. This gangstalking syndicate is one of Satan's masterpieces. Once a target is housebound and living in isolation, a 24/7 surveillance is successfully set up by using various electronics and community watch groups. It only takes two neighbors to keep a surveyed target under control by watching him come and go. In my case, neighborhood groups have set up a private Wi-Fi network around my home, so they can, simultaneously, listen to conversations I may be having with another perp. They do this over their cell phones. The instigating perp turns his phone on, while the group tunes in to listen to whatever I say, as he fishes and baits me. We can learn how to transition out of their grips. For as much as we have been through, we owe it to ourselves to gain even a little dominion over what remains in our lives It is our duty to be careful not to side with the enemy, think garbage thoughts, say garbage things, and treat ourselves like garbage.

I care enough about myself to live apart from the world around me.

January 16

Gangstalking uses suicide to collect souls for Satan's kingdom.

It can take us years to learn how to care for ourselves, while we survive the many levels of gangstalking. We smarten up when we figure out how they are watching us; it is an essential countermove. A base of operations is set up close to the target—usually at a neighbor's house, so they can work together to create chaos and havoc. This is in operation when they stop to converse with us, using a private Wi-Fi network within the group. One will badmouth the other, with the intention of getting us to add something to the conversation. They love to bait us into saying something bad about another perp who is listening. What we say is either recorded or streamed live to further ignite their hatred. It is our job to learn how our neighbors have been strategically planted. As the person on the left complains about our dogs, the person on the right pretends to side with us by calling him a pain in the butt, and the person up front buffers it by saying they are both nuts. If we watch carefully, we see them interact with one another. We can transition out of their game, simply by knowing it exists. We no longer need to be bounced around from one perpetrator to the other.

Help me, Lord, to not be deceived as I find out Evil Company corrupts good habits (1 Corinthians 15:33).

January 17

Wisdom can reveal to us the shame and inner struggles of our perpetrators.

The Bible tells us that we can have wisdom, but we must ask Father God for it (James 1:5). When we receive the wisdom, we then reach another level of awareness. We can spot the subtle ones: local business owners, church goers, and even family members, who are all secretly involved in our demise. The cruel people who harass us will smile as they stab us in the heart. They stay clever in their maneuvers by speaking to us about a God they do not know. Their passive-aggressive nature promises us things that never come to fruition. Believing them only causes us more frustration and confusion. No matter how hard they try to hide their involvement, we can see a trait that they each carry amongst themselves: bondage of sin. We thought they had the upper hand, but they do not. These players are affixed to their actions that eat away at their soul. Some are in so deeply they cannot see straight. Our wisdom will show us what no one else can see, and some of these things can be truly disgraceful.

One day at a time, I continue to live, learn, and grow.

January 18

The confidence we have in Jesus is viewed by the perpetrators who watch us.

There are demons that function through our perpetrators. Some perps might be able to get out from being a gangstalker by choice, while others are already owned by demons that must be cast out. Gangstalkers belong to Satan by bondage, not by freedom. Liberty is where the Spirit of the Lord is. TIs can endure many gangstalking tactics due to the mercy we have already received from God. If we look carefully, we can see where His mercy keeps us from failing. The perpetrators see how the Lord blesses us when their nets catch other targeted individuals, but we continue to walk away unscathed. The blessing gives us the power to seek a profound life, whether perpetrators target us or not.

Today, I will see my situation in a different light. My burden has been wrapped in a blessing.

January 19

We are in the grips of evil and there is only one way out.

We have two options: commit suicide or give our lives over to the care of God. This does not mean that everything becomes a cakewalk after we surrender. Once we hook up with Jesus, we can expect the devil to turn up the heat. While we are in a relationship with the Lord, we get the tools we need: grace, mercy, and divine protection. We do not have to stay dwarfed in a spiritual war; manifested through gangstalkers who are trying to kill us. When we choose to give our life to God, we leave the battle for Him to fight. Once we have this power around us, and we are using His Word to activate our angels, the devil and his cohorts are defeated.

Lord, you give me the tools I need to survive. I know that the more often I turn to you, the more I please you.

January 20

We thank the Lord for cutting off our enemies and destroying all those who afflict our inner-self (Psalms 143:8).

We confess divine results when we read Psalm 109 and Psalm 37 aloud. Let the perpetrators listen. Let them laugh amongst themselves. Few will have the good sense to fear the works we are calling forth. It is just a matter of time before the Lord fights our battle for us. Someday, the wicked will cry out to The Lord, but it will be too late, and He will not respond to them. When we plant God's promises in our heart, we can just sit back and watch Him work. Popcorn?

Just for today, I will get into the Word of God. I refuse to worry about anything.

January 21

This is a war of witchcraft, Satanism, gangstalking, and electronic harassment for the reaping of souls. TIs fight the battle from the front lines.

Voodoo witches and Satan worshippers work curses at night while their victims sleep. The witching hour is generally between midnight and 4:00 am. Witchcraft is a system. Witches put black magic curses on people while they are asleep, and their defenses are weak. Gangstalkers are also prone to perform most of their sneaky work between 2:00 and 3:30 in the morning. Planting good seeds in our heart is like planting vegetable seeds in a garden; they must have sunshine and water to grow. We guard the garden by fighting off scavengers and by pulling out entangling weeds that would destroy it. We ought to be as zealous about keeping good things nurtured in our heart and not getting entangled in the bitterness or hatred that dominates this world.

I bind and rebuke any bewitchment that would keep me from obeying the truth. (Galatians 3:1)

January 22

Having courage is a decision, not a feeling.

We must beware of the dirty deeds done to us by gangstalkers before these seeds get planted in our heart. Whatever grows in our heart will eventually come out of our mouth. With Satan knowing about God's Law of Confession, he goes to great lengths to plant seeds of hatred, bitterness, resentment, and despondency. He wants us to do three things: fear it, believe it, and speak it. When we start speaking negative things, Satan and his cohorts can legally act upon them. Without God's help, we are not capable of keeping bad seeds from sprouting, especially, those seeds of bitterness, when we are blind-sighted, deceived, or played a patsy.

Lord, let every root of bitterness be cut from my life (Hebrews 12:15).

January 23

Gangstalking: It is not that we have accepted it, but that we have learned to live with it.

God promises us that He will never leave us once we let Him into our lives. He will be with us through the floods, fires, and storms. When it looks like there is no hope, we must press on. Harassing people, with the intention that their own despondency will trigger them to commit suicide, is evil ingenious. We are seeing eviler people in the world than ever. Gangstalking has become a nationwide epidemic with many people falling prey to becoming targeted individuals. This battle is not ours. It belongs to the Lord.

Today, I may face a tough or painful situation, but I know that my loving God is with me to comfort and guide me toward peace.

January 24

Gangstalkers want custody of our mind.

Our mind is where we house arguments, theories, and reasoning. It is the enemy's playground and a place where we can be driven insane. *The Helmet of Salvation* (Ephesians 6:13-18) is a spiritual weapon where we put on the Mind of Christ. We do not allow the doings of gangstalkers and electronic harassment to invade our cognizance. We must fight hard to not dwell on our situation and on the cruel things being done to us. Rerunning thoughts that keep looping around in our mind become mental strongholds. In 2 Corinthians 10:5, we are to *cast down arguments and every high thing that exalts itself against the knowledge of God.* This is our instruction for warfare: to keep our mind on things from above instead of on our circumstances. We stay steadfast at praying in the spirit to win back our mind.

When wrong thoughts ignite a flame that spreads like wildfire, praying in the spirit can bring us what feels like a soft rain shower.

January 25

Targeted individuals are emotionally overwhelmed by never-ending annoyances and aggravation.

Angels are extreme warriors that do not only hearken to God's Word, but to the *voice* of God's Word. That means we can call them in, whenever we need help. However, if we do not speak God's Word, they cannot make a move to help us. If we are unsure what to verbalize, we can just read Psalm 91 aloud—words for divine protection. It also behooves us to take one verse that pertains to our situation and memorize it; we recite it to call in those angels that have been assigned to us. Moreover, we should put a harness on our constant complaining about what gangstalkers are doing to us. Moaning and groaning will not activate God's supernatural power, but rather pull in more of Satan's work. We use divine words to fight against those evil things that are too big for us to manage.

Today, I have powerful angelic help available to me. I will activate it by speaking the Word of God.

January 26

Inactivity is activity toward nothing; it allows the enemy to win over our lives.

Some TIs do not want to rely on God for the spiritual tactics needed to win the war. We want to have a hissy while stuffing our reality behind drugs and alcohol. We have a choice to try everything else before we give God a try. Our life has totally changed since we were put on a nationwide hate list. It is painful feeling badly about who we are. We move through each day alone, battling in a war we know little about. If we decide to try God, we will see that He has a good plan for our life. His plan is to give us hope and a future (see Jeremiah 29:11). Because life comes to us in pieces, we do not always see the big picture, so we tend to give up before fulfilling our destiny. Having patience is the key.

Today, I will begin to do what I believe God wants me to do. I do not have to do it all in one day, as I know this may take a lifetime.

January 27

They cannot break me because they did not make me.

Gangstalkers naturally rise in the morning with plans to ruin someone's day. They are the gatekeepers to our prison. They work in the background of our lives and, some of them, we will never see. We have become broken-hearted people. We have lost our freedom, our loved ones, and our good name. We are held captive behind invisible walls, secretly put in place as confines, to keep us under scrutiny and control. Although, we can heal once we surrender to our role in life, most of us will continue to kick and scream and balk at this option. Naturally, life will never be as we once knew it, but what higher calling is there than to keep someone from committing suicide? Letting another target know that they are not alone can be enough to save the day. The feeling of belonging is so empowering, it can be the difference between life and death.

By not hurting myself today, I can make a difference in another person's life.

January 28

Human trafficking is an anti-Christ spirit of slavery.

It is painful to learn how people control others for profit. We hear what the media tells us, but we do not see the secretive part of it: the upper-class, suburban high-school boy who secretly belongs to an underground crime ring. He will be promoted for simply luring fifteen-year-old boys and girls to a secret place where another batch of people take over: specialists who torture and paralyze these young people by scaring them half to death. We do not see their shame as they return to their suburban homes to live in silent terror from what they have just experienced. We do not know the depth of their helplessness, as they believe that any resistance will result in the death of their family. For years, they will live in a silent prison of degradation. They will follow orders and stay quiet, while others profit off their despair. In our controlled world of being gang stalked, we get pushed aside for looking crazy, and we eventually become quiet. Reading this book is a step toward breaking that silence. It is our job to shine the light for those who are still in darkness. We have a gift that they do not have: wisdom. No decent work comes from doing nothing, and really, we have nothing to lose for trying.

Today, I will trust that I am moving toward God's plan for my life, in which He protects me every step of the way.

January 29

We all have a breaking point.

Feeling lethargic is a direct result of getting repeatedly beaten down. Pushing ourselves to exhaustion is their way of breaking us. It may not happen quickly, but we can have a breakdown from constantly taking three steps forward and two back. Time is of no importance to the perpetrators who strategically dismantle the lives of targeted individuals. Someone new will come onboard whenever they get tired. Learning counter moves to their actions can become empowering for us. When we get tired of putting on the armor of God (Ephesians 6), we do it again and again. When we do not think we can go on, we do it some more. Persistency and consistency are our ingredients for survival. We *will* have victories. There *will* be days that we enjoy life. We *will* laugh again.

Today, I will use spiritual tools to beat this evil system.

January 30

Bill Winston's church radiated a power that at first was too much to handle. The first time I walked in, I wanted to turn around and run out. The devil did not want me to learn about the powerful Word of God, but rather to stay hopeless and despondent as a target of gangstalking and harassment, isolated in my little area of life.

Nothing can beat the Word of God because it fits into hopeless environments and impossible situations. It does not matter if we are on a harassment list for a lifetime of punishment. God has us in a place where we must have a personal relationship with Him. He knows exactly what we are going through—years of getting beaten down, having things taken away, and living isolated without anyone in our corner. When we meditate on scripture, we change our image from how the haters want us to view ourselves to something powerful and almighty. The Word of God is all-powerful and designed to rule. It tells us what we can do, who we are, and what we can have. When we meditate on powerful scriptures, we oppose the evil energy that has been put around us by people who stalk us. If only we meditate on the Word of God, it will change many things. Darkness cannot exist where there is light.

Today, I will choose a scripture to meditate on. As I memorize it, I will launch into a spiritual battle where I eventually win.

January 31

If the world has written you off, hang on, because Jesus is looking for you.

In Narcotics Anonymous, I always heard, "Don't leave five minutes before the miracle." The thing is: We never know when we have five minutes left of anything. The day that my dad died, I knew he was on his way out, but I did not know that he would leave during the five minutes I left his bedside. The morning my dog, Mama, died, I got up to make breakfast for her and Prettygirl like I did any other morning. But this day, it would turn out to be the worst day of my life. After I had just buried both dogs, a smug gangstalking neighbor, who had been covertly watching me in my home, wanted to buy my travel trailer for a thousand dollars less than what I was asking. I had become the community bottom feeder. She used that one day—that very moment—when sheer and utter despair had made it hard for me to even breathe, as an opportunity to take advantage of me. She got me on the phone just to take away the precious little energy that I was surviving on. Life will hit us harder than any punch ever will, but the audacity of gangstalkers can be like pounding the last nail in the coffin. Life does not tell us when we have three more reps left, or two more laps remaining, or even when we are close to the other side. We should just keep moving like we are walking our last block. We cannot give up, because we may be just around the corner from our breakthrough. We could be close to when God plans to change our circumstances, or when we suddenly get elevated and double honored like His Word promises us in Isaiah 61:7.

Today, I will pick myself up and stand one more time.

February 1

Hopelessness is a heavy weight that burdens our soul, but with God there is hope in the impossible.

There are Lambs and Worlders functioning together in a universal trend. The Lambs are the pure hearts that will see God. His seal is upon us. The Worlders are the earth dwellers—the perpetrators and gangstalkers who have sold their soul to the dark side. It is spiritual and multi-dimensional that these things are happening in unison around the globe. If we have any doubts, the World Wide Web has countless stories of targeted individuals, living on the other side of the world, who reveal uncanny stories that are parallel to our everyday lives. Many of us have become shut-ins to simply avoid being triggered by everyday stimuli or harassed by perpetrators as we get our car serviced, buy groceries, or run to pick up a lawn mower part. There is comfort in knowing that we are not alone. The mobbing that was executed on us in the dog food isle today is the same scheme implemented on other TIs around the world.

Today, I get through a jolting trigger by seeking shelter and then focusing my eyes on Jesus—the Lamb of God.

February 2

To win battles, you do not need weapons; you beat the soul of the enemy.
—General George S. Patton

Some targeted individuals are tortured with directed-energy weapons (DEWs) that were initially formed as an experiment during World War II. This technology was designed by the US government to simulate mental illness and delusion by using electromagnetic energy. It is now being used on innocent civilians through the walls of our home. For those of us who are not targets of DEW, we need to be grateful and pray for those who suffer this way. We are human beings, and just like Jesus' apostles, we all have our limits. Without the power of the Lord working in us, we are not immune to brokenness.

Today, I will lift my eyes onto the hills for the Lord who comes to help me (Psalm 121:1-2).

February 3

We walk by faith, not by sight.

I recently heard a story told by a well-known preacher. It went something like this: During World War II, there was a marine who had become disoriented after several explosions had separated him from his unit. He ran for his life with the enemy pack right behind him. He came upon a cave where he hid inside and prayed to the Lord to spare his life. Just then, a spider mysteriously dropped down in the entrance of the cave and began spinning a large web over the opening. For several hours the marine sat and watched the spider spin his web. He could hear the troops getting closer, until they were near the opening of the cave. "No sense in checking over here," the enemy soldier yelled. "No one could have gotten passed this web."

We never know how God is going to help us. We may not know how to get out of our situation, but we must never lose hope by judging the way things appear. What looks foolish to us might be the hand of God making the crooked places straight.

Lord, let the nets they have hid catch themselves, and into their own destruction let them fall.

February 4

You must never give up; there is just so much they can do.
—My dad

It is easy to believe that nothing good will ever happen. While we are under illegal surveillance, many roadblocks are strategically set up to stop everything we attempt. We eventually stop trying because we assume it will not work out anyway. This is exactly what our enemies want us to do. They want us to lose all hope and give up on our dreams. How dare they play god with our lives! They are *not* God, and their ability to destroy us *is* limited. The reality is: The lion that roars at us doesn't have any teeth and is kept on a leash. The real danger brews when we focus on suicide. This plan of escape does not lead us to a better place. It is a bad and final decision that leaves us with no options at all. When we hand everything over to the Lord, all things are possible. When we walk with God, being outnumbered means nothing. He knows all things and has all power. He may not stop what is going on, but He will walk us through it. Hopelessness is a ploy used on God's people (Lambs) by Worlders[4]. When we are hopeless, we not only close the door for God to work in our lives, but death starts to become attractive to us. We must learn to outsmart our perpetrators by asking Jesus to walk with us and help us in everything we do.

Help, Lord, for no one is faithful anymore; those who are loyal have vanished from the human race (Psalm 12:1 [NIV]).

---

4 Worlders: carnal people who are earth dwellers. They love being a part of the world's ways and are not interested in knowing God.

February 5

We need to stop digging when we find ourselves in a rut.

It can get overwhelmingly frustrating when everything we try does not work out. This goes for trying to sell our vehicle, trade something in, receive mail, apply for jobs online, inquire about things using the telephone, or better ourselves in any way. Our moves are blocked. This type of persecution is to make us sit with no resources, friends, or money; while the more we try, the more we lose. It is a form of solitary confinement. To live a life with any sense of peace, we must take a deep breath and surrender. Acceptance is the answer to all our problems. This can be tough for a Type A personality—someone who likes to set goals, fix problems, and get things done. When we feel overpowered, we should ask God for an understanding of peace during our persecution. This is what we must strive for—acceptance and peace of mind, so that we do not attempt suicide.

Father, I thank You that You have delivered me from my enemies, which are continually before me.

February 6

The gangstalkers cannot feed on themselves, for they are already dead.

We have been set up to feel alone, but we are not alone; it is all an illusion caused by isolation. We have more support in the spirit realm around us than we think. The haters that use us as their lifeline are also scalping the souls of other TIs. They cannot feed from an empty plate, so they must look for the vital energy of those who are oppressed, to feed off their oomph. At this very moment, there is someone ready to hang themselves, slice their wrists, jump off a bridge, or lay across railroad tracks. We must pray for them and thank the Lord that we are still alive. We are ready to do His work. We must come out of silence to let others know they are not alone. This is also how we keep ourselves from acting on suicidal thoughts.

Comfort them, comfort them, my people, says the Lord (Isaiah 40:1).

February 7

We do not have to self-destruct from what pathetic people have done to us.

The fact that no one from the churches has ever prepared us for this persecution is criminal. The idea that people who have the title of pastor or reverend take part in high-fiving one another and laughing at our demise is bitterly sick. Priests who take part in our soft kill[5] are pure evil. The so-called holy rollers who discredit us through gangstalking and policing are pathetic. God's wrath toward them is sheer repulsion. Some of us are shut-ins because we trusted these people due to their positions. In return, they've helped in hurting us. These are bad crimes committed by so-called good people who run the community. They are the worst kind of predators. They do not think they have done anything wrong, but they secretly fear that someday there will be a reprisal, particularly, if the TI cannot be forced to move away.

You, Lord, will keep the needy safe, and will protect us forever from the wicked, who freely strut about when what is vile is honored by the human race (Psalms 12:7-8 [NIV]).

---

5 Soft kill: a method of destroying someone by ruining their reputation, blocking their income, and disarming them of resources and support.

February 8

With Godly principles we live better lives than they do.

The Internet helps us to connect with others and see that organized stalking is widespread. It is prevalent everywhere, including Germany, Tibet, UK, Japan, Canada, and the United States. Satan wants to win the world and has been busy recruiting, planning, and getting nervous about Jesus coming back. Those who follow the great deceiver, Satan, are also deceived. We are the Chosen Ones who must comfort those who are persecuted to the point of suicide. God will supply our needs, as we wear His protective armor and go into the trenches. The Bible tells us that we must put on the whole armor of God (see Ephesians 6:11). We must follow this action step as we dangerously battle for souls, including our own.

I stand in the evil day having my loins girded about with truth, and I have the Breastplate of Righteousness. My feet are shod with the gospel of peace. I take the Shield of Faith. I am covered with the Helmet of Salvation, and I use the Sword of the Spirit, which is the Word of God (Ephesians 6:13-17).

February 9

We are more important than this world makes us out to be.

The Bible tells us to guard our heart by putting on the Breastplate of Integrity (Ephesians 6:14 [Amp]). This does not mean that we walk around thinking we are *all that*. We practice integrity because we are the righteousness of God through His Son, Jesus. Having this faith gives us confidence and boldness. If we do not guard our heart, it can easily take on resentment, hatred, and anger. We cannot have access to heavenly kingdom power[6] if our heart is full of wickedness. We must also protect our heart from further breaking. We cannot walk around with a broken heart when we have work to do. We are not able to strive for excellence or function to the best of our ability with a broken heart—a condition we live with, but do not hear much about. When we engage in spiritual warfare, we must have hatred for evil spirits, not people. Jesus did not hate people. He hated evil. He commanded it to come out of possessed people because everything must bow down to Jesus. We have access to this power when we use His name, but our heart must be like His. We must function with a pure heart to have access to His might.

Today, I will picture myself putting on the Breastplate of Righteousness. This is heavy armor that covers and protects my chest. I will use it to protect my heart when the enemy tries to stab me with hatred and bitterness.

---

[6] Heavenly kingdom power: a spiritual reality where the rule of God presides.

February 10

God has us covered in every way for us to make it through this time.

In all forms of organized stalking, harassment, and torture, whether it be through energy weapons or a government agency designed to weed and seed undesirable people from a community, our way of thinking gets attacked. We cannot allow insanity to enter us, for we need to have our wits about us. The Helmet of Salvation covers our ears, eyes, nose, and mouth—those gateways through which we absorb things into our psyche. Demons tremble at the name of Jesus when we speak it with biblical scripture. So, we bind the strongman and rebuke his demons in Jesus' name. Targeted Individuals are the Lord's end-times warriors. Just as Satan has his soldiers set up in the world's system, Almighty God has also set us in place.

I break all agreements with hell in the name of Jesus (Isaiah 28:18).

February 11

We are to put on the whole armor of God for offensive fighting.

There were two TIs giving their testimony on the internet. One was frantically hiding behind sunglasses with a towel over her head while she nervously made her video. Fear got the best of her as she warned the world that evil was coming in all forms—even up from the ground in her backyard. "They are coming," she exclaimed. "Be ready. They are coming."

The other TI fought back by walking up to his stalkers to film them with his video camera. He put on the Breastplate of Righteousness before he proclaimed, "I am a human angel of The Lord." His Helmet of Salvation was in place as he confronted his enemies. His film portrayed the similarities of his stalkers: their eyes looked dead and their facial expressions were robotic. Some of us see it in our stalkers, while others are afraid to look. God's plan does not include us running away from our enemy. If it did, our armor would cover our backside. The full armor of God covers only our front. We are to run toward our enemies, not away from them (see Ephesians 6).

Today, I can be like either target above. The choice is mine.

February 12

We must go through hell to get to Heaven.

A middle-aged woman woke up in a hospital after being unconscious for three days. Her life would never be the same. As she lay alone in her hospital bed, she could hear the voices of what she assumed were the third-shift nurses down the hall, talking trash about her. Even after leaving the hospital, she continued to hear these voices. Skilled people are involved in conducting operations and overseeing that these up-to-date psychological weapons are administered to the public. The professionals involved in perpetrating these victims blend in society as everyday folk. They appear to look and act normal but secretly devote their passion to the Luciferian One World Order, working behind the scenes to destroy God's people. Voice to Skull (V2K) technology is probably the cause for this woman's demise. Similar victims are claiming to be tortured through implants and satellite technology. There will be a great surprise for these evildoers—the Luciferian gangstalkers—at God's appointed time. It is promised in the bible to come upon them suddenly.

Today, I will pick a scripture from the Word of God and recite it. I will overcome evil by knowing Who made me and to Whom I belong.

February 13

Idol hands belong to the devil.

We can sit where we are and sulk, or we can put on our armor and fight this battle. We cannot fight it by filing complaints with the FBI or taking vengeance into our own hands by spraying bullets everywhere. All the darkness in the world today is from a spiritual war going on between heaven and hell. People on Earth are suffering Satan's concerns of being in chains for one thousand years when Jesus returns. His time is running out, and so he has pulled out his biggest guns: Isis, chemical and electronic warfare, pornography, human trafficking, pedophilia, and gangstalking.

When Satan was Lucifer—God's most beautiful archangel, his pride caused him to get kicked out of Heaven, at which time, one third of the angels went with him. These fallen angels are the demons controlling the world today. The good news is: There are more of God's angelic warriors around us than demons. They are waiting to hear scripture come out of our mouth, so they can perk up and come to our rescue. God created them that way. That is why nothing happens when we complain our plead for help. David, the shepherd boy, hollered out scripture as he fought Goliath. The angels had his back and he won.

I pray for angels to be released to war against any spirit in the heavens that has been assigned to block my prayers from being answered (Daniel 10:12-13).

February 14

A practical working knowledge of reality is that all evil is connected, and the only way out is through Jesus.

When life gets us down, it behooves us to reach out and do something for someone else, even a needy animal. It changes our thoughts when we stop thinking about ourselves and what the lowlifes are doing to us. God is then able to take those things that were meant for evil and use them for good. We wonder if this applies to us even while our neighbors spy on us. Yes, but it takes discipline to smile when we walk outside. It takes everything we can muster up to get out of bed some mornings. It is hard to appear happy when we are not taking care of ourselves. When we are troubled, we need to carry on with baby steps toward self-care, so we can care for another. It is all spiritual, not terrestrial.

Today, I choose to be blessed instead of annoyed; I choose life instead of death.

February 15

God has called us out from the world.

All gangstalking and harassment recruits have different motives. Our stages of gangstalking can fluctuate from low-level street gangs up to the federal judicial system. These people feel important when other members look up to them. When lies spread like wildfire about a target, these vigilantes feel like they are doing something good for the world by removing undesirables. Satan has deceived these people. No matter from what level we are targeted, it is always done through mind control. Whether they want us to become experiments or commit suicide, it is an invasion of our lives. Some TIs find reprieve in wearing a hat lined with videotape or covering their ceilings with aluminum foil. It is all done in a desperate attempt to stop harmful Directed Energy Weapons from piercing through to their bodies. While isolated and without a friend in the world, we must try to stay centered in something greater than ourselves like Jesus. The Holy Bible was written through the apostles by the Holy Spirit; it has the answers we need. God made man. God made the devil. If they are persecuting us, God still made them. He has all the power. Jesus loves people so much that he died for us, promising to send us the Holy Spirit to guide us in all things. If, in fact, these are the end times, we should follow the written instructions left by our Creator. He knew these days were coming.

I rebuke all spirits of madness and confusion that would try to oppress my mind, in the name of Jesus (Ecclesiastes 7:7).

February 16

A target's life is made to be difficult by player-haters.

I am sitting in a 1970 Shasta travel trailer with no running water. I am grateful that I could pay for two weeks at a nice RV park where I am dwarfed by million-dollar motor homes. How lucky I am to look out the window and not have to see twenty trailers like mine. As I voyaged away from the brutal Chicago winters, I met a man who came to Wal-Mart for his daily coffee. He was a breath of fresh air, since he seemed intelligent and was polite to me. We talked as I had my oil changed in the truck. He admired my little retro travel trailer and wished he had one to break the wind. He had been living in a tent under a nearby bridge for nine months, since his company had closed due to the economy. His pride would not let him live with his oldest daughter. It was by choice that he lived under the bridge. He wanted to survive on his own, even if it meant dying. Whenever I get gloomy about my little trailer, I think of that man living under the bridge, trying to block the wind with canopies, while he would read novels by lantern. Life is hard with just the natural ebb and flow of life. The Lord will punish those who oppress others as He blesses the oppressed. Look at what God did to Lucifer for thinking he was better than God. Imagine what God will do to those perpetrators who have taken the gift God gave us—our life—and sabotaged it.

In the name of Jesus, I bind and cast out any spirit that would try to tear apart my life in any manner. (Mark 9:20)

February 17

You've got to get on top of it.
—Robert Blake

Having our things sabotaged is a personal violation. Our stuff means something to us, even if it is not expensive. Reaching into our closet for a shirt can turn our insides out, when we notice that everything we own has little tears. Finding a broken zipper on a new pair of pants or finding only one shoe to a pair can ruin our day. Having our furniture moved is infuriating. These mind games are designed to keep us off balance, when something goes missing and then reappears weeks later. It is a way the group lets us know they are watching us and are in control of our lives. After everything is either ruined or stolen, we begin to look at personal possessions as not having much meaning anymore. It is interesting how our perception changes. Our peace of mind becomes top priority, because life is not worth living without it. We cannot just end our lives if we believe that God needs us. We are here to help the world. Getting saved (reborn) seals the covenant relationship we have with Jesus and our Father. We work with them as they protect and guide us.

God, hide me from the secret counsel of the wicked.

February 18

The enemy looks for our vulnerabilities.

God uses ordinary people to carry out His purposes. We receive power through the Holy Spirit (Acts 1:8), who lives in us. This is how God does amazing things through us. After years of harassment, we desperately need something good to happen in our lives. Sometimes, taking a hot shower can be the highlight of our day. It is easy to spiral into depression when we develop habitual thinking about staying in bed all day. Some mornings, we might have to fight for a reason to get up. We've got to keep our head on straight, knowing we are not in this black hole because we willingly jumped into it. We have an army of player-haters who creep around the corners of our lives, hunting for cracks in our foundation where we might be vulnerable. They will not let anything take place that we want for ourselves. This form of oppression causes targets to kill themselves, but these perpetrators are not worth our energy. We mustn't commit suicide. It is simply not the way.

There are spiritual principles not of this world that I can live by today. I am a world overcomer. The favor of God surrounds me like a shield. The Holy Spirit dwells within me and directs me. My faith is the victory that overcomes this world.

February 19

If we pray to the Father according to His will, He hears us.

When Martha told Jesus that her brother Lazarus had died, Jesus waited four days before He responded. He put His ministry on the line when He called out for Lazarus to rise and come out of the tomb. Jesus always went to His Father in prayer first before he tackled anything. Then Jesus would thank Him for hearing His request. We can learn from this principle if we want to receive answered prayer. A petition prayer is when we take a Bible verse to God and ask Him for what we need. We must have faith that He hears us while we pray. We stand on God's Word by believing what it says.

Heavenly Father, I need Your Holy Spirit to help me to not dwell on what they are doing to me. By faith, I am not enslaved any longer. Help me to ignore those who spy on me. Help me to get on in life with the purpose you have for me. Father, I give You thanks for granting this prayer request, in Jesus' name. Amen.

February 20

Something good is going to happen to me and through me.

It is a fabulous thing when God intercedes and makes something good happen for us. The times in-between can be dark and long-suffering. This is when we continue to stand in faith by praising and thanking God for His blessings. These acts are like making small deposits into a bank account. The day comes when there is finally enough to draw from. God remembers all our small deposits of forgiveness, gratitude, kindness, worship, and friendship with Him. The only thing God forgets are the sins we confess and repent.

I will not conform to lowlife. I get a daily reprieve from insanity by keeping my eyes on what God wants me to do.

February 21

They think they are pushing us down, but really, they are pushing us up.

Their primary weapon is through deceptive mind games. Waking up in the morning to find all the dishes removed from the cabinets and placed on the counter is beyond upsetting. This kind of foolishness is a form of their arrogance; it seeps through the cracks of their existence, and it is easy to spot when you know what to look for. These ridiculous mind games give the target a mindset of powerlessness. It is so far-fetched that we are afraid to tell anyone about it, so we hang onto the secret and allow it to fester. Really, we are more inconvenienced than anything, because now we must put all the dishes back in the cupboards. A chemical or poison might have been sprayed on them, so they all need to be washed first. *Oh well, the cabinets needed some wiping down anyway.* What we really want to do is change the locks, install chains, and put bars in the windows, but we take care of ourselves the best we can. We take care of our pets. We continue to keep our focus on God and try to stay grateful and joyful. Sounds crazy? It is the opposite of how our enemy wants us to be. It is the only solution that works for us.

I do not fret or have anxiety about anything because God helps me to deal wisely in all the affairs of my life.

February 22

When I saw the movie, The Enemy of the State, *I cried out to my mom, "Look! This has been happening to me!"*

We were not born into this position by accident, and what a tough job it can be. The Good Lord has had His hand on us since before we were born because TIs are part of His End-Time Plan. As warriors, trendsetters, and strivers, we are designed to go it alone, against the norm. What a prestigious position! It is an honor to stand apart from the average Joe Schmoe. TIs are light years ahead of most people, but God's ways are not our ways, and His thoughts are not our thoughts. We are in this world, but not of it. And so, we must be coordinated with the Holy Spirit, who is our umbilical cord to Heaven. He softly tells us things that are to come, and whether we should go left or right at the crossroads of life.

Greater is He who is in me than he who is in the world. I can do all things through Christ who strengthens me. Alone, it would be impossible, but with God, all things are possible.

February 23

Each person is a listening device.
—Zeph Daniel

We know when we are being listened to. We know why neighbors approach us for a meaningless conversation with their cell phones nearby, so the group can tune in on their private network. Are we paranoid? Hardly, but it looks that way. The Mark of the Beast is a one-minded government where, if we do not comply, we will not be able to buy, sell, or trade. The Book of Revelation tells us all about it. People have somehow ignored that sixty-sixth book of the Bible. Satan might let us study the first sixty-five, but not the last book. Most pastors do not preach it, for fear of losing parishioners; most church goers want to hear from a feel-good preacher. The last book of the Bible uses symbols and can be difficult to understand. Even though it tells us there is a blessing in reading the Book of Revelation, we wind up putting it aside. Suppressing this important reading is a savvy move on the devil's part. Satan stays on top of us through our ignorance. He does not want us to know things. If he can keep us in the dark, he can keep us from having victory over him and this world.

I bind and rebuke all wrath the devil has directed against my life (Revelation 12:12).

February 24

There was a time when citizens had privacy.

Since the destruction of the United States' Twin Towers on September 11, 2001, the number of Americans watched by the government seems to be increasing. They still check our mail, phone calls, and e-mails, and they even log the books we check out at public libraries. It is all part of the plan for the New World Order (NWO)—a one-world government. U.S security agents have secretly infiltrated citizen organizations to spy on our activities to create databases on us. The government's success in ruining lives has a lot to do with their secrecy. The more secrecy involved, the more unaccountability we have, and the more unaccountability we have, the more mistakes are made. People start acting on their own behalf with their own interests in the forefront. With no laws against gangstalking, there is a lot of wiggle room for corrupt and evil gang activity. Hair-raising, lifelong penalties are put on people in retaliation for someone getting their feelings hurt. The continual electronic observation executed by neighbors is to control and dominate us. We have become prisoners in our own homes in America. It is the new Holocaust.

The Lord is my Helper—I will not fear, dread, or be terrified.

February 25

At some point, we will be running for our lives.

Organized stalking is like Communism, where government officials get people to go along with them. They may not go along voluntarily but concur out of fear. Any fear-based decision already has an evil bully-like element to it. TIs are entangled in an underground network of corrupt government surveillance for a life of total depravity. The greater our deprivation, the more they can victimize us. It is all about power. We can find similarities to this evil phenomenon in the Bible. King Solomon had put David under government surveillance. He sent messengers to David's house to watch him with plans of killing him in the morning (1 Samuel). But David had God's anointing on his life and always managed to escape. We cannot just sit around like a mouse in a cage. While our enemies keep us isolated, with no friends or family, we must be ready to get out of Dodge at any given moment. God will help us, but we must first help ourselves.

[Father, I ask you to help me, as I have been trying to do this myself.] Deliver me from the snare of the fowler and set me free. You are a shield to me, and under your wings I seek refuge (Psalm 91).

February 26

We have got to laugh to keep from crying.

We waste a lot of time when we look to people to save us. Our hope should be in the Living God who has power over all, not in people who can further deceive us. Our Heavenly Father would never want us to be bound by our enemies' plan of destruction, so we must pray for fellow TIs. We must not think this is about gangstalkers sabotaging only our lives but understand that this is worldwide spiritual warfare. It is about who gets the glory, Jesus or Satan? If we give Jesus the glory, we realize we are nothing without Him. We get victory in return when we give glory to God because Satan has already been conquered in the spirit realm.

Today, I will give God thanks for all my blessings, for I know they are from Him.

February 27

Gangstalkers feed on our fear and trauma; let them starve to death.

Fear will negate God's ability to deliver us. Deliver us from what? Deliver us from anything. We must not be afraid! Whenever we go anywhere on behalf of the Lord, we stay divinely protected. It has been this way since the beginning of time. Jesus says, *Fear Not.*

Lord, deliver me from men who are like lions (1 Chronicles 11:22).

February 28

Opposition means promotion is coming.

At 5 a.m., a teenage boy rolled up on a bicycle, wearing a full-face ski mask in the middle of summer. From across the silent street, he slowly and fiercely screamed: *This—is—not—your—world!* He then quietly rode away. Life as a TI can be bizarre, but we must not allow ourselves to stagger under the heavy load of these experiences. Throwing off the anxious thoughts and oppressive burdens that gangstalkers throw our way is done in one smooth thrust, as we decide to trust in the Lord for everything.

Today, I can get past anything thrown at me; I get relief by dropping the heavy load of being targeted.

February 29

God asks no man whether he will accept life. This is not the choice. You must take it. The only choice is how.
—Henry Ward Beecher

By Universal Law, the only way for us to be truly happy is to help others, but we are so isolated that we hardly have a chance. In the beginning phase of my gangstalking, I ran around with buckets of ice water for the loyal junkyard dogs that were often left to fend for themselves. I did this daily, finding such joy in watching them drink water like an alcoholic would guzzle down a cold beer. This mission became my daily passion, and I was on fire every morning. Something that was so minimized and disregarded within the community had become humungous for me. It utterly fulfilled me. I had found Paradise at the bottom of the barrel.

Today, I will not despise a small beginning.

A Bonus Reading

I threw my cell phone out the car window and onto a residential side street; I was sick of it. Within four days, it was back in my possession. A homeless man who walked around the Chicago neighborhood had found it. He handed it over to another guy—an unemployed man who had recently lost his car and his bicycle. He walked to a store to charge the phone, so he could locate me. My mother went to get it. The man told her, "It was the right thing to do." God reminded me of something regarding people that I had forgotten about.

God uses those whom we least expect to open our eyes. Once we find out that gangstalkers use our cell phones as intercoms to listen to us throughout the day; track us with GPS; read our text messages; intercept and redirect our calls; and answer our voice messages, we want to throw our cell phones away. Getting rid of our phone can stop a lot of harassment and become a huge turning point for us. We take everything apart to look for bugs while never realizing our cell phone could be the culprit, as it is constantly at our side. After losing everything, followed by years of torture, it is astounding that God would work through two homeless men to return a cell phone. Even after all empathy for humankind is gone, God makes a move. The power of good is so strong, it can wipe away the residuals left by evil.

I would have lost heart, unless I had believed that I would see the goodness of the Lord in the land of the living (Psalm 27:13 NKJV).

March 1

The simple act of being someone's friend can change their brain chemistry.
—from *The Soloist*

We grow quiet after realizing that things come back to bite us whenever we speak aloud. We know they are secretly listening in, so we stop talking. We begin to think a lot and become accustomed to living in our head; this is not good. For some of us, we even stop talking to our pets; again, not good. When a targeted individual is enmeshed in nationwide gangs and dirty-cop networks, it is difficult to succeed in life. Our every move is under constant surveillance and on public display. We are kept isolated for brainwashing. If you keep a man in the woods by himself, chances are he will change.

The same goes for us. The Lord knew these days would come and has given us everything we need to survive. He is our refuge and will shelter us in the storm. We are special; hence, the kingdom of darkness is trying to destroy us because we have an assignment to do. When we are doing what we should do, we stay under God's protection.

Lord, deliver me out from the hand of wicked and unreasonable men (2 Thessalonians 3:2).

March 2

Without justice, evil will get more evil.
—Dr. Bill Winston

Constant surveillance is a tool; the underworld of gangstalking and harassment would not be successful without it. Cameras, cell phones, fake Wi-Fi towers, thermal imaging, and trackers are only a few devices used to keep us under control. They need to watch us to stop any boundless thinking and liberated power of influence that we might have. The more information they can gather through surveillance, the more successful they are at controlling our moves. Through Remote Neural Monitoring (RNM)—a thought broadcasting system—the government can investigate our thoughts before ordering peon street soldiers to mess with us. These soldiers are also under control and scrutinized for the execution of these commands. Nobody gets out of this thing unscathed. Targets are complaining that with RNM, gangstalkers can make a mockery of our lives. We are between a hard place and a harder place. We are watched all day, while our thoughts are being monitored, and then we are mocked for thinking the way we do. Who would ever have thought?

The enemy will not eat my flesh, break my bones, and put me in his cauldron (Micah3:3).

March 3

Obstacles should not stop us; they were meant to expand us.

Even while our lives are scrutinized, we can still connect to other TIs through the Internet. Public computers are still available at local libraries and most cell phones have Internet service. We can search for information regarding counterspy equipment or listen to stories by other targets. We get a handle on how our neighborhood uses a private Wi-Fi tower to network with one another around our home. We can also share this information with other TIs. We get ideas and find solutions to similar problems like: what to do with a shared wall between our apartment and our landlord's place? We watch a video on how a target simply tapes cheap headphones to the adjoining wall, while turning on the connected radio, real low. It acts as a sound barrier whether the channel is tuned to music or news, and it will not bother us in our environment because we cannot hear it. We will soon know if it works by our landlord's behavior. Property owners are strong links in the chain of gangstalking. We must be careful not to get too smart or we might end up without a rental. We could be back in our parents' basement, or in an abandoned van in their yard, or a pitched tent in the woods. The group's main concern is to have access to us. They do not care where we live. We should share any counterspy tactics, coping skills, and helpful information with fellow TIs. It could save a life.

God, let me increase in wisdom and stature (Luke 2:52).

March 4

We must not be timid or embarrassed to command evil spirits from our lives. Jesus talked at demons. We can too.

As we learn about different spirits, we can discern which ones are around us. It seems like a lot of them gather around our home to harass us. However, it is the Hittite spirit that pretends to be a friend. Usually, this is someone who associates with us somehow. This spirit is full of schemes and will bait us and then set us up, so they can steal our personal energy. When this spirit is working through a perpetrator, he will do evil things to us with a smile on his face as he stabs us in the back. When we see these evil things happening nearby, we can verbally thwart our enemy with the power of Jesus' name.

You, Hittite spirit, I take authority over you, in the name of Jesus. You will not bring deception or wickedness to my life any longer. You will not disguise yourself as a friendly neighbor or someone who cares about me. I command you to cease your activity in my life right now, in Jesus' name. Amen.

March 5

I plead the blood of Jesus over my mind.

A Holocaust survivor remembers being grateful for lice. It was a lice infestation and disgusting living conditions that kept the German Nazi guards away from a wooden barrack at Auschwitz. These Jewish prisoners were not under constant watch, and so, they took advantage of the opportunity to encourage classroom education for the children.

Just for today, I can find something to be thankful for.

March 6

Having to relocate every year is a process of elimination.

Perpetrators love it when we just sit and do nothing. They prefer us to exist on lower energy frequencies like sadness and hopelessness, while they use our creative and joyful energy for themselves. It is like breaking the spirit of a dog by keeping him chained, while loose dogs play around him. Learned helplessness is a by-product of this passive-aggressive abuse. Each place that we call home seems to get smaller, as does our world. We are squashed into mere existence, while being kept as an energy source for the demonic spirits that work through our perpetrators. Their deeply embedded hooks make it impossible to free ourselves from their entanglement. The Bible refers to these spirits as "principalities in high places". We cannot fight them on a physical level, since they are spiritual beings and way too powerful. We must encourage ourselves to stand tall. We wait for the Lord to consume them with the breath of His mouth and destroy them with His brightness (2 Thessalonians 2:8).

Lord, punish those who try to oppress me (Jeremiah 30:20).

March 7

The Word of God is like a lamp onto our path.

There is nothing a dark spirit can say to the Word of God. There is nothing it can do except disappear in the light. The Living Words of the Bible are the weapons we use to survive in any dark place, at any given time. When the Spirit of Truth abides in us, He shows us those things we were not able to see before. It is like a light goes on and we no longer doubt ourselves. With the Holy Spirit, we do not have to question the V2K that is pretending to be the Voice of God in our head. We can recognize these thoughts and ideas as being manufactured. We can cast them down in the name of Jesus without having any doubt about ourselves.

The Spirit of truth abides in me and teaches me all things. Therefore, He guides me into all truth.

March 8

The storm may be over, but the muck needs time to settle.

Our perpetrators will take everything good that we have done and use it for themselves. They will take the creative energies from our accomplishments and apply them to their own life. Though they hate us, they cannot live without us. They are like vampires that need the blood of a living creature to survive. Targeted individuals have, unfortunately, become bottom feeders to the high-ranking demons that possess our perps. We must verbally cast the millstone around their neck and command that everything they touch turn to dust! They do not have the authority to rob us of our accomplishments, and they must cease and desist from our life. So be it, in the Almighty Name of Jesus. God has amazing grace that has kept us, sustained us, and given us the things we need for our calling. People of God should not back down or slide away from their purpose. We might be called to save lives. We might be called to slay dragons.

When people despise me, it is a confirmation that whatever God has called me to do will be my greatness.

March 9

A condensed version of the serenity prayer: "F–it!"

It is not so much about the practicing of faith, as it is in making a choice to walk in it or not. When our tolerance level gets to the point of combustion, it is better for us to do a cut version of the serenity prayer than to get into trouble. That is, we throw our hands up and say *forget it!* We do not need to wind up in a dire situation behind our actions. The haters will bully and suppress us in hopes that we self-destruct. F–them, too!

It is okay to take the easy road today.

March 10

We must somehow learn to survive this, or we won't.

The concept of thoughts having energy hit the West Coast recovery scene, big time, in the 1990s. The teachings of a new and hip physician swept through the 12-step programs like wildfire. It seemed everyone in recovery was talking about how we attract those things that we think about. Dr. Deepak Chopra spoke about atoms, leptons, nuclear forces, and our thoughts having energy. The same concept is found in the Bible. God's Words are the Sword of the Spirit because they are alive. There is a battle for our soul taking place right now in the spirit realm. As we recite scripture aloud, our words are slaying dragons in this unseen world. Our faith can protect us from anything that comes to hurt us or tries to take us out. We fight back with words that have spiritual energy to annihilate our opponent.

Today, I will fight the good fight of faith by confessing the Word of God (1Timothy 6:12).

March 11

We must ignore the voices of insults and horrors.

Multitudes of people are complaining about the invasive technology of Voice to Skull (V2K). Some TIs deal with auditory voice frequencies in their ear canals: voices that talk nonsense by repeating words like freak, loser, slut, and faggot, to name a few. TIs who suffer like this must be extraordinary people to be nominated for such an elaborate operation of silencing. God knew these perilous times would come, and He made sure to give us a heads up about them in the Bible. Everything seems to be in there: stalking, mobbing, betrayal, smear campaigns, bullying, oppression, isolation, suicide, hatred, violation, running, hiding, hunting, and killing. The Bible also displays heroic stories of overcoming, escaping, and rising above circumstances. Jesus proclaimed that His sheep know His voice, and the voice of a stranger, they will not follow. It is plain and simple: When we hear other voices, we should ignore them.

I bind and rebuke the spirit of double mindedness, in the name of Jesus (James 1:8).

March 12

Gangstalking perpetrators are all one-minded.

A tragic story hit the evening news about a grandmother who took her grandchild to the shopping mall, only to push the child off a tier. The child died at the hospital. It was someone who the child trusted that tricked her into plunging to her death. Deception and wickedness are spirits functioning within our gangstalking neighborhood. When we must deal with someone to either service our home, automobile, or to just cut our hair, we are apt to run into these evil spirits of trickery. Gangstalkers act friendly, funny, and loving, but all the while they are planning to push us off a tier and trick us into plunging to our death. Really, we cannot trust any of them.

But the Lord your God will deliver them over to you and will inflict defeat upon them until they are destroyed (Deuteronomy 7:23).

March 13

Just because we expect integrity from others does not mean they have it.

There is a characteristic trait that an undercover cop or gangstalking perpetrator must retain to keep up a front for the sake of destroying someone down the road. To invite a person over for dinner is a form of politeness and a sacred practice in many cultures. The idea of being phony while breaking bread with someone is outrageous. Regardless of their status in life, gangstalkers do not have integrity. Whether they come over for dinner to unlock the bathroom window, so that another member can steal selected items, or they sit on their throne of knowledge but say nothing, makes them all the same: They lack integrity. They do not have morals, principles, or values. The sooner we accept this, the better off we are.

Lord, help me to see that sometimes, I am better off alone, while depending on the Holy Spirit for my next move.

March 14

Many church people are just plain fake while hiding together under the hidden evil of dark spirits; surely, they are spiritual fakes.

There are spirits in the church that are not of God. They are not difficult to spot: those clingy spirits of heaviness and discouragement with sister spirits of oppression and control. However, the most mean, perverted, and demonic spirits are often found with the daily church goers—those who read passages from the pulpit on Sunday mornings or assist the pastor in some way. Nothing is as demonic as when a TI reaches out in sheer and utter desperation, but no one from the church grabs hold of them. It is beyond words: the pain of barely existing after a brutal assault, without one parishioner extending a helping hand. This is the ugly underbelly of community gangstalking as it flourishes in broad daylight. We must press ahead and not allow Satan's demons to constrict us or weigh us down. With the all-seeing eye of God's Holy Spirit, we must make ourselves get up, pick up, and look up, before we can shake this one off.

If anyone does attack you, it will not be my doing; whoever attacks you will surrender to you (Isaiah 54:15 [NIV].)

March 15

Those who follow others, sacrifice themselves in shadows that do not belong to them.
—Russ Dizdar

Surprise! It's gangstalking in *Alice's Wonderland*. Just when we did not think things could get any more bizarre, yet another level of gangstalking unfolds before our very eyes. We watch in perplexity as a neighbor invests an exorbitant amount of time and energy to impersonate us. Everything about us is copied to a T: hair color, style of clothing, personal hobbies, and even home and garden purchases like a shed or a back deck. It is a sick and twisted level of obsession that develops, when a perp with a flimsy character loses control, while observing a targeted individual. It is along the same lines as a private detective falling in love with a subject that he has been assigned to watch, but with an added component of envy and danger. This can easily happen to an empty vessel or weak-minded gangstalking voyeur, who is overly zealous to finally become somebody within the group. It reminds me of the movie *Single White Female* with Bridget Fonda, where a woman goes on a killing spree while obsessed with taking over her roommate's identity. Nevertheless, it can be alarming, since we do not know their next move or if we will be killed for our identity. In some cultures, like with the Fijian tribe members, the practice of eating the bodies of rival warriors—which is a revolting act to us—is a sacred ritual to depict total victory: a finality, if you will. We wonder, *does this obsessed perp plan to eat me for total consumption of my soul?* A perp can get jealous of a TI receiving too much attention from the group. Most gangstalking perps were once empty vessels. Now demon-possessed, they have an insatiable need to feed off us. It is not a time to get discouraged, nor to be bullied into paranoia. We double up on our prayers and speak scriptures aloud. We speak *at* the problem using Jesus' name. Changing our thought-focus will alter our mood and experience, as we cling to God for dear life.

Dear friends do not be surprised at the fiery ordeal that has come on you to test you, as though something strange were happening to you. (1 Peter 4:12 NIV)

March 16

I will not die, but I will live, and proclaim what the Lord has done (Psalm 118:17).

We are kept in isolation and desolation for years. Nobody talks to us, unless they have plans to set us up for something. Gangstalking is like any other form of oppression and slavery: It has been around for centuries and merely wears a different mask. During the Civil War, plantation owners would feed their families the best parts of chickens, hogs, and cattle. They would send the guts and intestines down to the slaves' quarters. This was done on purpose: to feed the slaves those foods which could not strengthen them, for fear if they were fed healthy foods, they would become strong enough to escape. Likewise, we must keep our spirit strong, in case we are attacked with beams of electromagnetic energy that will weaken our body and mind. Jesus taught us about taking authority and how practicing His teachings would strengthen us. If we feed on the Word of God, we become strong in the power of His might; hence, our spirit can take over in times of physical and mental torture. Our spirit is *of* God, and He will help us to distinguish what thoughts are real and how our body should be functioning. A strong spirit, anchored in God's Word, will keep us from buying into those electronically induced thoughts and emotions that are not ours.

Today, I make a conscious choice about how I perceive my world. I recognize how powerful my spirit can be.

March 17

Ambulances and firetrucks are big contributors in gangstalking noise campaigns.

I used to wonder why some 911-calls did not arrive in time and innocent people had to die.

No one can control the wind or stop his own death. No soldier is released in times of war, and evil does not set free those who do evil (Ecclesiastes 8:8.)

March 18

We are up against pure evil wanting to take us out.

Life with the Lord—whom we turn to when we are in deep trouble—may confront us with new challenges. At first, we may have our doubts about God when He does not fix our situation. In time, we receive eye-opening knowledge on how to live amid the persecutors around us. We must still live our lives: play catch with the dogs; hang laundry on the line; finish reading a book. Sometimes, when we get a reprieve from the harassment, we begin to slack off on our relationship with God. We stop praying, reading warfare prayers, listening to encouraging preachers, and reading inspirational books. The reprieve does not last long. We are soon challenged with new problems: relocation, vehicle breakdown, an overcharge on a utility bill, or severe headaches and ringing in our ears. We quickly see how we need a relationship with the Holy Spirit. We cannot meet the many challenges of being a targeted individual without Him.

Today, I jump back on the bandwagon of spiritual growth, so that I will be guarded and guided through life.

March 19

There are some battles not worth fighting.

We must renew our mind by practicing a new way of thinking, instead of trying to sway gangstalkers from messing with us. Why? Because it doesn't work. When we waste our time with gangstalking informants, we end up with the short end of the stick, every time. Their main goal is to kill us by suicide. Our best bet is to ignore them. Without a doubt, after many smiles and friendly conversations, they will throw us a curveball from left field, e.g., while we are kept occupied, another member will go into our house to lace our food with tiny amounts of poison. We have not had the full flavor of being targeted, until we have experienced being attacked with drugs and poisons. They will do this to us, while wearing a smile on their face. For our own good, we should keep people at a distance.

Today, I will set aside my ordinary routine to refresh my mind through rest, change, and meditation.

March 20

A handler will always give a gift to their assigned target. We must beware of attached curses.

A friendship cannot be our source of happiness or sorrow. We are neither the slave nor keeper of our enemy. We are pursued by people who thrive off our energy, joy, and life purpose. They strive to steal it from us, leaving us to barely survive. To hell with them.

I will not try to get certain people to like me. I do not have to learn through bitter experience that trying to change the mind of an enemy is fruitless.

March 21

You are either with me or against me.
—Jesus Christ

Jesus, too, was a targeted individual of gangstalkers and hate groups.

I realize that it is not beneficial to hate them because they hate me, or to become evil because they are.

March 22

Gangstalkers will brutalize us with the very things we want.

After a decade of harassment, I prayed aloud for my own modest home—somewhere, I would not be forced to move from every two years. How dare my neighbors listen to my prayers and then set me up! A realtor in Southern Illinois offered his cabin to me on a land contract. Before the closing of Escrow, he invited me to spray wash and paint the cabin, as well as replace a large picture window, since he and his brother would help me. The deal turned out to be *three card Monty*. His game plan was to use me to upgrade his cabin, before sending me on my way. When perpetrators hone in on our emotions, we can find ourselves exhausted from being conned, manipulated, and used. We must always guard ourselves from giving away more than we can handle. These bullies can be anyone from a realtor, lawyer, reverend, tree cutter, stump remover, gang member, or stay-at-home mom. They come in all sizes and from all levels of society. They work together to lure us in, before setting us up for failure. We work at letting go of people, places, and things.

They will be paid back with harm for the harm they have done. Their idea of pleasure is to carouse in broad daylight. They are blots and blemishes, reveling in their pleasures while they feast with you (2 Peter 2:13 [NIV]).

March 23

It is challenging to start any process of healing when the knockdowns never end.

Jay was a quiet, thirty-five-year-old man, who installed custom glass for a living. He drove a nice truck and lived in a great beachside apartment. At some point, this handsome man had been deliberately introduced to crystal methamphetamine. He thought he had died and gone to Heaven when he suddenly had friends who wanted to do things with him. His apartment was always full of people who were partying and having fun. After the group had gotten him for everything he had, they cut off all contact with him. He stood alone in his barren apartment, unemployed and broken. He had nothing left to his name except a mean habit to kick. The bitterness of being used as a patsy kept him from moving ahead. The Bible warns us to guard our heart. Oh, how bitterness can destroy us faster than anything. Our bitterness will stand between us and any blessings. We must strengthen ourselves with the Word of God. It is the only thing guaranteed to work, because we are not fighting against flesh and blood but against principalities that rule the air: demonic spirits, we cannot see.

Father deliver me from the manifestations of my enemies. They tear me in their wrath. They hate me for no reason. They gnash me in their teeth. They sharpen their eyes upon me (Job 5: 4-31).

March 24

We should not curse the storm that is developing us into greatness.

Being gang stalked is like being thrown out to sea in uncharted waters, with no knowledge of sailing. Our unrealistic expectations of how others should treat us can spiral our emotions into an abyss of depression. We must take accountability for our own course, even when we drift. Our own self-care must always be on the top of the list. We sit at the gates of hell, as they beat our soul into submission and watch us slowly die. They do not care that this could take years. They do not give up, until we have been expunged.

I am responsible to find a new way of life for myself. I can do it by following the spiritual warfare strategies taught by Jesus. With new tools, I can responsibly climb out from the pit of despair.

March 25

Justice is very important to the heart of God.

Satan is busy building his own laws, trying to get Godly people to bow down to them. Church folk are the first to bow down to Satan when they take part in community gangstalking. They either sell out for mere favors, or they agree to participate to be a part of the community involvement. Still, it's always astounding to see a church-going Christian participate in organized gangstalking. The devil wants them as badly as he wants us. The closer we are to God, the more of a threat we are to the kingdom of darkness. We could never be so heartless as to drive a person to suicide, while secretly watching the whole thing unfold. The Lord will deal with these people His own way. If a reborn Christian decides to become a perpetrator, he is doing it while knowing God. We pity these pathetic souls that will come against the wrath of God. It is one thing to sin while not knowing Jesus; it is another thing to murder one of his sheep while knowing Him.

I do not have to concern myself with payback. The Lord says, "Vengeance belongs to me, and I will recompense" (Romans 12:19).

March 26

Gangstalkers are not only sent in to destroy us but to also watch God's anointing on our life.

The justice system is a main ally of demonic abuse. Targeted Individuals are at the center of local police networks that entangle us in legalities at our local courthouse. High-tech surveillance equipment overpowers us, as these organizations tamper with our lives through air waves for audio and video spying. The closest we get to having any proof of this is when our computer spyware alerts us: Your email is being concurrently used from another location. These militant and mafia-like groups are not interested in destroying terrorists who are threatening our nation, but rather those citizens whose names have been put on a Weed and Seed list.[7] National involvement means federal funding and federal involvement. These crimes are run by spiritual principalities in high places: Satanists.

Lord, let those who seek after my soul be ashamed and confounded. Let those who desire my hurt be turned backward and put to confusion (Psalm 70:2).

---

[7] Operation Weed and Seed is a multi-agency strategy that weeds out socially undesirable people living in local communities.

March 27

Baptism is a step toward Heaven, while we wait in the bowels of hell.

Water baptism is a refreshing life saver and can help us to endure persecution by strengthening our spirit. A strong spirit helps us to undergo things like having to move every two years and winding up with worse neighbors than before. Relocation is number two on the list for life's most stressful events. Number one is death. Baptism by immersion can be empowering for those who suffer from psychotronic assaults. When our body is in a weakened state, and our mind is not functioning as it should, we must rely on our spirit to get us through the day. Jesus refers to the Holy Spirit as our comforter. We should, too.

My body may collapse, but they won't break my spirit.

March 28

I never drank alcohol before I became gang stalked. I learned how to drink by throwing back a shot of ice-cold whisky and then quickly washing it down with Coca Cola to bypass the awful taste. I would feel it burn my insides as it went down, and my body would quiver while it wanted to reject the poison. I just wanted to change the way I felt and numb the pain of loneliness.

I was standing in a checkout line, drunk on whiskey, while feeling compelled to unload on the woman behind me. "They follow me everywhere," I blurted out. "I can't get rid of them." Her eyes grew like saucers, and her body jerked so hard, it was like someone pushed her from behind. To this day, I believe that it was either an angel behind her or the Holy Spirit inside her. She quickly fumbled in her purse to write something down, before handing me a small card with these written words: Read Psalms 18, 37, and 91 aloud. After staring into my eyes for a few seconds, she then whispered, "He sees everything you are going through." We never know how God is going to come through for us. He puts people in places to do things. When we do not see Him working in our lives, He is working things out backstage.

Lord, thank You for instructing me in the ways I should choose (Psalm 25:12).

March 29

Gangstalking stays in constant motion, while we stay stuck.

Since our adversaries want to take us out and make it look like an accident, we are always in a life-or-death situation. Satan is the deceiver of all time, and our perpetrators have sold their souls to him. Everything is secretive. Most of our perps do not know us, and we do not know them. However, if we happen to associate with them, they will not talk about it, nor will they give off their involvement. The deception does not stop with them rerouting our emails or watching us through spy cameras around our home. It would be nothing out of the ordinary for them to misinform our family in the cause of our death. Making a homicide look like an accident is not a big stretch. There are members who do nothing but loosen every nut and bolt on a vehicle, so the target loses control while driving. It looks like an accident and nobody gets blamed. The people involved will offer their condolences at our funeral, while hiding any involvement in the ending of our life.

Today, I will not be ignorant. I will not let myself believe that evil spirits have boundaries.

March 30

Jesus supplies our needs, for us to blossom.

We can live beyond the Hit. We can rise above their military methods of pursuit: bullying and casting burdens on us. We can blossom, even while we do not receive kindness from anyone. We can bloom through the deprivation of relationships, romance, kisses, and hugs. The removal of these things is to cause us to suffer—and die—before our time. If we are, in fact, end-time warriors, these methods of torture are to push us to live on a higher level of consciousness. For us to survive, we need to create an environment where we can safely flourish. If we begin to do the things we can, the Lord will do those things we cannot. He is our soul provider.

I will not be afraid of ten thousand that have set themselves against me, because You, God, are a shield for me (Psalm 3:1-6).

March 31

When we stare at what is wrong in our lives, it distracts us from what God would have us do.

Recently, I began questioning whether I had taken a wrong turn in my life, or if I was destined to live a life of gangstalking for a higher purpose. To go from living a life of receiving honor and respect and love from my bodybuilding fans to a life filled with hatred and repulsion from people seems too puffed up for one person to have caused. One Saturday night, an audacious, alcoholic Catholic priest sternly stared at me from his podium for what seemed like 30 seconds before he began his sermon with, "Some things we can blame ourselves for." He was basically saying it was my fault that the community inflicted their hate crimes on me: extortion, rape, and burglary. Of course, he had to do this during mass, in front of a church full of locals. Gangstalking perps infiltrate everywhere. I had become privy to the spiritual fakes and the involvement in secret societies, within that small community church. God had called me out because the Holy Spirit's presence was not there. As a child, I learned to endure extreme measures while being raised by a strict Sicilian father. His love, rage, and violence were critical in my early development. Years later, my heavy-weight training, coupled with a lifestyle of deprivation, was also extreme. Being gang stalked is an awesome cross for anyone to carry. I pick it up and follow Jesus, who told me to deny myself (I learned to put aside worldly cravings to become a champion) and take up my cross (which is big and heavy, but I am strong) and follow Him (whom I have known my whole life). I have concluded that I am here to carry this burden for the Lord.

Today, I take my eyes off what I think is wrong and lay them on Who I am following.

April 1

Once you focus on something and give it meaning, it produces an emotion. These emotions filter what we do and trigger actions or even non-actions.
—Tony Robbins

Our mindset is something we can govern, no matter what we are going through. Our thought life can be a redeeming quality, particularly each time we get knocked down. The demons that control our perpetrators live off our energy, while they study us like lab rats and leave us depleted. Mostly, they like to harass us in public. Sometimes, we do not get a chance to regroup in between the episodes of harassment, so we struggle to discipline our thoughts each time we get assaulted. When we practice the mindset of pleasing

God and not the world, we can make a habit of thinking suitable thoughts. Then we do not have to fight to regroup after each strike. By preparing our mindset, we can keep a level of peace while we overcome another round of cruel punishment.

This Book of the Law shall not depart out of my mouth, but I shall meditate on it day and night. For then, I shall make my way prosperous, and then I shall deal wisely and have good success (Joshua 1:8 [AMP]).

April 2

The burden of suffering seems to be a tombstone hung around our necks. Yet in reality it is simply the weight necessary to hold the diver down while he is searching for pearls.
—Julius Richter

When God calls us to do something, it is not unusual to find excuses why we cannot do it. Most of us are living lower than ever, after years of being gang stalked. How could we fulfill a calling from God? We might be living without running water, or our computer is old and slow, or we are watched too closely—how do we pull it off? In the Book of Judges, the Israelites were oppressed by the people of the East, known as the Midianites. The Israelites were made to live in caves, while the Midianites set up tents all around them, so they could be watched. This is similar to how we live, with perpetrators as our neighbors. The Israelites got knocked down every time they did something good for themselves. Just as oppressed and harassed as we are today, the Israelites were outnumbered, overpowered, and impoverished. Whenever they planted vegetable seeds in their gardens, the Midianites snuck over and pulled up the roots. Another example of finding excuses is when the Lord told Gideon to save Israel. Gideon told God why he could not do such an important thing: first, his bloodline was poor, and secondly, he was the least important of his family. The Lord assured Gideon that He would surely be with him in whatever he called him to do (Judges 6:16). Our excuses may sound legitimate to us, but nothing is impossible with God. If He calls us to do something, He will supply all our needs, and we will be under an umbrella of protection. This does not mean that our calling will be a cakewalk. We will always have tribulation in this unjust and evil world. We overcome it by our faith.

God, help me to see that it is because of my position that you are calling me, and not that I am unable to do it because of my position.

April 3

They have prepared a net for my steps; my soul is bowed down; they have dug a pit before me; into the midst of it they themselves have fallen (Psalm 57:6).

It is not uncommon that Satan would send messengers and evil spirits to keep us from our destiny. He did it with Apostle Paul, which he called *"a thorn in the flesh"* (2 Corinthians 12:7). Paul preached the Gospel everywhere he went, while winning souls for the kingdom of God. At the same time, Satan sent him an evil spirit of temptation. Some people assume it was Lust that Paul begged God to remove, but the Bible does not say. God assured Paul, He would give him the strength needed whenever he was too weak to resist. We can relate to how Paul must have felt. Here we are: living with no privacy; constantly harassed and feeling the frustration of having our life deliberately railroaded. Our options look bleak. We could turn to alcohol to numb our pain, but it might interfere with our relationship with God. Satan sends those temptations to distract us and keep us from our duty. We cannot allow the devil to talk us out of the very reason we are here.

Today, I lay aside the pain of being targeted as I renounce the spirits of bitterness and oppression. Father, I thank you for removing any mental strongholds, so I can think and see more clearly.

April 4

He tells us, "Be still, and know that I am God."

In a world where people strive to stay busy, God will, ever so gently, get our attention one way or another. Being still can take great patience, when it looks and feels like procrastination and laziness. We are living in a time when we cannot pause for a second while driving without someone honking their horn at us. The noisy hustle and bustle of our lives drowns out God's ever-soft voice. Even if we are isolated and living in silence, our negative thinking can be the noise that blocks us from hearing Him. We pray for a certain thing, but we often do not wait to hear back from God. Instead, we are directed by our own thinking, so we quickly jump up and go on our way. We waste a lot of time and energy by not being still. We need to wait for God to respond to our prayers.

Today, I will make time to be quiet, understanding that the Holy Spirit whispers while the devil uses a loud speaker.

April 5

We learn discomfort and how to stay alive through it.

We stand stronger by ourselves than if we were to get caught up in the mix of things. The world has let us down. We cannot function like other worldly players especially, if we have been straight jacketed.[8] People seem to make a mess of things that should be joyous for us. Our problems are no longer resolved with worldly solutions. We must tackle our dilemma, supernaturally, while we use kingdom principles like Jesus' name; the Blood of Jesus; a life of prayer; speaking in tongues; worship; and confessing scriptures aloud. Satan rules over this world by deceiving many people who live in the darkness of ignorance. His ways are twisted to look like God's ways, when they are not. He has even hoodwinked gangstalkers into believing that they are not under some sort of observation themselves. So, we stop worrying about this fallen world and start learning the ways of God. No man will be able to close doors that God opens, nor open doors that He closes.

He who walks uprightly walks securely, but he who takes a crooked way shall be found out and punished (Proverbs 10:9 [AMP]).

---

8 Straight jacketing: when the entire county is organized as a tactical unit, and the targeted individual is harassed and stalked by what will appear to be the entire world; leaving him/her isolated and helpless.

April 6

None of us know what tomorrow will bring; woe to them, who think they do.

The Lord despises the proud and haughty person who thinks they are bigger than Him. The wicked ones are the gangstalkers who violate and hurt people for the sake of belonging to a group. Their vicious acts are laced with an arrogance that blatantly shouts, *there is nothing you can do about it!* These people are very much *of* the world, running around like they know what tomorrow holds. In fact, their mindset is that they will make tomorrow better by doing whatever they want today. These people will face destruction. The Bible refers to them as scoffers—the wicked ones.

Lord, let them be confounded and troubled forever. Let them be put to shame and perish. (Psalm 83:17)

April 7

You got to take the hits and keep getting up; you got to keep moving forward.

I started my bodybuilding career watching all the *Rocky* sequels over and over for inspiration. I trained in a huge gym where 5-gallon buckets were strategically placed to catch the water whenever it rained. It was nothing fancy, just old-school, hardcore weight training. We didn't wear spandex, but rather cotton sweats and knit caps. I jumped rope in my basement, while I washed my sweat clothes and let the cold rinse water stay in the sink tubs for soaking my shins afterwards. Those were the days when I had nothing but heart. As I went from winning state competitions to national titles, I turned professional and won the World Championships. Watching Rocky Balboa was a huge part of my success. Ironically, fifteen years later, around the time the last Rocky movie was in the making, I was being targeted and held hostage near the Long Beach, California junkyards. While street gangs worked on stealing my storage unit, including my collection of movies, awards, and bodybuilding memorabilia, I would interact daily with a group of twenty-some people that lived in the area. They pretended to be friendly, while they had their eyes set on my material valuables, as well as on my soul. They lived in warehouses and containers. One couple lived on a trucking yard in the cab of a broken-down big rig.

One night, I came to my senses and realized that they wanted to turn me into a desperate woman. I was down there long enough to watch them do it to other women who turned tricks for a hit of crack or a line of crystal meth. It had been two years of taking their punches and getting back up. Each beating was worse than the last one, and I had lost everything, including a tooth. I was hearing underlying messages from the locals that I had overstayed my welcome and that it was high time for me to get rolling. Being tough with a high threshold for pain was great for winning bodybuilding championships, but I was out of my element. Taking too many punches would leave these haters no other choice than to murder me. They could do it, too, by drugging us and setting my trailer on fire, with all three of us locked in it. We could easily be drugged and thrown into a container where nobody could hear us for miles or sent off in the back of a big rig for parts unknown, to never be seen again. For less drama, they could simply dig a hole and throw us in it or drop us into the nearby ocean, with God knows what else is out there. Hell, they could burn me at the stake and nobody would talk. Anything was possible in "hell's gateway". They had already drugged me and my dogs, while causing us several close calls that could have left any one of us maimed for life. Through all their efforts, they never got what they really wanted: my soul. I never sold it, and I never gave it away. Every day, I thank God that I am blessed and that I can never be cursed. To this day, I do not feel badly about myself. I feel sad that those creeps do what they do, to people not as blessed as me—those men, women, and children who never make it out because they do not get back up.

For though the righteous fall seven times, they rise again, but the wicked stumble when calamity strikes (Proverbs 24:16).

April 8

There are six things the Lord hates, and the seventh is detestable to him: a person who stirs up conflict in the community (Proverbs 6:16-19 [NIV]).

We seem to attract one-minded people, no matter where we live. In my case, I am dealing with a female neighbor who has just reached the highlight of her life by becoming an organized gangstalking perpetrator. Since childhood, she daydreamed about playing Special Agent 99 from *Get Smart* and is now overly eager to begin her spying debut. She starts off overly friendly, only to stab me with occasional and subtle verbal insults. Each time, her eyes exhibit the lustful fulfillment of a starving hyena, feeding on a carcass. Perps will use the technique of reeling us in with kindness and then softly abusing us in increments. This game is supernatural and nothing other than demonic. I start to watch her as she comes and goes in her everyday life. I can clearly see the weight of misery on her, because when a human being engages in behavior that is morally wrong, it takes its toll. Although Satan runs this world, it still belongs to God, and He has His way of dealing with sin. We can examine the unfolding of a perpetrator's self-destruction with our gift of discernment, which we obtain and maintain by knowing the Holy Spirit. We can watch the entanglement of our enemy's feet as they get caught in their own net (Psalm 57:6). When we follow kingdom principles (that is, we work under God's Laws) and live by a different standard of rules, we will watch our enemies hang themselves with the rope they meant for us. This is how God works. He takes those things that were meant for evil and turns them around for our good.

Cursed is the one who attacks his neighbor secretly (Deuteronomy 27:24).

April 9

The Holy Spirit led me to what I needed to know. I thanked God and praised Jesus all the way home.

Every now and then, we need a two-day reprieve from the insanity, and we can have it if we play our cards right. It is good for us to fast from all the hatred, redundant community-watching, telephone-redirecting, street theater, and the endless mind games that organized stalkers bring to the table. We must never discuss our plans of escape, since they hear everything we talk about. If we can quickly and quietly disconnect from everything, it will usually take the group a couple days to hook back into us. Cell phones are our number one enemy, given that they help our perps track us; read our texts; hear our conversations; and listen to our daily moves. Taking off with our cell phone is fine, if we remove the battery. We can still carry it with us for an emergency. Two days of fasting from the craziness, incorporated with relaxation and prayer, can bring healing to our body, mind, and the whole essence of our being. It can help us to function at a higher level of energy and, maybe even, find the answer to an unsolved matter.

Lord, I know that when I fast in secret, you reward me openly (Matthew 6:18).

April 10

God has supernatural solutions to our problems, even before we know what they are.

The Bible offers us solutions to get our hopes up, when we have no hope left and everything looks impossible. Here are some impossible situations that prove nothing is too hard for God:

Apostle Peter was in jail, expecting to be executed the following morning, when God sent angels to rescue him. When the guards mysteriously fell asleep, an angel escorted Peter out of his cell. The next day, no one could figure out what had happened. A lot of times, when God has His hand on something, there are no logical explanations. Case in point: God sent an angel to tell Mary that she would become pregnant while remaining a virgin; thus, deriving the name, the Virgin Mary, Mother of Jesus. Joseph wanted to back out of their marriage, as he struggled with his faith. Again, there was nothing rational, since it was a supernatural event through the Holy Spirit.

Abraham and Sarah desperately wanted a child, and God made it happen when they were biologically too old for it to be humanly possible.

And the three Hebrew men who were tied up in a furnace so hot that it killed the guards standing on the outside came out not even smelling like smoke.

Finally, there was Daniel, who had been thrown to the lions. God sent angels to the den to keep them from opening their mouths.

These stories were written to give people like us the hope we need for battling the ancient-old strategies and evil tactics of gangstalking.

Father, I thank you for always making a way where there is no way.

April 11

We let The Word do the work.

During these perilous times, the devil is coming at us with everything possible to cause us new levels of devastation, despair, and hopelessness. We are seeing things happen in the world that have never taken place before. It seems everything is on display for all to see. And, of course, the suicide rate is higher than ever. Satan's goal is to lure souls away from God. The art of gangstalking is finely tuned and functioning in plain view, while it remains invisible to the untrained eye. We are up against pure evil with no worldly solutions for it. We must seek solace through Jesus Christ who was sent to Earth to save us. His Father gave us to Him, as a gift, and that makes us important, for we belong to Jesus. The principles governed by God's Kingdom are ideal for people sentenced to a lifetime of bullying, harassment, and oppression. The Word of God is for such a time as this as it brings us hope and peace because it has its own power—the power of God.

When I do not know what to do, I must confess aloud the Word of God and let it go to work for me. The Word has its own power; things will change as I speak it.

April 12

A beautiful woman in her early twenties lay motionless on an elaborate air mattress in an exceptional care unit. Nurse assistants are the ones who must rotate invalids every two hours to prevent bedsores. Her big, mahogany brown eyes are wide open, but as motionless as the rest of her. Her eyes do not follow us, nor do they blink. I wonder if she even knows we are there? It was truly the saddest thing I had ever seen. I was young at the time, and unhappy with my life, but I soon became grateful for it.

Even targeted individuals are more fortunate than some unhealthy people. That does not make our journey less bumpy, but it reminds us to keep our thinking in perspective. We can waltz into a nursing home that smells like urine and soon be grateful to not live there. Even our personal injuries or illnesses could be more debilitating than they are. Still, gangstalking has many of us living in basements, attics, or out of our vehicles. Trying to create mental stimulation can be frustrating when our outgoing phone calls are redirected, and our every move on the Internet is controlled. Our world becomes small, as it closes in on us from sensory deprivation. We are like prisoners in solitary confinement. This level of oppression can flip us out. Keeping our thinking in its proper perspective can become our daily reprieve from insanity. It also does not allow the perpetrators to win. In the Book of Philippians, Chapter 4, Apostle Paul teaches us to be content in whatever circumstances we find ourselves. It is possible, but not without effort. Life is much easier when we want what we have.

I will not spiral down into the abyss of no return by getting mad about the things I do not have. Today, I will read Philippians, Chapter 4, as a gift to myself.

April 13

Most of us have Type-A personalities for being trendsetters, go-getters, shakers, and movers.

Confinement is frustrating and crazy-making. We see it all the time with chained and neglected animals. They suffer from the deprivation of getting their needs and wants met. As targeted individuals, we go through similar punishment. The frustration of having our goals fraudulently held up, sabotaged, blocked, stolen, or destroyed, can take us out. Our enemies have all the time in the world to kick back and watch us put forth effort, while they patiently wait for us to burn out. We cannot survive such a lifestyle without the help of God. He gives us the grace we need for endurance and staying power. How can we not love a just God who gives us protection by grace? God is watching everything we go through, while the rest of the world lets us down.

Today, I will command things by using Bible scripture; it will release armies of angels to my rescue, to fight my battles for me.

April 14

If thou attend to thyself and to God, thou wilt be little moved by what thou perceive outside thee.
—Thomas à Kempis

No matter what state park we live in or what church we attend, we look like desperate misfits seeking refuge from the storm. Locals wonder where we came from and why we are there. People who show instability in residency or have no current work record—or have student loans without the completion of a degree—just seem to have something wrong with them. After a while, we have little to say about our past and even less about our future. We bounce around from one awful place to another. People are leery to have contact with us, for we may be emotionally unstable or—for lack of a better word—crazy. We do not have any recent success stories to share with anyone, as everything we have attempted has been sabotaged. We do not have any goals and are still recovering from our last beating. We feel less than others, which causes us to feel shameful about who we are. The whole situation makes us sad. This mental state of feeling like a misfit is part of their brainwashing and mind control program.

Lord, looking like a misfit is probably the thing that has bothered me the most. Please take this burden from me.

April 15

Do not fear any of those things which you are about to suffer.
—Jesus Christ

There is no privacy anymore, especially for those of us watched like science experiments in our own home. We not only put up with gangstalkers who tamper with everything, organize noise campaigns, and spread fake news to further alienate us from society; now, we must protect ourselves from Extremely Low Frequency (ELF) radio waves that can manipulate our brain. These ELF waves can cause us to dive into a depression, fly into a rage, or become paralyzed with debilitating thoughts of fear, to name just a few. This is electromagnetic radiation—harassment with no boundaries. The devil is nervous about running out of time before Jesus returns and has pulled out his big guns. We are not here by accident. The Lord has us here as his mighty warriors. We must persevere.

Lord, those who want to kill me set their traps, those who would harm me talk of my ruin; all day long they scheme and lie (Psalm 38:12).

April 16

Stealing a car made for a desperate escape out of the tight grips of corrupt law enforcement and dangerous satanic gangstalkers around the junkyards of Long Beach, California. A week later, my dogs and I sat on a mattress in an attic apartment, 3000-miles away. All I knew to do was listen to radio and television evangelists. I figured it would help keep me alive, keep the devil away, and maybe even reform those who were eavesdropping.

Well-seasoned TIs are highly attuned to living with tapped phones, spyware-infected computers, neighborhood espionage, two-faced family members, and even a pet that might not be acting normal. Although we know something is going on, what are we going to do about it? We realize our employer is in on it and that he secretly listens to us through the microphone on his phone. It bothers us. Our landlord accidently says something that tips us off that he secretly spies on us, or a sibling is trying to set us up by insisting that we drive her to her drug connection. It is all done under the game of "taking orders from headquarters". When we know something is going on, we do not need to convince anyone of it. We need to reach into our grab bag of spiritual principles and deal with it the best we can. What we really want to do to these people could get us into trouble. There are two ways of handling them: One way will put us away for good, which is what they want; the other way is lighter because we give it to God, so it does not become more of a burden. We get off the ride, crawl out of the box, or simply turn around and walk away. We stay focused on something to do with God: a good movie or a great sermon. Anything about God has its own power that causes evil to not hang around.

Lord, help me to not go over the deep end. I pray to stay responsible to myself by taking care of myself, today.

April 17

Learning to become attuned to our surroundings is an art that takes practice.

The wisdom we receive from angels, dreams, and the Holy Spirit is not from this world. Since we spend much of our days alone, we are in perfect position to practice becoming attuned to our surroundings. In the Book of Matthew, Joseph was not going to wed Mary when he found out she was pregnant. God sent an angel to Joseph in a dream to inform him that Mary was, indeed, carrying the Son of God (conceived supernaturally) and to marry her. Angels continued to come to Joseph in his dreams to direct him on how to keep Mary and Jesus from harm's way. The things that were happening in his life were not of this world. He had to go along with the unnatural plan of God, which was totally against everything he knew. When Joseph obeyed God, he and his family stayed under the supernatural umbrella of protection. Even when nothing makes any sense to us, we can be protected by staying connected.

He that handles a matter wisely shall find good (Proverbs 16:20).

April 18

Tribulation is what makes heroes.

Most of us have had enough heroism for one lifetime, but we should never knock it.

The roads that lead to great achievements have been paved with much tribulation.

April 19

The devil has lured us to the doors of hell, waiting for us to pull the trigger and step inside.

It does not help us to stay affixed to the shady works of our government. Once we know the basics rules of gangstalking, the rest is redundant. Granted, we need knowledge of the weapons we are up against, but most of us need to cut back some. We have been at this awhile and have no need to further study the topic of gangstalking. After all, we tend to bring into our lives what we focus on most. We should study kingdom principles and incorporate them in our lives. Let the government, gangstalkers, and wicked people do what they do. We face the secrecy behind the game anyway, which only encourages us to become our own worst enemy when we try to figure everything out. It is a twisted and distorted form of attack, designed by Satan. So, we take our eyes off *them* and focus our attention on the gifts God gave us. We need to know the promises He made us and the authority we have using Jesus' name. It is our job to refocus our attention on the Creator of Heaven and off the creatures that creep on the earth.

The Lord laughs at the wicked, for He sees that their own day of defeat is coming. The swords of the wicked shall enter their own hearts, and their bows shall be broken (Psalm 37:15).

April 20

We are not to complain about the music but rather learn to dance to our own tune.

It is not for us to omit the sound because we do not like the melody. God has not written the music for our life with a plan. It should not surprise us when God uses Satan in a way that will create something good for all people. He takes those things meant for evil and uses them for good. That is just how He is. We are not the composer of our life; we are the actors in a play. We must keep our ears open for new notes being added to our song. When Jesus walked on the water toward His disciples, He told them not to be afraid. Peter asked Jesus if he could walk out to Him. Jesus said, "Come." So, Peter walked on the water, keeping his eyes on Jesus. As soon as he began to focus on the high winds and the treacherous waters beneath him, he began to sink. It takes just a split second of taking our eyes off the Master, to miss a beat and get our toes stepped on. We should keep our eyes on Jesus, always.

Today, I will try to stay focused on the Lord and not become distracted by the world around me.

April 21

Deep down, we keep waiting for someone to rescue us. Whether it is the "Cinderella Complex," or "Peter Pan Syndrome," it is just a fairy-tale with hopes for a happy ending.

Everyone loves the underdog: the hero who shows up at the last minute; the vigilante who gets revenge in ways we can only dream of. Hollywood is made up of these protagonists, making millions of dollars off people who look for a two-hour escape from reality. We are living in a time when the natural world is running out of ways to make things happen. People are even becoming leery of taking prescription drugs, with their lengthy list of side effects. Our natural intellect craves for something more than this world can offer, leading many curious seekers to tarot card readings and other forms of the occult. What we need to do is get back to the God who created us and who will meet every need we have. Living a supernatural life is based on having the faith that separates us from the limitations of this world. There are things God cannot do for us until we believe they are possible.

Today, I pray for help in strengthening my belief system.

April 22

God has deliberately planted us among the wicked.

Some days, we cannot seem to escape the heaviness from all the hatred around us; causing us to have energy leaks by engulfing us. We feel as if we are wearing a terrycloth bathrobe while trying to swim laps. It bogs us down. We do not even try making friends because we do not trust anyone. Plus, it is no fun watching others excel while we are constrained to sit and rot. The wear and tear of nothingness is a complete and utter burnout. We simply do not have the tenacity we did six years ago. Being stalked and harassed for decades is no toil for the perps. When they get tired of us, another one zealously hails through the revolving door. It is tough to fathom a beginning, middle, and an end to this persecution. After years of harassment, we naturally become conditioned to negative thinking. We have thoughts like: *the dogs are older, and I still don't have my own place; enrolling in classes is fruitless because education won't help me; I won't get hired if I apply for the job; I can't join a dating service—it's just another setup for intimate infiltration; the car needs to be serviced, but the mechanic will ruin something else.* It never ends. It is a masterminded system for complete soul destruction. If we are not careful, we can burn out and simply stop attempting anything. This crime is beyond any level of justice. This is something that we must conquer through the supernatural and by staying on top of our thinking.

Rejoice not against me, my enemy; when I fall I shall arise; when I sit in darkness, the Lord shall be a light unto me (Micah 7:8).

April 23

Some days, we survive by simply resting.

The shepherd journeys across fields with a staff. Forest trail hikers use walking sticks. Elders manage with a cane to get from point A to point B. The Lord's rod and staff—they comfort us. The rod is to teach us, and the staff gently keeps us in line. It does us good to memorize Psalm 23 and use it as a weapon when necessary.

My strength comes from quietness and trust in You, Lord (Isaiah 30:15).

April 24

My emotional growth seems to have stopped at the time my life was stolen. For years, I would keep returning to that period to recapture and rebuild it.

Instead of focusing on what we used to have, we should focus on something we have right now, even if it is a pet. Perpetrators will often use something from our past to make us jealous, mourn, or feel sad and distressed. If our world halted while we were in college, the perpetrators will choose that period to upset us. One of the tribe will show up to tell us that they just graduated from college. They will have earned, none other than, the same degree we were working toward; that is, before our life was ripped out from under us. It is a bogus story, with the intention to crush our spirit. Our perpetrators feed off our reactions. Many of them are voyeurs and, by being a part of gangstalking, they have legal access to the criminal and perverted world of voyeurism.[9] Meanwhile, if there is something we can no longer do, we must focus on something we can do. This simple adjustment in our thinking can help to rebuild and restore us.

Right now, I am content and emotionally stable.

---

9 Voyeurism: the derivation of satisfaction by watching people secretly, especially when those being watched are undressed or engaging in private activity. A voyeur is a person who enthusiastically and obsessively observes details of a sensational subject's life.

April 25

Being gang stalked is like having a monkey on our back. When it is not there, it is hiding under the bed.

Evil is evil. Haters are going to hate. Burglars will steal. We need to get over it and stop looking at those living around us. Gangstalkers survive by feeding off their abused. They are not worthy of living rent-free in our head. God's Word tells us to think on those things that are pure, lovely, and noble (Philippians 4:6-8). We must think on those things that are good and worthy of praise. We need to rebuke evil thoughts from our mind, so we do not pull in more of what we are thinking.

Today, I give my thought life to Jesus Christ.

April 26

A synchronized view of what is happening as it happens, driven by inner compulsions to connect within a group are signs of the hive mind mentality.[10]

When we realize our environment is wired for sound, we tend to talk less. We even stop praying aloud, since the perps will use our prayers to set us up for another nose dive. We think we are getting answers from above when, in fact, our prayers are being intercepted by our neighbors. We are reeled in by the evil forces around us. It is a baiting trick, carefully designed by the microbes that live at the bottom of a septic tank. A group of hive-minded perps will put forth weeks of effort to "cluster feed" off one reaction from a target. It is always better to pray in the spirit, so the perps do not understand. When we are saved (reborn) and filled with the Holy Spirit, we get the gift of speaking in tongues, also known as "praying in the spirit." Not even the devil can figure out what we are saying, let alone lowlife perpetrators. Praying in tongues keeps the communication between our spirit and God. It can be quite satisfying when we can do something powerful that our enemy cannot use against us. Praying this way is a slick and courageous move on our part, using the highest form of power available to man.

Today, I will consider becoming born again in the Holy Spirit, which will give me the gift of speaking in tongues. This way, I can keep my prayers private.

---

10 Hive mind: a group mind in which the linked individuals have no identity or free will and are possessed/mind controlled as extensions of the hive mind. The concept of the hive mind is an intelligent version of real-life super organisms such as an ant colony or beehive.

April 27

It is hard to believe that existence as a targeted individual could turn out to be a blessing.

We hear that God's Chosen Ones will disappear from the earth when the rapture takes place. Some scholars say the rapture might be from a nuclear bomb; we see a flash and poof, there's Jesus! But, no one really knows. The Bible says, Jesus will first raise the dead and then meet us in mid-air. The left behinds—people who do not know the Lord or who have refused Him—will still be on earth through the seven-year tribulation. During this time, they will either accept Jesus as their Savior, to be hated, persecuted, tortured and killed; or they will get chipped—take the Mark of the Beast and belong to Satan and the Antichrist New World Order (NWO). Surely, those who take the mark will burn in hell, because it is their final decision, and a time when Jesus will no longer save them (Revelation 14:9-11). A lot of us want to die now to end the daily torment of living, but suicide does not change anything. We will still have to answer to God about the murder we commit. Some researchers believe: if we commit suicide, we will have to come back to relive this life; while others claim we will be punished because it is a mortal sin to commit suicide. Either way, our time here is not forever. We must hang on for our ultimate reward in Eternity. Getting the facts on the bigger picture should give us hope and reason to stick around. We are in the middle of an end-time spiritual battle, ultimately, won by Jesus, so we must get right with Him. (See Salvation Prayer)

Today, I will try to live a balanced life, so I do not open a door for Satan to come in and devour me.

April 28

Gangstalkers spend a lot of time planning their attack; it is the worst violation of our human rights.

Gangstalkers love to keep us so busy, our head spins. A target can stay busy just picking up pieces from one catastrophe to the next. If we get injured in the process, we must take care of that too. No one cares. If we need to go to court for a traffic ticket, the group will make sure we do not appear. If we do not make it to court, then we must hide, since there will be a warrant out for our arrest. If we are arrested on a Thursday, they lock us up until Monday. In four days, an army of gangstalkers can do a lot of damage. Our house and car keys are with our belongings at the police station, so they have access to our keys, too. With so many dope fiends, police officers, and gangsters involved, the chance of returning to our life, unscathed, is highly unlikely. Trying to create some sort of balance is a normal struggle for anybody, but targets must find balance between sanity and insanity. Our only choice is to fit God into the mess of things. We do not have to talk aloud; we can sit and talk to Him without making a peep. Our heart rate will calm down as we regain our perspective. In the middle of them taking us down, we should look up to stay strong.

Thank You, Lord, for gathering my enemies out of the lands of the South, East, North and West (Psalm 107:3).

April 29

People who take the Mark of the Beast are also hive-minded.

My residency had stepped up from living in Wal-Mart parking lots to camping out in state parks with hookups. Minus the dunce hat, I was now a sitting duck as, I later learned, law enforcement runs the state parks. It is not normal to be the focal point of so much hatred. We should understand, this degree of constant abuse from people is demonic. The players have this incredible knack to act the same, as they all have a one-mindedness toward us. They are nice in the beginning, which is a way of reeling us in. Then around Day Five, something derogatory is either said or done. The people who are set up around us seem to display a split personality. They intermingle with us, and then use some form of deception to torture us. Satan is the master of lies and deception, so naturally, his army of soldiers would use deception as a weapon. The Mark of the Beast is not "666" tattooed on their forehead, but rather a mark on their mind: a way of thinking.

These have one mind and shall give their power and strength unto the beast (Revelation 17:13).

April 30

We do not need to carry around hatred, anger, and self-pity, just because we are targets.

The Lord says, we should love our neighbor as we love ourselves. He teaches us that if we walk in the kind of love that God has for us, we surmount above what the world offers. If our neighbors are rude and full of hatred, it should not affect how we act toward them. Perhaps our neighbors cannot get their car out of a snow bank. It would blow their mind if we showed up to save the day, being that we would be the least likely to help. We may not even receive some verbal thanks, but we can walk away feeling good. They do not like it when we feed off them! The Bible says that being good to our enemies is like pouring hot coals over their head (Proverbs 25:22). There are forces in the world that cannot overpower us if we walk in love. It frees us from carrying around the heavy burden of hatred. We can keep God at the forefront of our mind and walk above the evil ways of the world. The Lord tells us to wear the world like a loose garment. This is all easier said than done.

Lord, lead me safely, and I will not fear. Let the sea overwhelm my enemies (Psalm 78).

A Bonus Reading

Some days, I live in quiet desperation; other days, I just live quietly.

When I was in Lourdes, France, I saw a young boy begging for money while holding a sign that read, *Hungry*. After spotting him several times, I questioned our tour guide. "Never mind him," he said. "He is owned by the Mafia." My heart sank at the way he nonchalantly said it; like it was a matter of fact—that the boy was a lost cause. Heaviness engulfed me, and I was overwhelmed with an unshakeable sadness. Locals will occasionally look at me, strangely, where I live. No one talks to me. Some just curiously stare, while others appear fearful and try to avoid me altogether. A few people seem entertained, as they display the global hive mind look: empty glossy eyes and rapturous smirk. The most disturbing are the folks who well up with tears and appear to be consumed with a heaviness by my presence. What I think they feel is what I felt in France with the little boy who was a lost cause. I deny the idea that I am owned by the underworld, although, it is obvious by my isolated lifestyle that someone stole my life: physically, mentally, sexually, and spiritually. Like the transmuting of a human being, I have been unable to do things; banned and kept from having a normal life. It is the clear levels of hatred that I do not understand. I know that in Ritual Satanic Abuse (RSA), they break down personalities to rebuild them, but in gangstalking they just break us down. However, at the junkyards, strange men went out of their way to approach me for sexual services like I was a prostitute. I assume this was the brainwashing stage. It was amazing since no one ever approached me like that during my world travels as a famous athlete, but while living on the streets in my Jeep, I seemed to be attractive enough to be paid. It was sheer folly: the number of men who took orders in executing this element of gangstalking called "street theatre".[11]

They cannot have me since I know Who I belong to: The King of kings and the Lord of lords.

---

11 Street theatre: harassment skits or staged events directed at or near a target, performed by gangstalkers in public places.

May 1

The devil used to wait outside the church; now, he goes inside and sits down.

Gangstalkers will regularly bait, dupe, mislead, and set us up. They come in all sizes and colors and from all occupations and social economics. Some of them have biblical names, recite scriptures, and are even reborn. The most dangerous ones are those we trust because they go to our church. I was conned into buying a small cabin in Southern Illinois and swindled out of several thousand dollars, before I was back on the road to nowhere. My two dogs were with me as we headed south, pulling a fifteen-foot camper trailer. It had become obvious, but not soon enough, that the realtor was a gangstalker and had been set in position way before I ever introduced myself. The entire process of having my money extorted took four weeks. During which time, as odd as it seems, the Christian realtor Daniel had introduced me to several police officers on various occasions. He told me they were clients looking to buy land. He invited me to tag along whenever he showed them property. The Lord abhors those who use Him to reel in His children for the sake of being abused. It is better to be a Christ-hater than to be someone who knows God and is a hypocrite. We are living in a time where people will do anything in place of serving God. Some do it for drugs; others help to ruin another person's life just to feel important. It is like raping a child for self-seeking gratification. It is despicable in the eyes of the Lord.

The Lord will give them according to their deeds; and according to the wickedness of their endeavors (Psalm 28:4).

May 2

Trading anger for courage is a good thing.

When people are angry, they lose their grip on any common sense they may have had. Our enemy wants us to lose control, so we end up in jail, an institution, or six feet under. It is an ingenious concept: using the law of attraction to cause a person to bring himself down. TIs can be harassed by fifty people at a time, especially if the perpetrators want to rob him/her. A lot of us have had everything taken away. Getting revenge sounds great but hardly possible with 24/7 surveillance. Possessing a negative state of mind, by focusing on all the evil around us, brings us more of what we do not want: oppression and frustration. Eventually, we lose our chutzpah. Although wounded, we do recover, but with truckloads of anger. We can continue to fight and win our battles by approaching our life in an intelligent manner: turning our frustration into the fuel needed to persevere. We do this by turning our heavy load of anger into courage.

Today, I will live beyond the hatred.

May 3

Why do you keep fighting, when you know all hope is lost?
—from *Legion*

Just as Satan has called out his demons to perform devious tricks and wiles, The Lord has called us out of civilian life to serve Him. As soldiers, we are in constant battle with evil. It is written that Satan loses this war and gets locked up for a thousand years in the pit of hell. Still, the beginning of sorrows must first take place: a time preceding the great tribulation. In the 2010 supernatural thriller *Legion*, Archangel Michael comes to Earth to fight Beelzebub, the Lord of the flies and head of the dwelling. Michael has a heart that is kind and merciful. As a General in the Lord's army, he must battle Satan and the fallen angels to save humanity. Although he perseveres to war against the enemy, his heart is made of love for mankind. This great dichotomy demonstrates that we can be kind-hearted, yet vehemently war against those wanting to kill us.

So, have no fear of them; for nothing is concealed that will not be revealed, or kept secret that will not become known (Matthew 10:26).

May 4

A man is sleeping under a bridge as he struggles to write his third book on gangstalking and organized harassment. Blacklisted from making money and blocked from finding a place to lay his bones, he persists. He gives me strength to continue with my two dogs in our fifteen-foot travel trailer.

We are all called to do something during this time. For targeted individuals, it seems like we are constantly blocked and must fight raw evil at every corner. We proceed ahead without knowing why, except that we must. Some of us do not know where our next meal will come from, or where we will sleep, or if we will return home from our trip to the store, as any number of things could happen to us. Considering that the police officers are heavily involved, we could have our vehicle impounded in a snap of a finger for no good reason. We could be driving one minute and left standing on a street corner the next. We can be unjustly arrested, maimed or killed at any given moment by anybody. Daily schemes and overpriced services can cause us major setbacks. Our bodies cannot handle this kind of ongoing stress. We can only hope to complete our earthly work before our time is up. If it were not for hope, our heart would break. We can afford to lose every possession we have, except our faith in having a purpose. If we are alive, there is hope for us.

[There is no exemption] but he who is joined to all the living has hope—for a living dog is better than a dead lion (Ecclesiastes 9:4 [AMP]).

May 5

This know also, that in the last days perilous times shall come (2 Timothy).

As we serve God in our calling, we will experience storms, roadblocks, fires, and instabilities. Normal life is full of these trials, but we know little rest. We have no reprieve from toil while our perpetrators keep us confined and oppressed. It is smoother sailing if we just opt to sit in our apartments, trailers, or boxes, while they watch us like guinea pigs. Once we try to make a move—even order something on the telephone—gangstalking perps will harass us by blocking our efforts, to make us want to give up. Enough! When we succumb to doing nothing because we will be messed with; when we stop using our phones since they are tapped; when we do not speak aloud in our home because we are being listened to; and when we refuse to go outside because we are watched, we participate in their lowlife plan. This is not how God wants us to live. We must be smart and learn news ways of doing things. We must never take part in any illegal behavior, since we are watched 24/7 by people who have law enforcement backing them. Let us not give the enemy more ammunition. However, when we stop talking, singing, going outside, or even praying, we are helping the enemy to imprison us. When we are saved, we live under the kingdom of God—a higher place than Earth, with its own governmental laws. Not everyone called by God is chosen, but those of us who are can rejoice under the umbrella of protection that He offers us. Let the enemy listen. Let them watch. We will not stoop down to a lower way of thinking because we walk on a higher level; one that they do not have access to.

Today, I may just dance like no one is watching.

May 6

We carry this burden with no earthly way out.

Targeted Individuals cannot rely on humanity for anything. Such a predicament lands us on a course where we must totally rely on God. Jesus is our only means of hope for freedom. He uses our trouble to make us strong. Our burdens help us to develop wings of eagles. These birds never fly in the storm, but rather soar far above it. Being like an eagle is like taking the higher road, flying far above gangstalkers, who are like crows and cannot reach such heights. The only way a crow can fly with an eagle is if the eagle lowers himself.

I will trust in the Lord and find new strength. I will soar high on wings, like eagles; I shall run and not grow weary; I shall walk and not be faint (Isaiah 40:31).

May 7

An evil spirit is like a sub-personality; it can see through the eyes of the human vessel it abides in. Some TIs have discernment for this.

Satan's battle is with God, not us. It is all about his ego and pride, which got him kicked out of heaven in the first place. For each soul he wins, he hurts God. It is important to realize how special we are. A lifetime of gangstalking and harassment elevates us into a special class of survivors. We are people in constant need of supernatural help from the Almighty Creator of Heaven and Earth, who sees all things. When we give our life to Him, His seal is on us. It may not stop the gangstalking, but we get to survive with His intervened grace. We can look forward to His promises. He is easy to love when we realize just how much he cares for us. Our perps want us to commit suicide or to cause us a debilitating accident. When we become soldiers for the Lord, we put on the whole armor of God, so we can fight with spiritual weapons. The motive behind evil spirits is to get us to think that God does not exist in our life, because with Him in our life, they cannot win our soul. When we recite biblical scriptures and use proper warfare prayers, we fight according to God's Word, and Satan remains a defeated foe.

Lord, show me a token for good, that they which hate me may see and be ashamed. (Psalm 86:17)

May 8

Jesus has already been rejected by this world, when he was in it but not of it.

We have seen our lives stripped of everything that we have worked a lifetime to achieve. Our family and friends have fallen away. We are no longer allowed to make a living to live comfortably. Our sense of humor went the way of the buffalo, and our good looks seem to be a faint memory of another life. The thumb of gangstalking crushes us underneath the normal ways of living. Jesus Christ builds His kingdom from disheartened people with torn apart lives. Heaven is full of dejected and unsuccessful pieces of this world. God can mold us when we finally break and become disheartened. In our dark and broken times, He gives us our mindful peace.

I can do something today that might seem impossible if I had to keep it up for a lifetime.

May 9

The beginning phase of gangstalking is always the worst, when we expect someone to help us.

My sister stomped around her suburban apartment, murmuring and complaining as she rummaged for a cigarette. There was not even a butt in a dirty ashtray. Meanwhile, the apartment manager asked her to tag along to run errands. Theresa locked the front door and double-checked it before hopping into the car. When they returned two hours later, she unlocked her door and stepped inside. She got a strange feeling of someone having been there while she was gone. Staring directly at her from the bookcase was a Marlboro-100 cigarette, as though it were asking, *how could you have missed me?* She knew it was not there earlier when she thoroughly combed the joint. Plus, it was not even her brand. Of course, nobody believed her story about the mysterious cigarette just appearing out of nowhere. Our cell phone is a weapon for perpetrators. Theresa had already seen it turn on by itself. She noticed the battery needed charging even when she was not using it, and sometimes, it was hot when she'd pick it up. These are signs that our phone is doubled as an open microphone—a makeshift baby monitor. The more information the perpetrators have on someone, the more ammunition they have for our harassment. The cockiness and audacity of leaving a cigarette out in the open was a clear and personal message: either come on our side or continue being harassed. Gangstalkers like to distract us from living our lives.

I will not allow fear and worry to alter my belief. Today, God will be my source of power.

May 10

Q: What is the first rule of battle?
A: Never reveal your position.
—from Snowden

Before the shepherd boy David slew Goliath, he had already achieved great victories by killing a bear and a lion with his bare hands. He privately recalled his past victories before he went to slay the giant in public. He remembered the times when the Lord gave him the strength he needed. We must remember the things God has done for us in the past, since He will do them for us again. We tell God that when He opens the door, we will walk through it, but He wants us to walk by faith first, and then He will open the door. This is how our faith works. Jesus told us that we cannot please the Father without having faith. It is time for us to go for it! It is time we stop being afraid of who will hear us and make fun of us. Who cares? We have been prepared for such a time as this: to slay the giants. God's armor covers only our front side to remind us that we should not run from our enemies. We face our problems head-on with our sword and shield.

Lord, help me to take one of your teachings today and put it to use.

May 11

We are already outside of the multitude.

When Jesus walked, people followed him. Those who stepped out from the crowd and diligently sought after Him got His attention and healing. A blind man resisted the orders to be quiet until Jesus stopped and gave him his sight. The one leper who stepped out of bounds to call out to Jesus was the leper who became clean. The woman with the "issue of blood" had crawled through the crowd to get her miracle healing. Only one thing was on her mind: *If I can just touch His garment, I will be healed.* There was also a lame man who was healed after being lowered through a roof where Jesus was teaching. It is simply okay for us to yell out, *J-e-s-u-s!* He will hear our cry and stop to comfort us.

Today, I will step out of the box. I will not fear what people think.

May 12

Jesus says, "Come as you are."

When the needy stepped out from the crowd and called out to Jesus, they did not care what others thought. Those who were told to be quiet yelled His name even louder. The leper man knew he was supposed to stay isolated in a leper colony because society prohibited him from being in public. He wore the clothes that lepers had to wear and hid his face from others. He did not try to change his clothes before he ran to find Jesus. He went as he was. God knows what we are going through. It is fine to seek Him just as we are. We might be targeted individuals due to a lifestyle we once lived. Maybe we committed murder while we were dealing drugs; or we gave up six babies during our ten years of using crystal meth; perhaps, we stole from the church. He already knows what we did. He invites us to come to Him just as we are.

Today, I will not let my troubles control me by dwelling on them.

May 13

Our desperate situation calls for desperate measures.

Imagine that you have a child who is possessed. Then one day, you hear that Jesus is passing through the area. Jesus: a man who claims to be the Son of God and has all authority, even over Satan. Jesus: the only One who could drive the demon out of your child. However, you are not of His race, religion, or creed. You are from a class of people that He did not plan to help. Others have told you that you have no opportunity with this man, Jesus. You have even heard that He dislikes your kind. The woman was a Canaanite and from the area where Jesus was passing through. Intimidation swept over her as she watched Him cut across the field with His disciples, but she knew she had to make her move. She ran after Him in desperation, for she knew He was the only One who could help her. At first, Jesus ignored her, while His disciples ordered her to go away, but her despair drove her to keep hollering His name while she ran after Him. Finally, Jesus stopped. The woman fell at His feet to tell Him about her son. In the middle of her extreme anxiety, Jesus insulted her by saying it was wrong for Him to feed His children's food to the dogs. Still, she was not going to leave without first getting her miracle. "But Lord," she replied, "even the dogs eat the crumbs that fall from their master's table." Her total powerlessness had become her strength, and Jesus granted her wish, telling her that her child was healed.

How much are we willing to go through to get what we want? The good news is: If we are wallowing in a mud hole, He is with us. He hears us from wherever we are. Jesus can heal us in an instant. He can change everything, no matter what.

I bind and rebuke all spirits of hatred and oppression that would manifest through harassment, in the name of Jesus.

May 14

Remember: God is within our innermost self, not in feelings and emotions from the outside world.

If we are saved, we should not worry or feel helpless, for we have the kingdom of God within us. Let us remember that no earthly circumstance can hinder the fulfillment of God's promises. No matter what things look like around us in this ever-changing world, we can trust that God's Word never changes. There is no circumstance in this world that will stay the same if we speak the name of Jesus over it. Great sorrow may surround us, but even then, every seed that gets sown is buried in sorrow anyway. When we speak the Word, it goes out like a two-sided sword, slicing through evil and wickedness. Some situations may worsen before they get better. Our job is to speak God's Word at our mountains. He will take care of the rest. It is that simple.

God shall let me see my desire on my enemies (Psalm 59:10).

May 15

We must stop letting circumstances write the ending to our story.

Our life has sadly lost its luster when we begin having problems with our phone beeping; people knowing about our personal life behind closed doors; our e-mails never reaching their destinations; and police officers showing up wherever we go. When we get overpowered by high-tech equipment like Voice-to-Skull (V2K) implants and directed energy weapons (DEW), we can struggle through the day to just stay alive. These government-sanctioned attacks are executed on us throughout the state and nation. It is a way to get rid of us in a silent way—murder that looks like suicide. This is the work of high-level demons and principalities. We are not built for this kind of thing, and certainly, we cannot carry this load alone. We must cast our care onto God, for He made us and cares for us. He sees what is happening to His precious children, and He will give us the grace we need. *My grace is enough for thee, for my strength is made perfect in [your] weakness (2 Corinthians 12:9).*

(Suggested scripture reading: Psalm 142.)

Today, I will recognize the most humbling thing: I am still being prepared.

May 16

Those who suffer are leading the army to peace.

When we realize we have an indispensable contribution—something priceless to offer others, it gives us reason to live. Having a mission can instigate us to celebrate our life in a distinct way. We suddenly see a higher purpose and reason for our pain. We no longer live aimlessly, lacking underlining passion in our lives. We trade in our focus on survival, and our strategies for making it through another day, emotionally, for a renewed mind. We begin to live a meaningful life through our deepest suffering and our silent yearning for something better.

Today, I will destroy the works of darkness by finding my purpose and destiny.

May 17

We must learn how to enjoy life without relying on other people for happiness.

When the storm is raging, we forget that our hardships are in direct correlation to our purpose in life. God does not give us problems according to our body weight or how strong we are in the gym; He gives them to us according to our destiny. When the harassment settles down, we might find ourselves unwilling to get involved with anyone, but it is highly unlikely. Human beings, by nature, find true happiness in sharing with others. It is normal for us to want someone special in our lives. The higher our consciousness, the more we walk alone. We learn the difference between loneliness and aloneness. God can yank people out of our lives as fast as they came in. We can find our acquaintances suddenly falling away for no reason. We do not know why. Maybe the organization scared them off. God sets us up to rely on only Him, so when people go away, He is still there.

Lord, I shall call upon you, and You will answer me. You will be with me in trouble (Psalm 91:15).

May 18

It really takes someone extraordinary to continue living while being hated by the majority and within all socio-economic groups.

How do we carry on with so much hatred from people? It is simply not possible for a single person to have so many enemies, worldwide. TIs are exceptional human beings, enduring more than any average, run-of-the-mill person ever could. How rare some of our painful insights can be, especially learning that a sibling—someone we grew up with—is one of our gangstalkers. It crushes our spirit to find out that our nephew, who we watched grow up, is now on board to soft kill us. The situation puts us in an elite class where we exist all by ourselves, while drinking from the bitter cup of suffering.

Lord, I know You favor me because my enemies do not triumph over me (Psalm 41:11).

May 19

Here I am, minding my own business, when someone slides into my life for a few hours, then goes storytelling to the leaders of my church. How could something so negative happen when I was doing everything right?

When we stay close to the Lord, He will work everything out. The devil always gets involved in whatever good we are doing. For instance, we finally belong to a local church where we praise and worship and do the things that please God. We begin to see miracles in our life from tithing and practicing kingdom principles. Someone says something to the pastor about us, which then leads him to revolve a sermon around our personal life. We know that false statements are sweeping through the congregation. We want to walk away because we have been offended. This is precisely what the gangstalkers want. Someone may say, "The difference between walking away or not is the difference between a milk toast Christian and a mature one." That is not necessarily true. Being involved in a church can be an ideal outlet for perpetrators to further hurt us. Furthermore, whenever we get attacked by the devil, it is a sure sign that we are doing something to upset him. It is a good sign when tribulation finds us. We should have concern when we are not bothering anyone, especially the evil doers.

In the name of Jesus, I remove all false burdens placed on me by people, leaders, or churches (1 Thessalonians 2:6).

May 20

Horses have horses, dogs have dogs, and rabbits have rabbits. So, any offspring of God are gods.

Not all of us are children of God. Many are called but only a few are chosen. Those of us who are chosen continually to grow in spirituality. How difficult it is to be a victim of isolation and an outcast of society, yet we press forward in life. In having had our dreams smashed, and our lives put to a halt, we find ourselves on a completely different course of action than someone with a normal life. How wonderful it is for children of God to have advantages that others do not. Protection is divine when we live under the covenant; we have the power to heal people, cast out demons, and call forth things by faith. We are the offspring of our Creator (Acts 17). We get seated next to King Jesus. That makes us royalty in God's eyes. Our inheritance is proportional to our image—that is, how we view ourselves; not the way haters want us to see ourselves. We can believe in God and never access what belongs to us, if we do not see ourselves as little gods—made in His image.

Today, I live by what I believe, not by what I see (2 Corinthians 5:7).

May 21

No human can separate truth from a lie when the devil is talking, unless they know the Word of God.

We all must deal with the strongman: the one who holds rulership in a demonic establishment. The Bible tells us that we must first bind the strongman, since no natural person is strong enough to beat the devil when he is using people through deception and manipulation. The devil knows who we are and will order attacks to destroy us if we are on an assignment for God. Gangstalkers want us to think we are nonentities, going nowhere. This demonic hold is from a Jebusite Spirit, influencing us to give up and end our lives, since we are, after all, a lost cause. This spirit tells us there is no way out and that man is more powerful than God. It whispers there are too many against us and life is over. It screams we are not important to God, so He will not save us. We cannot get rid of this spirit with anti-depressants or synthetic solutions. This spirit must be bound spiritually, using the weapons from our spiritual arsenal.

Prayer: You, Jebusite Spirit, I bind you and I command you to be removed from my life and cast into the sea. You and your cohorts are under my feet because Jesus says, "Come unto me, all ye that labor and are heavy laden and I will give you rest" (Matthew). I command you to cease your activity in my life, taking your heaviness and negativity with you. You will no longer instigate feelings of quitting or ending my life. I break your powers now, in Jesus' name.

May 22

This world is not as it was fifty years ago.

If we allow it, we can find something to steal our victory and peace of mind all day long. Our enemies work overtime on us in around-the-clock shifts. We must change our values and priorities, no matter what life dishes out to us, to live comfortably in today's world. It is meaningful for us to no longer live above our means, but to find comfort in saving a little money rather than spending it all. It also behooves us to want those things we already have. Sometimes, it is not the world that needs changing as much as it is in our attitudes.

I have an important part to play in the world. When I find it difficult to change my ways, I can turn my will and my attitude over to God. With Him, miracles can happen.

May 23

He will keep you if you want Him to.

TIs are people who have a bold heart. Every day, we fight off demons sent from the spirit world; those that jump in and out of the vessels of gangstalking perpetrators. Not everyone is as privileged as us—to be able to respond as warriors, while safely abiding under God's protection. He will always give us the victory through His gifts of courage and boldness. When we bring our issues to God, we get in covenant with Him, so we have no reason to quit or cave-in when the enemy turns the heat up.

I thank God for helping me to enjoy my life even a little.

May 24

He who despises his neighbor sins against God, his fellowman, and himself, but happy is he who is kind and merciful to the poor (Proverbs 14:21).

This scripture will negate the evil forces of any neighborhood operation from harming us. While neighbors are busy with organized stalking (listening, planning, and oppressing), we function on a different level of government—one that prevails over them. Kingdom principles are not *of* this world: confessing the Word of God aloud; speaking to demons with the Word of God; decreeing and declaring; binding and loosing; and praying in tongues. Spiritual warfare may initially feel uncomfortable, but we will begin to see the results that this world system cannot give us.

I release the sword of the Lord against the powers of hell (Judges 7:18).

May 25

In times of isolation and aloneness, we learn to become attuned to ourselves and the Holy Spirit who lives inside us.

Joseph probably kicked and screamed at the idea of uniting with Mary, who was already pregnant and claiming to be a virgin. Instead, he trusted in God and leaned on Him to take care of everything. Even though it takes practice to become attuned to ourselves and the supernatural ways of God, this is where we want to be. Like Joseph, we really do not have much of a choice. We stand at the door labeled, "No way. I cannot do this." We must decide to take a leap of faith and go for it! Everything we need has already been set into place.

Father, I thank You for saving me; I pray that Your mighty power might be known.

May 26

I have learned to be content in whatever state I find myself.

Gangstalkers try to bully us into inactivity, which is a nothingness we must fight off daily. Before deciding to hire a contractor to remodel our kitchen, we might be better off doing it ourselves. We could also try to be more like Apostle Peter in Philippians 4:11-12, by finding contentment with the way things are. Living as a targeted individual is completely different than living as a normal citizen. It is impossible to find even one person to whom we could tell our story. The people we hire and think are legitimate workers are closet perpetrators. They come in and out of our life through the revolving door of gangstalking. They turn out to be infiltrators with an agenda. We give our money to hired help who fix something with their right hand, while they purposely break something with their left. This kind of a rat race causes us to shoulder a huge amount of stress that we cannot continue to carry. There is a helpful scripture: *The Lord is my helper, and I will not fear what man shall do unto me (Hebrews 13:6)*. We must cast our cares onto the Lord because He cares for us.

I break every curse of trusting in man that would open my life to desert spirits (Jeremiah 17:5-6).

May 27

Acting on something can be the difference between life and death.

Emotional abuse worsens over time and wears us down. The enemy wants to make us bitter and full of resentment, so we become our own worst enemy. Having a bitter attitude blocks our blessings, and this is the way the enemy wins. We begin to dislike the way we look when we stop caring for ourselves; we gain weight, our hair is unkempt, and our clothes are outdated. Our tattered self begins to display "victim" on our sleeve. It happens to all of us who are living with the harassment of being gang stalked. We all struggle with thoughts of busting out of this life before our designated time. We sit and wonder if our life makes any sense at all. We can put on *the garment of praise* to replace the feeling of heaviness. If we do not want to go to a church to praise and worship, we can sing to the Lord in our own way. We must not stay inactive, especially if our joy is gone. Pressing forward, by taking baby steps, will save us from soaring too low in our time of misery.

Today, I put on the garment of praise for the spirit of heaviness (Isaiah 61:3).

May 28

God's eyes are on all our ways; they are not hidden from Him (Jeremiah 16:17).

God sees everything. Nothing gets past Him. He does not like when we are hurting from the cruelty of others. However, there is just so much the enemy can do to us. In the Book of Job, Satan wanted to test Job's faith. God allowed him to take everything away from Job, including his children, but he was not to kill him. Job even suffered from painful boils all over his body, but he kept his focus on God who, he knew, would not let the devil dish out more than he could handle. Sometimes, there are circumstances that we want to fix our eyes on, but we must ask God to help us to focus on Him, instead. No matter how badly a situation looks, there is a divine plan for us. God will help us through the eye of the storm, if we concentrate on Him.

Lord, my eyes are on You and not on my circumstances. I let go of past disappointments and trust my life to You.

May 29

When our mind tells us that we are lacking something that everyone else seems to have, the devil is at work.

The devil loves to deceive us by compelling us to think other people have it better than we do. This is one of his primary trickeries: getting us to take our eyes off the blessings that we *do* have. When we think like this, our gratitude is quick to go out the window. It only takes one little deceptive thought like this for us to be led into a downward spiral of self-pity and depression. Discouragement quickly floods in and, by the time we know it, we are in a full-blown funk—all from a lie the devil put in our mind, along with the temptation to compare our insides to someone else's outsides. Whenever we do this, we always end up with the short end of the stick.

The devil wants to rob me of my joy, but I will not fall for his wiles and schemes. Today, I look at the things I have and thank God for them.

May 30

If the hate does not take us out, the loneliness might.

Perpetrators will come in from all directions when we have something they want to take. If we stand rooted in God's word—pick a scripture, any scripture, and stand on it—our faith will be made manifest. The perps might get everything we own, without justice taking our side. They could publicly humiliate us to boot, but we will hang onto our soul since it is not up for grabs. Two weapons that the enemy will use to keep us from our destiny are sadness of the heart and a hurt spirit. Even if we are unenthusiastic about life, we must continue to display self-respect, or they will hone in on us and come in for the kill.

Jesus, I trust in Your mercy. I believe that my enemies will not say they have prevailed against me. Those that trouble me will not rejoice, for I will not be moved (Psalms 13:3-5).

May 31

To be a good soldier, you must know the enemy.

Following a ferocious upheaval caused by street gangs and corrupt law officials in Long Beach, California, I sat on a moldy mattress in a barren, rundown attic apartment in Tinley Park, Illinois. If ever I would have contemplated suicide, this would have been the time, but my two dogs gave me reason to live. So, I haphazardly flicked through the channels of an old television that had been left by former tenants. Call it fate, but I would soon be introduced to a spiritual warfare series of teachings by Dr. Bill Winston. He preached about principalities in law enforcement. He talked about how ranks of demons get pipelined down into certain territories within geographical regions that are overseen by the strongman; weird stuff that seemed to hit a cord with me, although I had never heard anyone ever talk about such things. I faithfully followed his ministry for the next seven years, applying spiritual principles to my life while silently battling the sadomasochistic underworld of gangstalking. When we know how Satan works, we can get a grip on how to better protect ourselves from the uncompromising evil practices of our enemies. Everything demonic seems to get used as a weapon for our destruction: deception, mind control, secrecy, as well as being lured and baited to be blind-sighted, tricked, and caught in a net. I was open to anything that would help me, so I got baptized and filled with the power of the Holy Spirit. Now, I am a soldier in the army for the kingdom of God. I have the weapons to blast through the evil forces that have come against me.

I will hope in the Lord and keep his way. He will exalt me to inherit the land; when the wicked are destroyed, I will see it (Psalm 37:34 [NIV]).

June 1

We are in so deeply that we accept our rut as a way of life.

Addiction can happen with anything to which we completely surrender ourselves. Any physical addiction can be the culprit in developing underlying beliefs that cause us to harbor negative emotional strongholds. Interestingly, organized gangstalking has a similar strategy for seizing someone's soul, since the more we feed something, the bigger it grows, whether it is good or bad. When we talk about how awful our life is, we can expect to receive more of it. Our perpetrators will use this mind-control tactic until we bond to a bad habit that will later lead us catering to a full-blown addiction. They will use anything they can to create chains around us; mostly our own thinking. The junk that we think and talk about can cause us to attract more of the same garbage. What a spectacular plan of darkness: they do something loathsome to us, and we take it in by focusing on the repugnancy of it. In time, voila! It grows into something humongous. Walking in faith and power comes from reading the Word of God (preferably aloud) throughout the day. Replacing our dark thoughts with Bible verses of hope and divine protection can change things in our physical world. Evil cannot stand to be around the Word of God, especially the name of Jesus. If we want something to die, we must first starve it and then fill in the void.

I decree and declare that evil spirits leave my life, as I hear and speak The Word (Matthew 8:16).

June 2

One night, I sat motionless in my trailer as perps changed out the tires underneath me. I knew they were up to no good, but I could not move.

Gangstalking perpetrators are big on poisoning and drugging their targets. They can easily do this by sprinkling chemicals around the house or by putting a little something on our toothbrush or pillow. The practice of administering drugs for mind-control permeates this underworld crime syndicate. We can easily have our own problems with drinking alcohol and using narcotics; we certainly do not need any help from them. It is too risky for us to score drugs because there is always the possibility that the drug deal will be a setup to land us in jail. We could also be tricked into receiving bunk—dope mixed with something else. Some of it is laced with chemicals to accelerate our addiction, to make us needier and more easily controlled. Remember: We do not have a friend in the world that we can trust. We should learn to live clean and sober, at least, most of the time. Having our faculties working properly will help us to handle situations better. We learn to trust our lives with only God. We must stay confident that we can do whatever we need to do, while staying in the present moment.

I bind and cast out all spirits of self-deception in the name of Jesus (1 Corinthians 3:18).

June 3

Gangstalkers draw up personal plans to encourage our suicide.

According to our own level of faith, our victory lies in our relationship with God, as does the reason for our existence. When we get a blessing, it is so we can be a blessing to someone else. God knows we cannot give away something that we do not have. If we are here to give money to the poor, we will be blessed with money to give. If we are blessed to preach the Gospel, we will be given a voice to do so. God gives each of us exactly what we need to fulfill our God-given destiny. If we want to tap into the riches that God has for us, we must decide to be a blessing to someone else, no matter how bleak our world looks. When we do so, we receive more than we ever gave away.

Today I will present myself well and abstain from speaking negative things about myself and others.

June 4

In your worst situation, speak the Word of God.
—Dr. Bill Winston

We should not stay in isolation, wondering what the organization will do next. We cannot run to the police and file complaints, nor talk ourselves blue to get someone to believe our bizarre story. We must attack evil with all the power and authority God has given us. We turn away from the world and seek the answers to why we are here. Inner reflection helps us to find ways to get through our life, one day at a time. We have the keys to God's Kingdom. We use our mouth to lock and unlock doors. We can bind evil spirits and loose angelic forces to work on our behalf. Jesus died on the cross to give us access to these powers. They are for us to use.

In Jesus' name, I bind, expose, and cast out any demon that would try, by stealth (undetected), to come into my life (2 Samuel 19:13).

June 5

We cannot navigate forward while staring in our rear-view mirror.

We've all kept copious chronicles on being gang stalked, harassed, drugged, poisoned, and robbed. We have sagas of complete and utter humiliation and experiences of seduction and abandonment, as well as numerous setups of being played a patsy. They are all sad and horrendous stories. They have left us with wounds that bleed and scars we see every day. We hear that time heals all wounds, but our condition only seems to worsen. We wonder: How can people do this to another human being? We become paralyzed with unhappiness when we further dwell on our past. It is another form of bondage. Apostle Paul tells us, *but this one thing I do, forgetting those things which are behind, and reaching forth unto those things which are before (Philippians 3:13).*

We change our mindset to break the chains that bind us. We pull ourselves up and out of the victim seat by replacing our disgusting thoughts of yesterday with scriptural promises about our future. By also doing something for someone else, we can experience a brief reprieve from feeling victimized. If we get active and passionate about doing something other than complaining, we allow God's army of angels to work in our life. The devil will constantly lie to us about how dreadful things are, while God wants us to have faith and believe in the future.

(Suggested scripture reading: Philippians 3:1-14).

God, send Your angels to smite the demons that come to destroy me (Isaiah 37:36).

June 6

The dark results of our endeavors are from spiritual wickedness in high places.

We see how gangstalking uses people in government positions to keep us down. Some of us end up with a fabricated rap sheet that has been blown out of proportion. We end up doing time for something we did not do. Hiring an attorney is possible, but as a target, getting them to do right by us is another song and dance. Harboring grief and sorrow can blast an opening for eviler things to come our way. We cannot let these emotions ruin us. We lose power and clear thinking when we wallow in the endless pit of these low-level feelings. Targeted individuals (TIs) must pray about everything. We take our problems to the Lord and leave them at His feet. We can learn innovative ways of moving onward and upward with supernatural strength. We cannot live life without any hope for our future. If we believe Jesus died on the cross and rose again, we not only have hope in all situations, we are divinely protected and guided through every storm. None of us get out of this thing alive.

Today, I loosen myself from every bond (Luke 13:16).

June 7

The battlefield is in our mind.

Sometimes, we think our battleground is where we live, especially, when we are harassed by our neighbors. We can move several times without finding any reprieve from their collective mind games. Unbeknownst to the rhyme or reason for "mirroring" (when a perp imitates a target), they seem all too eager to play a part in this mindless act. On the other hand, they will engage us in conversation, while the rest of the crew covertly listens in on a closed-circuit Wi-Fi network over their cell phones. While onstage, they appear manic and full of glee; this is their moment of fame in front of the group. The perps bring much negative energy unto themselves by engaging in these acts. We all have a personal responsibility to take ownership of the choices we make. Our neighboring perpetrators are secretly living in their own hell.

Today, I will speak the Word aloud. I do not need to have any emotions or thoughts about it. All I do is speak it and let it go to work for me.

June 8

We do the best we can with what we've got.
—My mom

We cannot allow the organization to drive us crazy by taking on everything they throw our way. Some of us are so tightly wound-up in their grips, we cannot sneeze without them knowing. Running does not work due to tracking devices. Making verbal plans does not work because of hearing devices. E-mailing is fruitless for reasons of cyber-bullying. Relocating just sets us up with new neighbors and landlords that have been assigned to us. Life is naturally messy, even without perps tampering with everything from our work clothes to the foods we eat. Simple, everyday life can be overwhelming! No human being can handle all the wicked arrows that fly at TIs from every side, year after year. God knows what we are going through. He sees the actions of our enemies. The Lord waits to hear from us, so He can act on our behalf. Throughout the day, we say aloud, "I cast this care onto the Lord, for He cares for me."

(Suggested scripture reading: 1 Peter 5:6.)

Lord, let your fire protect me and cover me (Exodus 14:24).

June 9

If we do not take care of ourselves, nobody else will.

Tearing apart our car after hearing a faint beep from under the dashboard can make us nuts. We hear a beep while driving from one county into another, and soon police cars zip around us from all directions. After several years of this unexplained wonder, we either come to grips with their tactics, or we end up losing our mind. Some targets commit suicide, which is the organization's ultimate plan for our destruction. Some of us have nervous breakdowns. This would never be God's plan for our life. They are from Satan's demons, working through people. The fact that we are drastically outnumbered can make us feel doomed. We must remember: Satan is a deceiver. He is the prince of deception and makes things appear in ways they are not. Jesus is the Prince of Peace. He gives us victory if we hold onto our faith, even when it looks like we are defeated.

Today, I prophesy to every dry bone in my life and I command it to rise up and live (Ezekiel 37:1-4).

June 10

When our soul is bouncing off walls and wondering how things will turn out, we need to refocus.

Perpetrators will use our beloved pets to hurt us. Haters will cause us unjustly problems with animal control and the courts, so we must be vigilant in covering ourselves from all angles. We keep our pets legal, while we post *Do Not Trespass* and *Beware of Dog* signs in the yard to legally protect ourselves from having them taken away for bad behavior. So our dogs bit a gangstalker who was prowling around the backyard. Good dogs! The perp may not suffer any repercussions for public drunkenness, trespassing, stalking, or falsifying a police report, but we will have to go to court to show proof of rabies shots. Six weeks later, when we receive a notice in the mailbox from animal control, we must not fear! This is all part of the harassment. There will be problems to solve, but they will not prosper. We walk into the courthouse muttering under our breaths, *No weapon formed against me shall prosper (Isaiah 54:17)*.

I rebuke all spirits of torment and fear because I have peace through the blood of Jesus (Colossians 1:20).

June 11

Wisdom makes prudence her dwelling, finding knowledge and discretion (Proverbs 8:12).

While perpetrators intentionally evoke hostility and rage in us, we cannot act stupidly or we will end up handcuffed and hauled off to jail. They have tactics, through staged public events, that could cause us legal problems. At least once, these outrageous episodes will catch us off guard. Having wisdom is a big key to our survival. We do not have the privilege of thinking aloud, nor can we use anger as an outlet, no matter what they do to us. We take care of ourselves by keeping a low profile. We stay away from large events and public places like taverns and nightclubs. Our safety comes from finding peace in the quietness of our life. Trading in human friendships for animal contact can be more rewarding, satisfying, and safer for us in the long run. Isolated targets need unconditional love, and there are many lonely animals just waiting to love us.

(Suggested scripture reading: Proverbs 8.)

God, let me receive and understand Your hidden wisdom (1 Corinthians 2:7).

June 12

We must be persistent in dealing with our enemies.

The power of the Holy Spirit is in every person who gets reborn (see Salvation Prayer). We can reroute demons by combining the wisdom of the Holy Spirit with the authority of Jesus' name, since the spirit realm recognizes both. We must not be afraid to use these powers against the evil spirits around us and at the demons controlling our perpetrators. God's grace gives us the ability to bind the works of darkness.

Lord, show forth Your salvation in my life from day to day (Psalm 96:2).

June 13

I am actively taking care of myself by not letting problems trouble me.

Jesus wants to restore everything we have lost. While our perpetrators relentlessly continue their attacks, we fight daily to keep ourselves together physically, mentally, emotionally, and spiritually. The level of stress we undertake is off the chain. We must get a grip on new ways to care for ourselves while living under such abnormal conditions. We need to take the time for rest and relaxation. By doing so, we honor God. We do not let our perpetrators see us defeated. In other words, we don't let them see us sweat. Even when energy beams are their weapon of choice, and we are physically attacked, we must keep our spirit strong. *Even though my body decays, my inward body keeps being renewed daily (2 Corinthians 4:16)*. We must keep ourselves spiritually fed every day. It is our spirit that goes on to live eternally, not our physical body. While we are in this world, we do our best to become a good representation of the Holy Spirit's power—something the perps do not possess, nor have access to.

In the name of Jesus, I command every organ in my body to function the way God intended (Psalms 139:14).

June 14

We must feed ourselves spiritually to be enabled to go the distance.

When we realize that we are in this thing alone, with no one to turn to, we can then let God in. The spirit realm has more help to offer us than this world ever could. We stumble around as spiritual babies, trying to learn how to function in our new way of life. There is nothing wrong with being a spiritual baby. We all start somewhere. As time goes on, the devil gets angrier, as do our gangstalkers, and so the pressure of being harassed increases. The madder Satan gets, the more dangerous our haters become because, let us not forget, they work for him during this time of disillusionment, war, depression, oppression, and spiritual wickedness. We, on the other hand, work for the Lord and take pride in the fact that we are special soldiers. Our calling is not to run and hide, but to stand and fight for what is right. We spiritually nourish ourselves to fight the good fight of faith, while being assured that God is in our back pocket.

(Suggested scripture reading: 2 Timothy 4:16-18.)

Lord, you have called me, and you will make my way prosperous (Isaiah 48:15).

June 15

God is planning things for our best, even when we are at our worst.

Targeted Individuals complain of having sudden mood swings for no apparent reason. Nothing has changed from this morning, except now, we are in a funk and harboring thoughts of murder. How can this be? Satellite harassment and electromagnetic waves can permeate through skin and bones to control our thoughts. The people behind these psychotronic weapons can even play with our bodily functions to make us think we are falling apart. Almighty God sees the horrible things being done to His people. He sees how they have taken our lives away—the very gift He has given us. This is not going unnoticed by our Maker. We must never act on thoughts of suicide or emotions of despair, as we may not be having our own thoughts and emotions. We must run to God and let Him wrap His loving arms around us, instead of allowing the cruel actions of others to further control us. *Vengeance is mine*, says the Lord in Romans 12:19. He will clear our name and repay our enemies in His own time, when we completely hand it over to Him.

I walk in holiness, and no lion can dwell in my life (Isaiah 35:9).

June 16

The pain of doing nothing is worse than the pain of falling short.

Our society has become more unsafe and less stable than ever. While we carry a heavy load, we must depend on God who is still in control. We stay stable in knowing that Jesus is always with us when we are under insidious attacks. Our faith must be strong, for we have nothing without it. Harassment groups use subtle strategies to take control of our lives, causing us to lack the privilege of finding temporary escapes. With 24/7 surveillance, we can suffer punishment and negative repercussions for any wrongdoing. If gangstalkers find out about our weaknesses—getting drunk, smoking weed, having a bad temper, or stealing—they will be sure to hone in on that area as leverage to bring us down. Yes. They will use sex, too. We must keep a strong spirit by clinging to Jesus, while we withdraw from the ways of this world.

(Suggested scripture reading: Ephesians 4:17-19.)

Lord, let the spirits of lust and perversion be destroyed with Your fire (Genesis 19:24).

June 17

How painful deception can be.

It is indescribably violating to show up at an event, take our dog to the veterinarian, or stop to refuel our vehicle and find ourselves in the middle of a "staged conversation" with a perpetrator. This is what they call a *Random Encounter*. It seems to be a meaningless waste of time and precisely their goal: to waste our time and energy. We are commonly so isolated and hungry for conversation that we get set-up every time. Organized gangstalkers will do anything to pull us away from ourselves. Their job is to inconvenience us and get in the way of our plans. God's Plans. These perpetrators have no concern for us, and by their facial expressions, they are overly stimulated at the opportunity to detain us. They want to impress the group—those who are watching and listening to their ten minutes on stage. People from all age groups, nationalities, and neighborhoods are involved in this community-oriented policing program. When we really have no idea what to do, we take our problems to God. We do what we can and leave the rest to Him.

Lord, let me be amazed at Your power (Luke 9:43).

June 18

Wisdom flows through us when we ask God for it.

How easy it is to go to the other side. It seems like a flimsy soul is all that separates good from evil. Let us imagine that a friend has been doing things to raise our antenna. We have sloughed it off several times, and we cannot continue to ignore it. We have held this person in high esteem, but now they've let us down. We thought they loved us, but they have been spying on us to gather information. The many times we broke bread together were only secret plots to use us. We must learn to put our trust in the Lord, not in our fellow man for darkness is after him, too. We can move on from the pain of it all, but not before we are at the Lord's feet, telling Him all about it. If we ask for wisdom, we will get it (James 1:5). Meanwhile, can we handle the truth?

Lord, let me receive and understand Your hidden wisdom (1 Corinthians 2:7).

June 19

(What they do)
(They smile in your face)
All the time, they want to take your place
The back stabbers
(Back stabbers)
—The O'Jays

A loved one asks us to stop talking negatively about certain people. Little do they know what our spirit discerns whenever we are around them. Quite frankly, we do not put anything past anyone, anymore. We have seen how low people can go while smiling and pumping our mitt. Gangstalkers will do whatever is necessary to be admired by the group. They sleep with a target just to gain access to personal files or plant something in their house. They have already sold their soul; so, to expect them to have scruples is ludicrous. Targeted individuals deal with the ugly side of human kind, which can be difficult for our loved ones to fathom. We should not be surprised when people do not understand. We see first-hand the dishonorable tactics performed by perps for reasons that are far less than personal gain. Some participate in unruly skits just for attention. A hardened conscience lets one do strange things. No one may ever believe what we go through and what we know. That is okay. The Lord sees it all.

Lord, let those who seek after my soul be ashamed and confounded; let those who desire my hurt be turned backward and put to confusion (Psalm 70:2).

June 20

We need to use spiritual tools to win this battle.

Satan uses lasciviousness by using those things that appear small and insignificant to catch his prey in a net. He does this to gangstalkers who use no restraints in their efforts to look good in front of other members. We must be aware of what lasciviousness is, so we can recognize it. It is the groundwork in creating bondages such as the addictions that make perpetrators act like puppets. They are addicted to the false sense of power that organized stalking gives them. Gangstalkers are deceived by the government; they believe they are working as important spies when, in fact, they are only a part of society's lowlife. Soon, they lose their soul and all emotion until they are back onstage in a staged conversation with a new target. Satan uses lasciviousness to grab them by the short hairs.

Today, I loosen my neck from all bands (Isaiah 52:2).

June 21

Gangstalking is the hidden evil—thriving in plain sight.

Some people frown on solitude and isolation. To endure a lifetime of it, we must learn to adapt to it. If we have been in this game awhile, we find ourselves living in deeper isolation every year, without the choices or regular options we used to have. At some point, we get honest with ourselves and accept that we have lost most of our vibrant personality along with any people skills we may have had. Displacement and aloneness is the reason. That is why entertainers stay active; so, they don't get rusty. We have become so busy with mere survival that everything else has taken a back seat. We can begin to change this by communicating through social media. By adding a short comment on a video that would receive us a response from someone, we begin to feel a part of something instead of being isolated and alone.

Lord, release Your warrior angels against the demonic princes (Daniel 10:20).

June 22

We either accept our life or jump off a cliff—which is what they want.

We have lost everything overnight. We feel like we have been plucked out of one life and placed in the outer limits of another. While gangstalking exists on a whole other level of consciousness, it takes us constant effort to keep from becoming brainwashed. Years of rudeness, control, stalking, and harassment can take its toll on us. We are not living this lifestyle because we are losers; someone, for whatever reason, put us on the organization's hit list. So be it. We must excel at living and enjoying life to the best of our ability, even when it is against all odds. The gates of hell shall not prevail against us.

Remember me, O Lord, with the favor that You bring unto Your children, and visit me with Your salvation (Psalm 106:4).

June 23

Gee, if we get rid of friends that we know are involved, we won't have anybody to talk to.

We tend to trust the people closest to us and should not be surprised when we are betrayed. It is usually the husband, wife, or a family member who becomes our handler—those who are appointed by the organization to manage our life through manipulation and abuse. That goes for some people we work with, since our handlers can get changed out. Having an employer take part in our demise can be heartbreaking—especially if they were our friends. It is less of a liability for an employer if we voluntarily leave our job, rather than get involuntarily fired; this is where workplace mobbing[12] comes in. We must always be on our toes and not let our head get in the way of what our instincts tell us. Sometimes we sense that the people we trust are not trustworthy, but we go against our own spirit of knowledge. We do not want to believe that someone, with whom we spend a lot of time, is a perpetrator in disguise. We keep sweeping circumstances under the rug, even when we know we shouldn't. We must listen to our gut about people and give ourselves more credit than we do. We can have confidence in knowing that God is directing our situation.

Lord, teach my hands to war and my fingers to fight (Psalm 144:1).

---

[12] Workplace mobbing: A systematic harassment by a group of individuals in the workplace is commonly set in motion to make us quit our job and become unemployed—for life.

June 24

This type of death is a silent murder—designed to get the job done without raising questions.

Beginners really deal with a lot, all at once. By having the rug pulled out from under us, we are left disarmed early in the game. The truckloads of hassles and problems can wear us down to the point of becoming emotionally bankrupt. The last thing we want our therapist to ask us is if we still see strange people following us. There is not much help in this world for the targeted individual. The gritty underworld of gangstalking exists in silence. It is well hidden, yet fully functioning in plain view. It is hard for others to believe us, even when we offer them proof. Any suicides will go down as being caused by mental problems. Although, we are harassed, isolated, and emotionally tortured, our death raises fewer eyebrows if it is reported as a suicide caused by mental anguish.

Today, I will learn a technique for self-care that helps me to feel better, for I cannot let myself spiral into despair.

June 25

Gangstalking thrives at the surface of the underworld where it does not alarm the rest of society.

Post-traumatic stress disorder, or PTSD, is an anxiety disorder that affects people who have lived through a traumatic event. This is known to be among soldiers who come home after serving in a battle. TIs are soldiers who fight a hidden war. We are without resources to aid us in rehabilitation. We also do not get a four-year term of service. We are sentenced to a lifetime of punishment. We endure an existence of aloneness with very little, if any, moral support. Some of us connect to others through the Internet, where we find support groups and learn of similar global events taking place. People who have lost their life's possessions in hurricanes and earthquakes can teach us that life goes on, even without our things. In a roundabout way, we can find help.

Lord, make darkness light before me (Isaiah 42:16).

June 26

We bounce around inside a circle of people who are all one.

The same gangstalking and harassment techniques are used nationwide. The training may have started with the Stasi-East Germany Secret Police. Hand signals similar to those used by baseball players help gangstalking informants covertly communicate with one another; this really makes them feel important. Perpetrators do their homework on a prospective target long before they pull out the starting pin. The more isolated the target is, the better of an opportunity for the group to perform their finest cruelty. The more vicious the attack is, the better entertainment it is for the members. It is like a form of sport harassment, if you will. Behind the scenes, gangstalkers can coerce events and, sadistically, orchestrate a target's life. Once the group gets what they want, they downshift from friendliness to complete alienation, hoping to run the TI out of the area. Sometimes, strong-arm tactics are used to force the target out of the state. This is important to the organization, especially, if they stole guns and vehicles, or a lot of money was extorted from the target. The community, including the cops, would want this type of TI as far away as possible. Wherever the target goes, the nationwide members will continue the harassment to prevent him from returning for his property, or worse—revenge. This level of victimization can cause us post-traumatic stress disorder, but we must find ways to heal. There is no reason for us to settle for a life of discouragement. No matter how many times we get knocked down, we must get back up. God always sees our determination. When we do everything we can, God will do those things we can't.

Today I will withstand the enemy; I know that people, throughout the world, are suffering like me.

June 27

They think it is funny when we get blind-sighted.

Perpetrators will portray themselves as being frustrated or combative to distract a target while he/she gets blind-sighted. The shocking trauma of such an unexpected attack can leave us hollowed out.[13] Gangstalkers will use the pathetic aftermath of such a commencement of hostilities for sheer amusement. They will, joyfully, bring their children to view the broken TI to point and laugh at as if they were screening a caged animal at the zoo. It is something out of a horror film. We are like prisoners of war in our own country by our own people.

Each time a target stands strong, resisting Satan's temptation to commit suicide—another soul is won for the kingdom of God. We must help others to rise above the wiles of getting pounced on by these gangstalking goons. As we expose this crime, we chip away at the kingdom of darkness.

With my eyes I will see the reward of the wicked (Psalm 91:8).

---

13 Hollowed-out: thrashed and left empty with no value, worth, or effectiveness.

June 28

We cannot solve our problems with the same level of thinking that created them.
—Albert Einstein

We cannot settle for natural knowledge by expecting to save ourselves with filing police reports, sending letters to the FBI, or hiring an attorney. These natural ways of the world will avail us nothing, so we must rise above them and seek Godly wisdom. Spending time in prayer and reading the Bible aloud will change and strengthen our energy. If we are targeted by hate groups that practice voodoo rituals and black magic witchcraft, we can expect to experience a bizarre and restricting heaviness in the atmosphere. We can reroute evil spirits by speaking Bible scriptures *at* them; we can also read the Book of Psalms aloud. This is a heavy-duty weapon in keeping ourselves unavailable to any evil energy or curses sent our way.

Lord, help me to use Your Word to reroute curses before they reach me.

June 29

We are not lost souls, for we each have an appointed time.

Fear belongs to Satan. It keeps us from doing what God wants us to do. Once we are in fear, we cut ourselves off from everything divine, because we are no longer light-hearted, nor are we open and receptive to anything good. Fear and deception are the backbone to gangstalking and used to torment and paralyze us. One technique is to get a target sensitive to everyday stimuli like sounds, colors, and regular occurrences. A person's name may bring up incredible fear from them hurting us badly in the past. A certain street may cause us fear from something awful happening there. The sound of helicopters might trigger a panic attack. Once we are negatively sensitized, the perpetrators can activate our emotions like a remote toy. Fear-based emotions can control our reactions anytime and anywhere; thus, making it easier for perps to exhibit "flagged" people in a crowd. As soon as we spiral into an area of fear, it is imperative to have access to spiritual tools. We should always keep a dialogue going with the Lord quietly and secretly under our breath. We learn to turn a thing over to God before it traps us.

The fear of man brings a snare; but whoever puts his trust in the Lord shall be safe (Proverbs 29:25).

June 30

Although, our life is not comfortable, it is still possible to have some sort of dignity.

One day in midsummer, I glanced across the field of my Georgia country property. At the end of the road was a pool full of kids, laughing and playing a heated game of water ball. I waved hello, expecting them to wave back, but they did not. Instead, they each, quickly and simultaneously, jumped out of the pool and ran into the house like they had just seen a ghost. I stood motionless, as the abrupt silence pierced my heart like a racing arrow. We wonder why people do not respond properly to us anymore. Nobody wants us around. If we were ten years old and our mom told us the person next door was in a mental hospital, we would act scared, too. We would duck out of sight if we believed she was a witch and would cast a spell on us. Little ones can reveal the truth about their parents, so innocently. If we are praying for wisdom, we may just get it through a child. We learn to pray for the misinformed. We know that the more we bless our enemies, the more we are blessed when they mistreat us. Again, we grab for tools that are spiritual, for they never fail us.

Today, I will rule over my oppressors (Psalm 14:2).

A Bonus Reading

It's another day in Paradise.
—Eddie Little

It had been a decade and I was still able to keep from returning to state parks and Walmart parking lots. I was, however, living in Chicago and driving around without a driver's license. The Long Beach Police Department had stripped me of my California Commercial Driver's License and ability to continue teaching California Comedy Traffic School long before I was escorted out of the state by LAPD helicopters. Everything had been tampered with by the time I left California, including my credit. What had started as a fix-it ticket for a missing tail light had grown into a suspended license with a $4,600 fine. So, I had to drive without a license; something, I had since I was sixteen years old. Now I was on the lam, running from justice like a fugitive. One night, a Chicago cop pulled me over because my license plate light was, supposedly, burned out. He stood at my window and asked to see my driver's license, proof of insurance, and registration. As I leaned over to make some time by shuffling papers in my glove box, I softly whispered, "Jesus, help me." At that very moment, I heard a call come over the officer's radio. He tapped my door with his hand and said, "This is your lucky day," before rushing off. I continued to drive nationwide without a driver's license for several years. It was not by luck that I never got caught. Had God's hand not been on me, I could have been taken to jail. I would have lost Mama and Prettygirl as well as our home, which was a trailer that I pulled behind us. These problems were not the results of using drugs or alcohol, since there was none of that. These were tragic, life-changing, legal problems that were strategically orchestrated by gangstalking rogue cops.

The Lord is good, especially in a day of distress (Nahum 1:7).

July 1

Maybe the root cause of our gangstalking will, one day, save a life.

Some days, it seems we cannot win for losing as our emotions are all over the place. We know they are just feelings that won't kill us, but we are still overly emotional. What used to not phase us seems to bother us these days. Every day that we live our lives the best we can, we win against those evil spirits that fight against us. Even on a difficult day, we can muster up something to feel good about. Just being part of God's bigger plan seems to give us reason to carry on. Who knows? Perhaps, the restraining order that we took out on a gangster will, one day, save the life of someone's mother or sister. We are a "work in progress" and must hang on to that good feeling minute by minute. We cannot allow ourselves to spiral into hopelessness and despair. The blessings from God cannot penetrate through to us when we are wallowing in frustration and negativity. No problem is too big for God. We must keep our eyes off worldly things and stay focused on the spiritual things that are unseen.

He who endures to the end will be saved. Lord, help me to go the distance.

July 2

We often forget to step out of the war zone in between battles.

We have been carrying unbearable weight on our shoulders and have developed tunnel vision from doing it for so long. If we focus only on our problems, we could be amid a blessing and not know it. We can get out of an emotional funk, instantly, if we can see it for what it really is: the devil's plan to distract us from God. We try to function in life with our eyes open. Nothing is done on blind faith, since the Bible tells us everything we need to know. It tells us about the promises we can rely on. The more we immerse ourselves in the spiritual warfare that gangstalking is, the better we can discern between the voice of God and that of Satan. Whether we want it or not, it is now our job, since gangstalking is a spiritual war of many battles.

Lord, let Your showers of blessings be upon my life (Ezekiel 34:26).

July 3

When we stay connected to Jesus, His Spirit will help us to instinctively know how to survive the next season of events.

We all have a story about running amok when our name first turned up on a target list. We were desperately seeking answers in the beginning as to why we were evicted from our apartment and why strange people were following us. We were constantly stopped by police for no reason. Strangers treated us rudely wherever we went. Plus, we had to suddenly fix a lot of broken things around our home or car, depending on where we were living. If we survived this first stage of confusion, then we had to decide if—and how—we would live. Although, we have gotten a handle on a few gangstalking rules like the basic characteristics of gangstalking perpetrators, along with some of their Stasi hand signals and a possible modus operandi, the temptation of suicide still hangs around the front door of our life. We hear it knocking. It's always there. We ignore it. We will become seasoned targets because we are among the chosen few destined to make it.

Thunder in the heavens against the enemy, O Lord (Psalm 18:13).

July 4

God is on His own schedule.

It is funny how we think we have surrendered until we *really* surrender. Trying to understand the mind games and deception used by harassment groups can be like traveling upstream for someone who is naive to the underworld. Even a little knowledge on how gangstalking operates can immensely help us in our survival. We may come from a family where no one was gang-affiliated, yet we find ourselves in the grips of street soldiers who take orders from their aunts and uncles. Our lifestyles are from two completely different worlds. It seems like there are bullies on one side of the tracks and patsies on the other. One side is aware of the gangstalking phenomenon, while the other side does not have a clue. If we cling to Jesus, we are guaranteed to win. It may not look like it from where we stand, but there are biblical promises that we can rely on. Our task is to let go and trust in Him.

I pray for the willingness to accept my life exactly as it is in this very moment.

July 5

The Holy Spirit works in us to distinguish truth through the smoke screens of our enemies.

Not all gangstalkers are willing participants. A nephew on parole would be forced by cops to play a part in our demise. We might have to confront him as to why he always has his cell phone nearby whenever we are talking. We understand that members listen in on staged conversations through the open microphone. Pulling a perpetrator's covers may also be shaming; sending him from a Mach-1 level of anger to Mach-10 in five seconds. This is how perps act when we let them know we are hip to their game. They get angry and aggressive as a ploy to distract us. They also act dramatic, since the group is watching and/or listening in. What really happens when we confront them is that the perpetrator gets cut from the group. This upsets the perp immensely, and we can clearly observe him take an emotional nose dive. He might even cry with it having nothing to do with us. Perps do not care about us, only their role within the group; it is fun for them to play someone, collectively. When the Holy Spirit comes upon us and we get anointed, we are given discernment—the gift of knowledge. When we get connected to the Holy Spirit, we understand things that used to baffle us. Sometimes we see things we wish we didn't.

God, let me have and walk in an excellent spirit today (Daniel 6:3).

July 6

God has a plan for our life, even when we feel it is over.

Imagine there are different regions in a city, all with various levels of consciousness. Stretch it out worldwide and envision it. The world has areas of darkness and other areas of light. Those regions that are cursed show nothing but darkness. Satan has a strongman in charge of those places. The strongman—a high-ranking demon—has many lower-level demons that obey him; thus, resembling how gangstalkers and street gangs function. These places of darkness are unusual, to say the least, and the presence of evil can be felt in the air. The people are weird, and the animals are even weirder. It is like entering another partition or dimension that soon compels us to want to hightail it out of there. God, obviously, does not give us all the details to our destiny at once because He wants us to depend on Him every step of the way.

Today, I will bind the strongman and spoil his goods (Matthew 12:29).

July 7

The Hidden Evil: an underground system run by the mob, government, and law enforcement.

All kinds of people make up community watch groups. These people are approached by men with badges—not necessarily law enforcement but impersonators. Fake files have been created on us, displaying family photos and the whole nine yards. Neighbors will be told that we are under surveillance for some awful thing we have done. We watch mothers hurry their kids indoors whenever we drive up or even walk the dog. People from cultures that are unfamiliar with gangstalking will react differently to these lies, based upon their worldly views and beliefs. Each of our neighbors will interpret what they hear about us in a different way, depending on where they come from. Some will continue to be polite to us, while others will show us their venom at once. We should be aware of the ideas and attitudes within other cultures, especially if we are targeted in a large city with mixed ethnicity. In smaller towns, country folk will blindly and eagerly jump on the gangstalking bandwagon simply for something to do. We must try to stay spiritually connected to God and stay receptive to His presence. We work at getting our spirit and mouth to work together to rebuke any evil intentions sent our way by the many peculiar people who suddenly seem to live all around us.

Lord, bless me indeed, and enlarge my coast. Let Your hand be with me and keep me from evil (1 Chronicles 4:10).

July 8

Something inside us says, it is time to roll; we leave a situation just moments before a catastrophe happens.

When we incline our ear unto wisdom and apply our heart to understanding (Proverbs 2:2), we begin to have divine interventions. We might bite our tongue during an intense argument before meekly walking away, or we could see a demon behind the person's eyes with whom we are having a conversation. This world has nothing to offer us. God is really the only one we can safely trust. Satan, the expert deceiver, has even deceived himself about his own powers and the prophecy of Jesus' return. He will be locked up for one thousand years when Jesus comes back. Now he is running frenziedly, causing worldwide chaos, since he is almost out of time. We should walk in confidence and stay grounded in God's Word, so that those who are deceived will not affect us.

In the name of Jesus, I release the whirlwind to scatter those who would conspire against me.

July 9

Watch what you pray for because you might just get it.

God will give us skillful knowledge and wisdom if we ask Him for it. Organized stalking is successful at ruining people's lives, partly because of the secrecy within the groups. The gangstalking perpetrators function under the authority of secret societies, while the targeted individuals rarely know any details of what is going on. When we do learn about our situation, we must remember that we asked God for wisdom. Yes, we got what we prayed for, whether we like it or not. Great disappointment comes from learning that someone is betraying us; this deception is deeply painful. We get our blessings and wisdom from God, not from anyone in this world.

Father, it is written in Proverbs 2:6 that you will give me wisdom in my situation. I am here in Jesus' name, boldly asking you for it. I believe I receive it. Amen.

January 10

We become stronger as time goes on.

We seek God in the middle of conflict. We find our confidence and assurance in Him. We rarely find it in the hands of anybody we know these days. We become grateful, by recalling the times that God was faithful in bringing us out of danger. When we are in trouble, the first place we need to be is clinging to Him, since we cannot handle these issues by ourselves. If God has brought us through danger once, He will do it again. We should always include Him in our ongoing safety strategies, so we can stand strong in the high winds. We thank Him in advance for His promise to fight our battles for us.

The name of Jesus is a strong tower. I run into it and I am safe (Proverbs 18:10).

July 11

There is evil among us in the most ordinary places.

There are gateways in this world that lead to dark and unholy realms. We tend to develop a keen sense of intuitiveness, ESP, a sixth sense, or a gut instinct about the underworld. There are times we wonder if our subconscious is playing games to fulfill some need we have. The reality is our subconscious mind helps us with what we need. Targeted individuals have extraordinary needs that most people do not understand. Folks do not have a clue as to how we live on the cutting edge, 24/7. If a person wants to have anything to do with us, they must accept our special needs. Some balk at our requests; therefore, letting us know up front that they will not meet them. This could force us into deeper isolation or even spiral us into depression. In time, we find ourselves better equipped to lay the groundwork for anyone who genuinely wants to get close to us. We do not complicate our life when we create personal boundaries. We simplify it. We must have our boundaries and personal needs honored by family members and outsiders if they want to be a part of our life. Period.

I can easily let go of people who do not care about my needs and wants.

July 12

Most of us have been stripped of all privileges and rightful dignity.

We have allowed our grief-stricken state of being to become woven into the tapestry of our lives. We justify feeling unhappy as better than not feeling at all. Some of us do not even question it anymore, for we expect to be disappointed. We must never live without the optimism and confidence of God's promises. The forces behind grief and sorrow are evil spirits sent from the dark side to further destroy us. Luciferians put curses on people by sending us these devastating demonic spirits to coax us into committing suicide. God made Satan as a beautiful archangel named Lucifer, but when his pride got in the way, God kicked him out of heaven. Just as there are people who follow Jesus, there are many more who follow and worship Lucifer. They believe in his powers because they are real. Evil spells and curses are spiritual and must be fought on a supernatural level. We will surely lose if we attempt to fight them on a natural level. We command the spirits to be removed from our life in Jesus' name and to be burned at the roots by the fire of God. We then fill that void with positive affirmations and scriptures. Reading from the Book of Psalms aloud will make darkness flee, for it cannot co-exist with the light of God's Word.

I trust You, Lord, that You are training me in steadiness. I am to always focus on You.

July 13

Oh, but I'll live on,
I'll be strong;
It's just not my cross to bear.
—The Allman Brothers

Many of us are targeted because someone refused to take responsibility for their own actions. We have been forced to carry something that is not ours to carry. There are lots of people who do not have the grace of God and are unable to look honestly at themselves. And without some sort of help, most people can only point a finger. We know we cannot change others, especially those who do not want to be changed. Also, it is ridiculous to try and stop our neighbors from harassing us by giving them gifts in a desperate attempt to get them to like us. If we focus too much on the stuff we cannot change, we miss what we should be doing in the line of God's will. When the time comes, we stand in front of God to give an account of our life. So, we do not let their actions control us by stealing our joy while we are still here on Earth. We do not spend our life upset about something we cannot do anything about. When we take responsibility for ourselves, we can make our own decisions. If we do not, nothing will change.

Today, I take my focus off the world and put it on myself, where I meet Jesus on my path.

July 14

It behooves us to learn how to protect ourselves.

We mustn't allow our life to become wasted. We need to do what we can to make it worth living. We cannot keep doing the same things over and over just because we are on a nationwide hate list. It is our responsibility to become knowledgeable on protecting ourselves. We know that perpetrators can remotely turn on our telephone receivers, using them as microphones to listen to our actions. It used to be that only the Feds could do that, but now anyone can download eavesdropping apps to their cell phones and computers. A TI can have more privacy by not carrying a cell phone everywhere. Most people have their cell phones within a foot of them all day and night. We even carry it with us into the bathroom. The telephone GPS is tracking us wherever we drive. Turning the Wi-Fi off and putting the phone on airplane mode is another way to block access to us, but not much. In the world of gangstalking, our cell phone has become an excellent surveillance and harassment tool. Removing the battery is the only way to successfully disconnect from the perps. Televisions are now being used for surveying the target in their home. A micro camera is set up behind the light on the front of the TV; this can be covered with a band-aid to block their viewing ability, while we can still use our remote control. Lately, people have been claiming that we are watched over the entire screen of our Smart TV. Our best bet is to completely unplug the unit from the wall when it is not in use.

God, let the hidden things be made manifest (Mark 4:22).

July 15

Many targets are hit with energy weapons from a base of operation near their home.

Sometimes, we do not feel good: Our head pounds for days with no relief from painkillers, or we cannot think straight due to our thoughts being in a state of confusion. Our eyes can burn so badly, we must lie down and close them because we cannot do anything else. Nausea and heartburn, as well as dizziness, can overtake us in an instant, causing us to have to sit still. And what about those swirls and flashes of colored lights that we see on occasion? We may even flip between feeling hot and cold throughout the day and night. Sometimes, we just don't feel good.

Lord, help me today to not cast my pearls before swine, or waste any of my precious time on evildoers. Please give me discernment through the Holy Spirit as to how I can better protect myself.

July 16

It takes effort to keep our energy focused on one thing.

Our enemies have specific goals to kill, steal, and destroy. Most perpetrators smile and act friendly, as they pretend to help us with something. Distracting us from our plans is one of their big time moves. If they can get us off course, they can keep us from our calling. The Bible is full of stories of Satan and his cohorts using lies and deception to destroy people. It is amazing how gullible people have become; how they believe any smut they hear about someone. If our perps keep setting fires for us to put out, we will spend all our time putting out fires. We are far better off getting rid of these so-called acquaintances. Our life might seem boring at first, but we will have less drama keeping us from our purpose.

I rebuke and destroy every trap the devil has set for me (Psalm 140:5).

July 17

We are not targeted for success; we are targeted to be destroyed.

The wisdom we pray for might not be pretty when we get it. We could learn about something that deeply hurts us like being deceived by a close friend or family member. Imagining that we could function better by doing drugs is not a way for us to think. We need to be extra cautious with everything we do, especially with what we ingest. Gangstalkers are control freaks; they are big on drugging and poisoning people and their animals. If we use street drugs, we may as well hand over our life, since the dope will probably be laced with something we did not bargain for. The Bible tells us to stay sober and vigilant because our enemy goes around like a roaring lion, looking for someone to eat. It is to our advantage to keep our mind functioning properly and not impair our judgment by drinking or using. We must take care of ourselves to stay healthy and whole. We ask God for His wisdom in making all big and small decisions.

In the name of Jesus, I bind and cast out all spirits of self-delusion, self-deception, and self-seduction caused by drinking and using.

July 18

Gangstalking perps take their role very seriously because it is important how they look to one another.

Our conscious contact with God is our only hope for survival. For the typical targeted individual, life becomes no laughing matter. We are quickly outnumbered when the local police infiltrate our social networks, systematically destroying any relationships we might have. We become disillusioned and hopeless when no one takes our back, and we are left stranded like a lone wolf. We begin to run from the law, ironically, without having done anything wrong. After we exhaust all worldly solutions, we finally go to Jesus. He knows what it is like to be kissed and betrayed. We go to Him when we think the only remedy is a handful of pills or a bottle of whiskey, since He knows about temptations from being hungry, lonely, and tired. He performed miracles in front of people who still did not believe what they saw. He healed the sick and helped hurting people and look what the world did to Him. They humiliated him, beat him, and then nailed Him to a cross. Jesus knows what it is like to be mistreated. When we try to move along, but the world is not interested in us anymore, we go talk to Jesus. Before we begin to talk things over with Him, we gift-wrap all our troubles and lay them at His feet. This way, there are no hindrances to keep us from hearing what He has to say.

Lord, surround me with Your shield of protection as I move through this day (Psalm 5:12).

July 19

We have a life. It is real. It may not be the one we want, but it is ours to embrace.

We ought to stop focusing on our mere existence and begin to enjoy the small things. Firstly, we stop comparing our life to gauge where we are. Our perpetrators are not as free as they look. They have sold themselves out and are in bondage to Satan. Even though our friends have disappeared, and we have lost many material things, we are still in charge of our behavior. Secondly, we must try to give ourselves the best life possible. We practice smiling wherever we go. We play with our dogs, shovel the snow, water the plants, wash the car, and get our mail with a smile on our face. This will irk our neighbors and show them that our spirit is not broken. We neither acknowledge them, nor engage in conversation with them, for we refuse to be set up to be distressed. We can completely bypass them by simply wearing earphones and sunglasses. We are alive. We have a life. We find a way.

I am sitting in heavenly places in Christ, far above all principality, power, might, and dominion (Ephesians 1:3).

July 20

There is one thing in life that is certain: things change.

People do not like change and will go out of their way to avoid it. It is normal for us to look at all the terrible violations and get melancholy over our losses. Having a resistant mindset toward change goes against the grain of how life works. We should invite change, look forward to it, and try to see it as positive. Our doom and gloom will grow to enormous heights as we focus on just the negative things in life. It hurts us when we only see things from a negative perspective. For example, we just moved into a new place. It does not belong to us, but it is where we rent. We can go months without appreciating the backyard, or that we live only a few miles from our mother, or that we found a landlord willing to take our pets. All we focus on is the fact that we are still throwing money away on rent. It takes effort to keep our attitude from going south, when we are deliberately being controlled and oppressed. We must make a habit of looking for the blessings in everything, because it is in the middle of our mess that God blesses us.

Let the heavens be opened over my life and let me see visions (Ezekiel 1:1).

July 21

We deny its effect on us—all those evil attempts at brainwashing.

Having discipline and setting boundaries in our life can prevent a lot of sad things from happening. We have thought, at one time or another, that living on the edge was exciting. Now all we want is to live in peace and quiet. Jesus wants us to have peace and will help us to set up boundaries to de-stress. Perhaps we need to stop going somewhere in particular, or we need to cut off a phony friendship. Accomplishing these things, one day at a time, exercises discipline in our self-care. We stay true to ourselves when we take responsibility for our own wellbeing. We must find our comfort zone and learn how to live within it, or we will never enjoy life. We take our eyes off *them* and focus on making our life worth living.

(Suggested scripture reading: Numbers 11:11-14.)

God, Send Your angels before me to prosper my way (Exodus 33:2).

July 22

We must find innovative ways of coping, functioning, and building a safe life that is peaceful.

Obtaining drugs to ease emotional pain is risky behavior. It is easier to turn to alcohol, but we cannot trust bartenders and servers either. Targeted individuals have horrific stories of being drugged at restaurants and clubs. Friendly waiters are notorious for spiking drinks. We really do not have the luxury of ordering alcoholic drinks, unless it is a bottle of wine—and opened at the table; this is a personal boundary we must insist on. We should always practice moderation in our actions. Suppressed anger can fester to dangerous levels when we are intoxicated, causing us more problems than it is worth. We are not alone; targets throughout the world go through the same feelings. No matter what, we can make it through another day—this day.

I decree: The enemy will not take my inheritance through oppression (Ezekiel 46:18).

July 23

When there is no more use for us, it is like getting out of Dodge City after the gunfight.

There is nothing more personal than getting run out of town, after having our life torn apart. We have lived through a lot of destruction already, but there are diverse levels a TI must endure. Every person that leaves our life seems to take a piece of our heart with them. The silence of being alone, throughout the years, seems to grow in unison with our loneliness. We have been jobless, penniless, and friendless while standing against monumental hardships and dilemmas by ourselves. We try to transition back into the real world, but no one seems to care about us. A code of silence keeps most uninvolved bystanders ignorant of any local crime ring of gangstalkers, while others are too afraid to not get involved. Other folks become influenced by the local sheriff's office or police department and become willing to help oust us from the area. We must encourage ourselves to practice the presence of Jesus. He understands us. We can always count on Him to be with us.

Today, I am a miracle in motion; watch me as I wave goodbye.

July 24

With our name on a nationwide list for lifetime punishment, we can sometimes feel it is entirely our fault.

If we are not dead, we might be forced to start over somewhere else. That is when reality hits hard. We feel ashamed that we have managed to cause all this trouble. *If only I hadn't dated that person or witnessed that crime; if I hadn't taken out that restraining order.* Shame can either keep us from knowing the truth or kick us into denial, where we forget the truth. Our shame can direct and control us if we do not shake it off. People make mistakes out of passion. We must forgive ourselves and throw away any dishonor. It surprises us that we might be carrying around our perpetrator's shame. It is not unusual for a victimizer to transfer his/her shame onto a victim. We do not need to do that anymore, and from now on, we let people carry their own stuff. It is time that our haters take responsibility for their own shortcomings.

Today, I will unravel the tight robe of shame from around me and kick it to the curb.

July 25

We have become the focal point of someone's resentment, jealousy, anger, or shame.

When we are living on the streets, personal hygiene takes a back seat to survival. We notice how old acquaintances look at us. Our shame builds up and we want to crawl in a hole, but we cannot. We have just crawled out of the trenches where we have been fighting for our life, and now we refuse to bow down to anyone. We have become aware of many things since fighting this war. If this is about punishment, we know we are the focal point of someone else's issues. They want us to carry their shame for something they did. Targeted individuals are heroic survivors—fighting a battle that we have never been trained for. We have gone through things that most people cannot wrap their mind around. We do not quit! We made it this far and can get back on track—step-by-step, one day at a time.

I may have lost the battle, but because my soul is not up for grabs, I will win the war.

July 26

How could someone like us help another person?

We are living in our parents' basement because our lives were taken away, and we have very little left. We are either unemployed due to smear campaigns, or we have a job where we suffer from "workplace mobbing"—another form of gangstalking. But, we made it through the initiation stage and are still here to talk about it. That makes us valuable. We can help other targets—newcomers—to get through the initial stage. The beginning is a fragile time when the bottom falls out and everything spins out of control, often leaving an innocent person hollowed out.

There are many ways we can help awaken society to this covert crime: we can blog/vlog on the internet, write books, make bumper stickers, put up flyers, call radio talk shows, design a website, or stand on a corner with a sign. We can place small index cards that list informative websites in public restrooms and laundromats or post signs on our property that read: *Stop community bullying/gangstalking*. If God calls on us to help troubled and oppressed souls, He will let us know how to do it. We can take something meant for evil and turn it around for something good. Helping someone else is a perfect mission for burnt-out old-timers. It gives us reason to press on.

I trust in the Lord with all my heart and lean not unto my own understanding. In all ways I acknowledge Him, and He shall direct my path (Proverbs 3:5-6).

July 27

Imagine, waking up in the morning to your unique purpose in life: to spoil someone's day.

There are gangstalkers who wake up each morning with a specific job to do. These perps have an assignment to cause hardship or heartbreak in someone's life. Their job is to hurt people, day-after-day and year-after-year. They are miserable human beings with hardened hearts. Most of them have hefty drug addictions to support, since they cannot stand themselves. They have sold their soul for a little something in this material world and now carry a personal curse. Gangstalking neighbors will never be something or someone they are not. They are being who they really are: dead and hollow inside. Satan has them existing in their own hell. Some of the old-school perpetrators wear the devil's torment like a wetsuit: tight and constraining. A trained eye can easily spot them as they look tired, worn-out, and constipated. Living our lives with a plan and purpose may have been thrown to the wind; however, until we start developing our faith, we will stay stuck where evil wants us. Faith is the only thing that will overcome this world. We must never lose it, or we will lose our way.

Now faith is the substance of things hoped for, and the evidence of things not seen (Hebrews 11:1).

July 28

Training our mind from focusing on them is like exercising a muscle we have never used.

We should learn to live for an audience of one—God, not the perps who listen and watch us all day. Feeling discouraged, upset, and blaming everyone else, will get us nowhere. First, we set our mind ahead of time to how we will think and feel if a certain situation arises; we then exercise our mind to think that way. Targeted individuals are up against many tricksters. There are tons of members who work shifts around us, and no matter how much progress we make, we need daily discipline to keep from talking about all the negativity surrounding us. Everything is a mind game. If they can break us in our mind, then they got us by the short hairs.

In the name of Jesus, I bind and rebuke every spirit that would try to distort, disturb, or disintegrate the development of my personality.

July 29

Some of the federal and state employees involved in gangstalking are sheriffs, police officers, feds, marshals, game wardens, fire fighters, and utility company employees. We are steadfast in our battle to stay alive.

Yes. We might be overburdened and starved for love, affection, and truth. No doubt, we are unemployed and homeless, too. The haters take us down to ground zero, with hopes that we kill ourselves. We sure wouldn't have far to go, being that we have been camped out at the gates of hell for years without anyone extending to us a helping hand. Silence is a form of consent. Priests and pastors who preach about Jesus and then watch as the community baits us into a trap are a special breed of evil. If the beast is, in fact, a government where all participants are one-minded, we must get busy learning what the Book of Revelation would have us to do. Suicide and homicide are of the devil. God is about choosing life.

Lord, deliver my soul from lying lips and a deceitful tongue (Psalm 120:2).

July 30

A person who lives within will always excel beyond.

We go through struggles that most people do not understand. Our developed senses are *on point* from all the games played around us. We become highly aware of the repetitive daily activities performed by our neighbors. We are *on the ball* about the guy next door, who just moved back in with his parents; he always seems to throw out the garbage whenever we are outside. We are also cued to the synchronicity of how one neighbor leaves, another one arrives. Never are both neighbors gone at the same time. Clearly, there are watch shifts. Our landlord will trip up and say something about our personal life—something that happens behind our closed doors that he shouldn't know about. We are aware of the unbearable fact that everything we say and do is monitored. The only way to live through this nightmare is to abide in the Holy Spirit. In His world, logic does not apply, and we do not have to try to figure everything out.

He who dwells in the secret place of the Most High, shall abide under the shadow of the Almighty (Psalm 91:1).

July 31

The hardest thing has been walking the straight line and not turning villain.

When I pull myself up from where I have been, despite my haters, I get to feel good about myself. After a perpetrator busted in my house through a doggy door and bullied me around, I shot off a 9mm pistol to scare him away. Since he had installed the doggy door some months earlier, he had been secretly using it to steal money and jewelry when I wasn't home. He must have installed cameras to see where I hid my father's inheritance, because he had helped himself to that, too. He had been covertly drugging me, while putting me on public display for scheduled feeding frenzies amongst the neighbors. With help from local deputy sheriffs, he stole the 2005 Chevrolet Suburban that my dad had left me, with only thirteen thousand miles on it. As this drug-infested demon ranted and raved at me, we fought in a knock-down fight for the pistol. After I got a hold of it, I could easily have put it to his head and pulled the trigger. I had every good reason known to man. But, for a split second, I saw how pathetic he really was—a slave to the underworld. He had sold his soul just to reach a little promotion on the streets. I could not allow myself to go down with the ship. The sheriff's deputies laughed at me whenever I called to have my pistol returned. I overheard comments from inside the criminal investigation department about how I needed shooting lessons; the deputies had fun with the fact that I shot up my house rather than the perpetrator. They didn't have a clue that my dad taught me how to shoot when I was a kid, so we could go deer hunting together. I had been shooting guns for years. They had no idea that I was one step ahead of the game by knowing that if I had shot this intruder, I would be in jail, without a ticket. As a target of this insidious gangstalking underworld, I must abide by a new set of rules, for the world's judicial system does not apply to me anymore, since my citizen rights have been taken away. It has been difficult to not act out of revenge; to not have a weak moment of acting in a way that anybody would. It has taken every ounce of strength to be bigger than my enemies and outsmart those who would love to put me away. None of which would be possible if I were not under the Almighty Hand of God.

I am beautiful, special, and stronger than all of them.

August 1

We are in the middle of a spiritual war between life and death.

Some of us expose our stories on *YouTube* to help us cope with the injustice of our attacks. By connecting with others, we notice a similar pattern of techniques that are being used around the globe. We read how some targets have moved to other states, only to find even less reprieve from the insanity. We discover that police officers and firefighters are involved nationwide, and that regular people get recruited into these harassment groups daily. We should never fully trust anyone over the Internet, either, as there are undercover perpetrators posing as targets. Spy sites reveal the many easy-to-buy spy gadgets like tracking and hearing devices, as well as an assortment of counter-spy hardware. Some of the targeted warriors, who have gone before us, teach us what works and what does not. Sadly, we read about people having committed suicide while their grieving families are still being targeted. By the end of the day, our gratitude grows for one thing or another. God gives us enough grace for each day, one day at a time. We do not get the grace today that we will need for tomorrow. Suicide is never God's plan for us. By connecting and sharing with others, we can wiggle our way out of having a victim mentality. We are worth the try.

I do not know what God's plan is for me, but I know He works through people. I have good reason to live today if I can stop another target from dying.

August 2

It is when we stand up on the inside that haters are attracted to us, since they want what we possess.

The very thing that makes God happy can be an attraction that causes us to be hated by others. Being anointed is threatening to those who are not, and possessing this quality is probably why we got the green light.[14] A recent study in domestic abuse claims that angry partners feel power and control over their mate's inner strength while they are physically beating them up. People who are exceptionally jealous or feel threatened by us seem to be much happier when watching us get squashed. One translation of the Bible reads: *Don't cast away your confidence, for payday is coming* (*Hebrews 10:35*). God will reward us if we stay strong on the inside. Even if we live in a wheelchair, or we are bedridden with an illness or disability, we can still stand up on the inside. The more we can endure without folding, the bigger will be our reward. We may not be free today, but someday very soon, we will see the Son of man coming in a cloud with power and great glory (Luke 21:27).

Today, I will not throw away my confidence as it will be richly rewarded (Hebrews 10:35).

---

14 Green light: the act of putting a hit out on a target. A term used when there is a price on your head; to give permission, or a go ahead, to move forward with a project or a whack job.

August 3

There is a part of us that would love to be Rambo for just one day.

We are often envied for the inner quality we possess. We lean on a higher power to help us decipher through the muck in our lives. The closer we stay to our Heavenly Father, the more inner strength we unleash; however, we can quickly lose it in public when perpetrators move in with *Directed Conversation*. This is when two perps get close to the target while carrying on a conversation about the target's private life. We are triggered[15] and will soon come apart at the seams. This attack is psychically brutal and executed to ruffle our feathers and zap us of our good energy. If we complain about it, we will look nuts, so we decide to stay indoors and become a part of the ever-growing population of people who are shut-ins. But are we safe? Maybe our private life is being transmitted over a closed-circuit video system via cable or satellite. No matter what is unleashing around us, we should feel proud to still be alive. The quieter we become, the better we can hear the voice of God, anyway. He will instruct us on our next move.

Today, I will continue to grow, despite it all.

---

15 Trigger: something that suddenly kicks off feelings of trauma, sadness, anxiety, or panic.

August 4

It takes 6 to 9 months for perpetrators to get their hooks deeply into our lives.

At first, there is a strategic guerrilla warfare[16] plan that is set in motion. They investigate where we work, bank, and go on weekends; who we see; what bills we have; how much money we have saved; and who might leave us what in their last will. Next, the rugs get pulled out from under us and our life falls apart in a domino effect. We have been tactically disarmed and displaced to be methodically stripped of everything in an ambush. We may even be drugged or poisoned. Once their goal has been successfully completed, they will want us gone. We will be totally cut off from the group, and if we don't quickly leave the area, the local cops will get involved to help speed things along. Life can get real quiet, fast. This is the end of the road for some targets as they commit suicide, understandably. The gangstalking crew that pulled the wool over us are well-seasoned. For them, we were merely a means to an end. They have been doing this to people for years; this is all they know and as far as they go. For us, we get a moment of reprieve, when we can pull ourselves up and wipe our nose, or even kick an addiction. Our actions toward surviving have been Herculean, and we should be proud of ourselves. We have been taken by the best of the best, and it took an army of them. We made it out alive. We will never be the same.

In the name of Jesus, I break any limitations and restrictions off my life that are placed there by evil spirits.

---

16 Guerrilla warfare: activities involved in a war, fought by small groups of soldiers.

August 5

This world offers lifeless ashes compared to where we spend eternity.

There might come a time when we are driven by a need for information. Maybe, it was because of smear campaigns[17] that our small business folded and our friends ran away, leaving us to stand alone. We might also have been robbed, exploited, or left with our credit ruined. It is possible, but highly unlikely that they tried to kill us before we moved away and have not been bothered since. A lot of us have tried to escape by relocating, only to face hell someplace else. No matter how much information we gather, or where we reposition ourselves, life will never be as we once knew it. So be it! As we broaden our mind and spirituality, we find joy in the fact that our time here is short.

I know how they work; therefore, I cannot be caught off guard. I work on my inner strength, and I get stronger with each struggle.

---

17 Smear campaign: a form of soft kill executed on a person by making false accusations and spreading lies.

August 6

Wake up! Community-policing groups are watching TIs in their homes on CCTV.[18]

Gangstalking neighbors collect personal information on how we live our daily lives to harass us. As pathetic as it has become, monitoring devices are now installed in our doorways to alert perps when we come and go. These devices are then synchronized to their cell phone SIM Card. Creepy neighbors can synchronize specific behaviors like calling their dog to whenever we walk out the front or back of our house. Surveillance through our satellite televisions also help them to work against us, since they are watching us live in—what we think is—the privacy of our own home. This sneaky, mafia-like, community network of neighbors will covertly run this game on us until they either break us or get rid of us completely. This is a very shaming tactic. We must approach these issues on both a logical and spiritual level. After we bind and rebuke these intrusive spirits in Jesus' name, we plead the blood of Jesus over our home. We then simply unplug the television. This long and drawn-out problem will quickly go away. After years of such violation and intrusion, we watch with discernment as the neighborhood not only mourns their loss of control, but they will purposely try to avoid us.

In the name of Jesus, I loosen myself from the demons that would try to frustrate and discourage me in my own home.

---

[18] Closed-circuit television (CCTV) is a camera surveillance system in which video signals from cameras are transmitted by cable or satellite to remote PCs, cell phones, tablets and Smart TVs.

August 7

We must be careful to stay as level-headed and unemotional as possible.

We can spend too much time rifling for tracking devices, wireless cameras, and bugs. A lot of energy is wasted when we try to gather incriminating evidence to prosecute a perpetrator. Illegal 24-hour surveillance does not allow us a safe place to keep important documents, pictures, film, or equipment. If we are so closely watched, how do we even set up a court date without them knowing? Our phone calls are recorded, and our email is controlled, so we forget that. If our vehicle does not start the day of a court hearing, we need to have a Plan B. Anything is possible if the police are in on it. They can easily make us miss an important court date, but even if they do not, then gangstalking-affiliated judges are certainly not hard to find; they are everywhere. We can spend a lot of time and energy preparing to fight for our rights, while gangstalking officials keep us spun like a top. On the other hand, we can always hand the garbage over to God and spend that time taking care of ourselves. Self-care is something we cannot do without. No clever work comes from working under confusion, anger, urgency, or fear. We need to have a sense of peace before we move ahead. Obtaining proper rest, eating good meals, and practicing spiritual care becomes a priority, even if we must fight for it.

Today, I will let go of the chaos and get honest with myself. I will get peaceful first, and then let my work and life emerge from there.

August 8

I have to wear earplugs in my home just to ignore their verbal assaults and am now going to the bathroom with a blanket covering me just to assure a little privacy!
—Alan Wilson

We are at a point of not trusting anyone. Like a child leans on a grown up, we must learn to trust ourselves. What does our gut tell us? We expect our mature side to take care of us when we are hungry, tired, angry, and lonely, but lately, we feel like a child with no say-so over anything. That part of us relies on our adult side for nurturing and meeting our needs. We must be there for ourselves, especially, since we are isolated with no friends or family support. Without us, who will keep groceries in the house, read us spiritual stories, or tuck us into bed? God directs us through the Holy Spirit, but He does not grocery shop for us. As we include Him in everything, He will help us with whatever we need to do for ourselves. We listen to our inner needs and try our best to meet them.

Today, I am first. I will do whatever I need to do for myself.

August 9

We cannot find joy in our life if we do not like who we are.

It is difficult to be around people we do not like. We will always be miserable if we dislike who we are, because we take ourselves everywhere we go. Getting mad for something we did in the past is also a waste of time and energy. We do not have the luxury of beating ourselves up, especially if we want to live with some sense of peace and joy. We only need to ask God once for forgiveness, not ten times. For most of us, the only love and kindness we get is from ourselves. The child within us goes through a lot of persecution and deserves our affection. We need to have peace with God and with our self, no matter how other people treat us.

I care very little if I am judged by you or by any human court; indeed, I do not even judge myself (1 Corinthians 4:3 [NIV]).

August 10

Untested faith is having no faith at all.

We cannot see the miracle by looking at the problem. We can become oblivious to our blessings by constantly looking at our messes. We become so wrapped up in all the spying and conspiracies around us, that it saturates us in despair. Keeping ourselves from plummeting into depression and self-pity only comes by focusing our attention away from our undesirable circumstances. The darker our lives become, the more entrapped and helpless we feel. Self-pity will lead us to depression and then to despair, until we want to die. The goal behind gangstalking is to pile enough misery on us until we commit suicide. There are some perpetrators who feel guilty about their evil actions, but in time, their hearts become hardened with practice. When we begin to have thoughts about suicide, or we notice ourselves leaning that way, hopefully, we have trained our mind to quickly focus on Jesus; this is how we progress in our healing. We ask God for what we need and thank Him for it, even before we see it.

Doubt: despairs, complains, and is sad.
Faith: rejoices, gives thanks, and is glad.

August 11

Focusing on the negative things is a sure way to develop a dangerous habit.

Our lifestyle can take some getting used to. We need to try different things and find what works best for us. Some things will work while other things won't. We must be patient with ourselves. There are no classes where we can learn how to do this thing. We do the best we can with what we have. Acceptance is the key to our serenity, which is the most important thing right now. We need to set aside time each day to practice having peace of mind. We will not survive for very long by being in a constant state of panic. We must learn to take our mind off our problems and focus on something positive like: we have a roof over our head; there is plenty of food to eat; or our pets are healthy and still with us. We must pull our mind away from the negative "goings on" around us, since our enemies want to rob us of any hope we might be retaining. We stay grateful for whatever is positive in our lives, for it is from God.

I rebuke all spirits of torment and fear, because I have peace through the blood of Jesus (Colossians 1:20).

August 12

When it comes to people doing something for us, we must presume nothing and be thankful for everything.

Our unreasonable expectations of people, places, and things can leave us in a constant state of disappointment. We can easily get our mind set on something we think should happen or on something we think we need. We become so fixed on receiving it, that we pout and dive into self-pity if we do not get it. If we walk around thinking the world owes us something because we are gang stalked, we block our ability to receive any blessings from God. The Bible teaches us that God resists the proud and gives to the humble. Whatever our current circumstances are, there is always something we can give thanks for. We might be homeless, but we can be thankful for our camper; we may be isolated and alone but grateful for our pets. Perhaps we are grieving the loss of a parent, we can be grateful that we still have the other one. This type of a thankful mindset qualifies us to receive grace from God: gifts and favor. We leave the door open for more things to come our way when we do not complain.

Today, I will be thankful for the trivial things. I will have an attitude of gratitude.

August 13

Reputation amongst gangstalkers is of utmost importance and, certainly, one would be full of glee if a target's suicide was on their watch.

Gangstalkers are quick to play sneaky games behind the scenes. They work a dangerous game of highs and lows with our emotions while covertly finagling something for us to get excited about, only to watch us come crashing down with disappointment. It works like this: you order a new pair of designer eyeglass frames as seen in a magazine. You think you are talking to the optician, but the call has been redirected and intercepted by the group. These conversations go on for weeks, until you receive word that the frames have arrived. You are excited when you get to the store but are soon let down. You ask about your frames, but nobody knows anything about them because you have not been talking to anyone from there. Our emotions are abruptly switched from anticipation and happiness to those of sheer exasperation and world-weariness. These games of emotional nose-dives are vicious. We must stay away from feeling sorry for ourselves, at all costs. Self-pity, depression, and despair are dangerous emotions, as they can easily lead us to commit a homicide. We can end up in an uncompromising situation behind these emotions, since they are from the devil and will cut us off from receiving God's Grace. We can be thankful for our experience, because now we can protect ourselves from it happening again. We make a pact to not do business over the telephone; thus, creating another protective boundary for ourselves.

Losing is out of the question today, if I know what game to play.

August 14

We have the right to get unstuck from what somebody did to us.

The negative stuff we hide in our heart has power over us, especially when we cannot talk about it. The fact that we have become targeted can make us feel shameful, particularly if we are denied the right to earn a living. There are many forms of abuse that can mess people up. A person who has their heart broken does not feel right about life in general. As targeted individuals, we run around all day with a broken heart from having our lives picked apart. Most of our perpetrators are people whom we will never meet; they work behind the scenes for the devil. We still have a true friend in Jesus, regardless. That is why we should spend time with Him. He doesn't give us ten things to do at once, but rather leads us step by step, giving us one assignment at a time. If we listen carefully, we will know what to do.

Lord, lead me in a plain path, because of my enemies (Psalm 27:11).

August 15

I think you try a little harder when you're scared; something that has always worked for me.
—Rocky Balboa

Luciferian gangstalkers will always gather for a feeding frenzy whenever a TI is violated in a drugging or rape. These predators have different strategies for different prey and will always get together to feed off the trauma. These sadists love to watch us squirm as we're slowly microwaved by Directed Energy Weapons. They also get together to watch us get sick after we've been poisoned. If a target commits suicide, the instigating perpetrator will be held in high esteem for having won the game. They deeply care about how they look in the eyes of their fellow perps and are rewarded among themselves, within the group. They may even show up at our funeral to say things like: *We are so sorry; it looks like he/she was more unstable than we thought. Did you know he was suicidal? Let us know, if there is anything we can do for you.* Our family members will not know they are being lied to by government perpetrators, who make a living this way.

Their sword shall enter their own heart, and their bows shall be broken (Psalm 37:15 NKJV).

August 16

I have chosen not to be erased.

It is interesting how the world views homeless people and those who have nothing. Gangstalking perpetrators will cause us to be homeless and then use us for their entertainment. Most people look for happiness while acting selfish, but happiness does not come that way. We cannot be happy and selfish at the same time. Being in isolation and away from activity, unfortunately keeps our eyes turned inward. We need to get ourselves off our mind. Trying to find a way to help people or to even bring comfort to needy animals is a big challenge for us. Being of service is the only way we are guaranteed to find contentment. God never stops working in us when we are willing to stay open to the good in life. It is important that we take part in whatever God puts in front of us. We need to do the best we can. The importance of this world decreases as our faith in God increases.

Today, with Your help, God, I cut the cords of the wicked from my life (Psalm 129:4).

August 17

It is difficult to ignore something we are aware of.

It is hard to ignore the undetected signs of gangstalking after becoming aware of them. We notice things that others disregard or take for granted. We can still go about our daily life, while aware that our neighbor's role is that of a community informant. When we are outside working, does he keep popping out to throw out garbage, get something out of the garage, or make trips to his car? If we are under an umbrella, having lunch with our mother, is he sitting outside in a nearby chair? He stays inside his house most of the time, but now that we are outside, there he is. He is assigned to us. Another clue is when our neighbor asks questions. If he is an informant, he will ask a ton of questions. He will act like he is our friend, when nothing could be farther from the truth. Just because we are hip to how perps operate, we must remember that many TIs don't have a clue. They may not be attuned to it and live in painful darkness. A Christian woman and her military husband had been targeted for ten years before someone told her about gangstalking. Everything they had questioned was finally answered when another TI shared information with them. Our goal should be to enlighten others. Where there is secrecy and darkness, we must let the truth be made known.

God, send out Your light and truth, and let them lead me (Psalm 43:3).

August 18

Neighbors. It is always the neighbors.

When we cut off all contact with nosey neighbors, someone else will soon be planted. We must always guard our heart, no matter how lonely we are. If we know how gangstalkers work, we can almost expect their next move. It can begin with our mysterious landlord, who has been married for twenty-two years, but is now living as a single man in the front house. Suddenly, he is overly friendly and goes out of his way to make conversation with us. He begins to get pushy and eventually comes on to us. It does not make a difference that our rent is paying his mortgage; he never raises a finger to help us with anything. These group members can be of any age, race, or creed. They are only out for themselves and the group. People who are too assertive and borderline desperate to make us a part of their life are usually up to no good. We can almost stand back and expect them to become even more forceful, as the group puts pressure on them. Even if we like someone, we must guard our heart because their efforts are not pure. They want to take advantage of us and use us as entertainment before we get dropped like hot coal. Their techniques are designed to break us down, especially if we stand strong on morals, principles, and values. We lean on God and ask him for the strength to stay away, since it is for our own good. God will also give us the strength we need to withstand the perp's angry attitude after we sidestep him.

It is by the grace of God that I can handle anything that comes my way. Sometimes, avoidance is the best policy.

August 19

God will create a way where there is no way.

A perpetrator will usually be planted within proximity to the targeted individual. He/she will usually come on the scene with a bang and want to get to know us. On the other hand, they might be someone disguised as our landlord's brother. This way, when the landlord is gone, the so-called brother can keep an eye on us. The landlord works during the day while the brother sleeps, since he works the graveyard shift. One leaves at 8:30 in the morning, and the other shows up at 9:15. Eight months later, *poof*, the brother has moved out. No movers. No unusual activity or noise. No goodbye; nothing. The whole thing was bogus. The next day, a forty-some-year-old man moves in next door, supposedly back in with his parents. The rear window blind used to stay open, but it now remains closed. The guy looks like a cop, dresses like a cop, walks like a cop, and sneaks around like a cop—he *probably is* a cop. Perhaps, he will use higher tech equipment like satellite Wi-Fi or thermal imaging. His plans might be to use microwave radiation while he secretly watches us. Who knows? No matter what is going on nearby, we must stay centered and take care of ourselves. It is not healthy for us to stay fixated on a change of activity around us. Once we learn of it, we need to refocus back onto God. Somehow, we must appreciate that there is a whole other world out there, besides them.

The Lord is the author of all. He is the only hook-up I need.

August 20

We can solve one problem and quickly get two more.

Although everybody has problems to solve, a targeted individual can become a professional problem fixer. The perpetrators maneuver through a revolving door-like system where one leaves and another shows up. Each member specializes in one thing or another. One might be a car mechanic to blow up our engine or a carpenter to bug our home. Let us not forget the thief, Don Juan, who flirts like there is no tomorrow. We should not be surprised when he helps himself to a piece of our jewelry—just a small token for his significant other. When we are isolated and without a friend in the world, the group will cause us to desperately need help from someone. It is another setup. Now, we are not only lonely but helpless. This is all done while the other members are being entertained from front-row seats. When the time is right, they will send someone in to victimize us some more. When he leaves, another one will show up. This abuse goes on for as long as it takes to complete their mission. If we do not have any valuables to steal, they will simply torment us until we commit suicide. We are not equipped, nor strong enough to fight such an army. We must let go and let God. We fight the good fight of faith (1 Timothy 6:12). It is good because we win.

Lord, deliver my soul from death, my eyes from tears, and my feet from falling (Psalm 116:8).

August 21

The bull's-eye is the mark for attack; where the vandalism takes place, the rape occurs, the extortion is completed, and the entertainment begins.

A whole decade can go by without us receiving one act of kindness from anyone. We grow vulnerable because of our deprivation of human contact. We must be careful to not rush or get pushed into a faux friendship. A perpetrator will use matters of the heart to form a relationship with us, to gain access to our life. They could have opened the door with a simple smile or a helping hand. It is *intimate infiltration.*[19] This cruel scheme is usually devastating and meant to take us out. Having personal boundaries set in place will save our life. When someone smiles at us, we can smile back. We can allow ourselves to embrace the warm feeling of a smile, before we leave it as just a smile. We ask God to keep us from receiving the kiss of death.

Faithful are the wounds of a friend, but deceitful is the kiss of any enemy (Proverbs 27:6).

---

19 Intimate Infiltration is a form of false intimacy performed by a perpetrator who is trying to get close to the target or people the target knows. If the attempt fails, the target's best friend may soon have a new significant other.

August 22

Their schemes are well-planned setups to minimize, embarrass, and utterly demoralize us.

It is common to accidentally slip into another vicious scheme. We must get back up, brush ourselves off, and refuse to buy into it. We are not victims because we have a need for victimization. We battle evil forces that neither fight fairly, nor are out in the open. Some of us are targets because of someone's envy—an ugly, yet powerful demonic spirit; or a perp is refusing to be accountable for his own actions, and we have become the scapegoat within the group. We need to be diligent about not losing our perspective of who we are, so we do not take on someone else's trash. We must also refrain from focusing on an obsessed perpetrator, who is wanting to transfer their jealousy onto us. We do not want our energy level to drop down to such a low vibrational frequency. It sounds passive, but spending five minutes a day to sit quietly and breathe deeply is something we need to practice for staying centered. We can deal with a bad day of dark feelings in ways that reflect self-responsibility rather than victimization. While we are in a whirlwind of negativity, we should take time out to get balanced and ask God for direction.

God, help me to not use gangstalking as an excuse to live below Your standards. Help me make the right decisions that will help me to either break this curse or live with it more comfortably.

August 23

The Word of God is a seed. Our heart is like soil. When we read scriptures aloud, it is like planting the seed of God into soil. The seed takes root and grows into a tree. The tree bears fruit. Things begin to change.

There is a solution in the Bible for everything. In fact, our stories are profoundly like David's writings in the Book of Psalms, in which there are accounts of persecution, hatred, deception, betrayal, wickedness, and even spying. After surviving years of torment, we are unsure of who or what to believe. We really cannot trust anyone, but we can always trust and rely on the Word of God. While other things change, the Word stays the same. It can send curses back to their senders; create walls of protection around our home and loved ones (including our pets); and help us to gain insight (discernment) on people, places, and situations. Confessing scriptures aloud is a great power available to us, yet few people do it. Once we get a handle on it, the powers of darkness will try to persuade us to stop. Some things may even begin to look worse before they get better; this is just Satan trying to discourage us. He will get us to talk about what the perps are doing, to cancel out what we have been calling forth. If we stand firm on speaking scriptures aloud, change will inevitably begin to happen. All we do is speak it and stay out of the way. The Word of God goes to work doing things we could only have imagined.

I release the sword out of my mouth against the enemy (Revelation 2:16).

August 24

By confessing Psalm 91 and Psalm 109, we call in God's angels to work for us.

Things have been done to us that make us question our lives. It is a terrible thing when friends, co-workers, and even family members become part of our gangstalking saga. At some point, they must have been approached by the organization to have become a part of a group set out to kill us. Perhaps their involvement was demanded, or they were made an offer they couldn't refuse. Being needed by the group adds fuel to the fire, causing a perp to become overly zealous about putting the kibosh to us. We sow our own seeds and reap the words we sow. After we begin to confess the Word of God each day, our perps may get taken by surprise when good things begin to happen for us. We must continue believing in God's promises. We do the footwork and leave the rest to Him. We go away with great faith in the Lord, who never leaves us.

Thanks be to God, who always causes me to triumph (2 Corinthians 2:14).

August 25

To ask for wisdom and then fall apart is weak and in bad taste.

If we are going to ask God to give us the skinny on someone, we must be able to cope with what He reveals to us. After we ask for wisdom, we may as well ask for help with digesting whatever it is that we find out. Facing some things may not be pleasant and cause us to be unhappy, or worse yet, enraged. Everything we go through is for a higher purpose. We ask Jesus to help us all day long, as we prepare ourselves to prevail. We are built to make it.

God, give me the spirit of wisdom and revelation, and let the eyes of my understanding be enlightened (Ephesians 1:17-18).

August 26

Don't let this make you bitter.
—Christopher "Stik" Sylbert

Being taken advantage of makes us mad. It is tough to not harbor anger toward haters who hurt us. Gangstalking is an evil masterpiece; to persecute a person, day in and day out, causing him to become ugly, bitter, unforgiving, and full of resentment. These are all blessing blockers that keep our prayers from being answered. Organized stalkers set out to control our lives and make us suffer. They know that anger eats people up from the inside out, and it is for that very reason they go out of their way to provoke us. Mercy and truth are powerful weapons used to protect us in the eyes of God and man. We must pray for the creeps that disrespect us. We must pray for the innocent bystanders who become perps out of fear of being targeted too. It is not easy to pray for them, but when we do, the channel for our own prayers will open back up. We do not want to stay stuck under the power of darkness. God will deal with our enemies.

Lord, you said, when we go into battle in our own land against an enemy who is oppressing us, we should sound a blast on the trumpets. Then we will be remembered by the Lord and rescued from our enemies (Numbers 10:9).

August 27

Sometimes God calms the storm, but other times, He calms our heart while we ride the waves.

We can unexpectedly find ourselves in the middle of a downpour with no place to go. A well-organized gangstalking group is also a thievery ring made up of street gangs, rogue cops, and dope fiends. If we live in the boonies or out in a dead zone, perps can covertly complete any mission without facing legal ramifications. The more helpless and isolated we are, the easier they can hone in on us. It is even better for them if we are caught off guard with no action plan. After we are hollowed out, they will try running us out of town. After a well-planned scheme goes off like a detonation in our life, it is not a time for us to be weak-hearted. We may get blown to pieces, but we cannot fold like a cheap suitcase. They must not get the best of us. Sometimes, the only thing to do is hang on and ride it out, even when we feel trapped with nowhere to go. Whatever storm we are in, we must not fear Satan, gangstalkers, or law enforcement. We only have one alternative when we find ourselves outnumbered: to stand strong on God's Word and resist the high winds. Resistance is a form of refusal to go along with their plan and challenges them to the core.

Lord, let my enemies be overthrown. Deal with them when You are mad (Jeremiah 18:23).

August 28

The source of our great suffering is that we are not like everybody else.

When we become controlled by other people, we run on low vibrational energies like fear and depression. Some days we are completely shut down and don't have a clue as to *how* we feel. Whether our torment is through gangstalking, electronic harassment, or human trafficking and sex slavery, it is being done to control our mind. Even if there are physical beatings involved, it boils down to one big mind game to instill fear in us, while they consume our energy as their own. They want to take away our self-esteem and make us as destitute as possible. The spirit of fear will then take on a life of its own. Once it gets instilled in us, it will flourish like a plant grows with water and sunlight. To "set our mind" means we have the power to make up our mind. God has given us such capabilities as mind focus. If our thoughts are being held hostage by someone, we can strengthen our mind with biblical scriptures. If we are watched and listened to 24/7, we can secretively speak to Jesus for help in our situation. God often works in mysterious ways. We will be given the grace to endure any circumstance as we are guided through a plan of escape. It is wise to include Jesus in all our thoughts and plans.

Today, I will dwell in safety; nothing shall make me afraid (Ezekiel 34:28).

August 29

After years of harassment, our struggles sit more quietly as we learn to stop complaining.

To complain means to remain. There are times when all we do is complain. Targets get frustrated and spin out of control from our constant negative emotions. During the beginning phases of being gang stalked, we are appalled at the audacity and rudeness of our enemies. We want to tell everyone, but it really changes nothing. Complaining just fuels and escalates our negativity. It takes us years of complaining and talking it out, before we can set up a comfort zone within our own personal boundaries. It is not that we give up; it is that we change our thinking which then changes our lives. We can find comfort in an uncomfortable world. We can seek purpose in a meaningless position. We can have love while surrounded by hatred. Our thoughts are energy, and we must make a habit of becoming aware of them, so we can change our thinking whenever necessary.

With my mouth, I will greatly extol the Lord… For he stands at the right hand of the needy one to save his life from those who condemn him (Psalm 109:30-31 NIV).

August 30

A lousy attitude with stinky thinking is like a brick wall: It can keep all good from permeating through it.

An attitude of gratitude can help us to feel happier throughout the day. By being thankful for the insignificant things, we open a way for good things to come in. It is amazing how many things we can be thankful for, even if we are living in an abandoned parking lot. The quickest route to the quicksand is to complain about our negative circumstances. In the face of it, we can pull ourselves up and look at life with appreciation. There are always things to be grateful for while we are praying for our life to be different.

In the name of Jesus, I bind and cast out all spirits of depression, despondency, despair, discouragement, and hopelessness.

August 31

God is not going to control our mind; He told us to do that.

After nearly two years of being hit from every direction, the remainder of my dad's inheritance was finally gone. Another perp came in to retrieve the cameras that were set up around the place. It was time for them to move on, now that they had located the hidden money and taken it all. I rarely left my house, so I was baited in letting someone come over. I also believe the perp came to punish me for moving the money from bank to bank, burying it in the ground, hiding it in the walls and making it hard for them to find. I felt like a criminal, trying to keep what was mine and I was exhausted! I had lawyers, judges, sheriff deputies, and what seemed like the entire world after the money my dad left me.

The night before Christmas Eve, a friendly perpetrator asked if he could bring me something for Christmas. I was in a weakened and needy state, and I foolishly allowed him to come over. We did not drink or smoke anything. I just remember him giving me a long hug at the door and handing me a Christmas card, which would later be taken by the sexual crimes department; never to be seen or talked about again. A few hours later, I woke up from my own blood-curdling screams. I found myself half naked on the bed with the perp behind me. I was being sexually assaulted with an instrument. Later I would learn that he was squeezing my cervix with either his hand or a vise grip. I had never experienced such pain in my life. I tried to crawl away, but I couldn't. I had been drugged and sexually violated in my own home, as well as exploited through some type of private remote viewing that, in just a few hours, the whole town would become privy to and use against me.

Sadly, at 57 years old, I had already been celibate for ten years, by choice, because of the vicious gangstalking games. For four days, I laid on the living room floor in the fetal position utterly mortified. I was in a daze that felt more like a coma: hollowed out and thrashed. Like a caged and wounded animal, the group covertly monitored my status over a closed-circuit TV network that I was unaware of at the time. They were feeding off my trauma, while living large on my money and any good energy they managed to rob from me. While watching me squirm, they were celebrating a job well-done. After two long years of time-consuming work, they had finally succeeded in raping me financially, emotionally, mentally, and physically. As they would say in Hollywood, *It's a wrap!*

A week later, after visiting two emergency rooms, I was finally beginning to heal from the cuts, bruises, and infections that were left between my legs. I had become the recipient of laughter and utter disgust around the township. Even the older women from my church struggled to keep the smirks off their faces. I could not believe this was my life! As far as I was concerned, I had landed on another planet with non-humans. The sexual degradation and insensitive comments made at the local health department by employees kept replaying in my mind. I could not stop the thoughts from looping all day and night, like a computer program. Letting these bad thoughts rerun in my mind could have destroyed me. I screamed at God to take them away and stop my head, but He told me to do something about them myself in 2 Corinthians 10:5—*Cast down thoughts and everything that is not from the Word of God.* This was true spiritual warfare. I needed a bouncer at the door of my mind and His name was Jesus. Together, without any friends, drugs, counseling, or an ounce of justice, I managed to fight the good fight of faith. Although, I did not win the battle this time, I knew I could win the war if I refused to think about homicide and dismiss any suicidal thoughts from entering my mind. It took me two years to realize that within that small quiet country town existed an underworld of secret societies that went back hundreds of years. This dark experience did not break my spirit, and it amazes me to this day how God pulled me through it.

Instead of your shame you shall have double honor (Isaiah 61:7).

September 1

God's favor will carry us through every terrorizing mind game.

Noticing a huge dog running toward us on the street can be alarming. Frantically, we pull in our pets and quickly slam the camper door behind us. We do not realize that what we just saw is not real, but rather an image from a nearby projector. Our distress is pure entertainment as it overwhelms the perps with delight. They are amused not so much to see us react in a normal manner, but at their ability to cause such a reaction. They also like to infiltrate certain sounds such as a crying child yelling for help or the rustling of leaves to insinuate someone is walking around outside. This was twenty years ago in Hollywood, when my neighbors were perps from the special effects industry; projecting images and sounds of helicopters circling above. One night, there were window shattering sounds of a freight train barreling through my back yard, yet there were no railroad tracks within 50 miles of my house. Today, there are other technologies that do similar but more brutal things like Voice-to-Skull (V2K) torture. The news media recently covered a story about a government agency having played voice recordings of a terrorist's mother while the prisoner sat with a gunnysack over his head. He was further tormented by sounds of his mother crying out his name and giving off the illusion that she was imprisoned just down the hall. These are military tactics.

No matter what is going on, God's Word never changes. Memorizing biblical verses can help us stay mentally strong. It helped Jesus when he was in the desert for forty days without food. When he was hungry, and the devil played mind games with Him, He would say aloud to Satan, "It is written..." before He recited a scripture. We should be like Jesus and stay focused on the Word where there is power, stability, and victory.

Today, I bind the spirit whereby the enemy is trying to distress me in my home.

September 2

All gangstalking strategies are from Satan and have been around since the beginning of time.

If the plan was to make us suffer for only a two-year period, there would still be emotional residue from all the abuse. A lifetime of dealing with constant setbacks and disappointments is a total drag. It is not a normal day if we do not take two steps forward and two back. Not only do we deal with failure but also the loss of having everyone and everything taken away from us. It could have been as innocent as storing our stuff in a storage unit and one day finding everything gone. We might have been falsely arrested and after spending a weekend in jail, found our apartment opportunely cleaned out. It is normal for us to feel defeated and remorseful. Pissed off! If we carry around our sorrow, we hinder our own future. We might try looking at the thousands of people who have lost everything in hurricanes, wildfires, and tsunamis. When it comes to loss, we are not alone. It is the way our things were taken that is concerning.

Father, deliver me and keep me from the enemies of the land—famine, pestilence, blasting, mildew, locusts, caterpillars, plagues, and sickness (1 Kings 8:37).

September 3

These dark times have Satan coming on strong, using huge armies of evil workers with high hopes of winning the world.

Life is not easy when everyone hates you. It takes all kinds to make the world go around, and these evil perpetrators and predators are just doing their job. It is most important that we learn to be happy with how God designed us. We can have peace within ourselves, even while we are constantly fixing things that have been broken on purpose. Managing our life is easier when we get along with ourselves. As targeted individuals, we face big obstacles in everything we set out to do. There is an army of perpetrators assigned to each one of us. Although, we are soldiers for the Lord, it is not always about saving the souls of others, as it is about saving our own. God always has our best interest at heart. He is always working things out behind the scenes.

Lord, you are my God who goes with me to fight against my enemies and to save me (Deuteronomy 20:4 KJV).

September 4

It's not what stands in front of you; it's who stands beside you.
—from *Only the Brave*

We are part of God's perfect plan, even if we do not like our situation. For a long time, we have unsuccessfully tried to get others to believe our story. Not everyone has had spiritual training on how evil runs this world. Some people are not interested in playing catch-up on the topic of gangstalking. We are lucky if we have one person to whom we can talk to, that is on our side. As we work on our spirituality—which has now become a necessity for survival—we will intuitively know what to do and how to do it. While we undertake God's assignment, we stay steadfast under a canopy for His divine protection. We may still go through the mud, fire, and high waters, but He will help us through it. Nothing shall by any means destroy us.

He heals the broken-hearted and binds up their wounds (Psalm 147:3 [NKJV]).

September 5

We are in the middle of a spiritual war, and for us to survive, we must use spiritual weapons.

Like trained soldiers go to war for their country, we must learn how to use our battlefield weapons. We speak the Word of God at the presence of evil; these spirits despise everything about God, especially the name of Jesus. In the sixth chapter of the Book of Ephesians, we learn how to properly dress for spiritual warfare, because whenever we have a victory, Satan will turn up the heat. This is often referred to as: *new level, new devil*. Being a soldier for the kingdom of God is not a runaway victory, but we get everything we need to be great warriors. We develop a high threshold for pain, which enables us to endure long bouts of fighting, since gangstalking is generally for a lifetime. It deeply saddens Jesus when one of us takes our own life, especially, if we are called to help those who are not as strong. We are the Chosen Ones—the selected few who fight in the frontline trenches. We accept this honor daily, while we stay physically fit, emotionally sound, and spiritually attuned.

God takes my most horrendous battlefield and turns it into my greatest blessing field. As I let go of mourning my disappointments, I begin believing in God for a fantastic future.

September 6

We battle an army of people who have designed a psychological warfare plan against us.

When perps try to drive us into a morbid state of depression and confusion, our first piece of protective armor should be the Helmet of Salvation to protect our mind. If we take on emotions of bitterness and venomous anger, we will lose the war at ground level. The target often blows up, assaults someone, winds up in jail, and is forced to pay costly fines. We can also get depressed by engaging in risky sexual behavior, not realizing that every partner sent in will further degrade, exploit, and abuse us. While we are feeling dejected and hopeless, we can easily turn to drugs and alcohol and get defeated early in the game. The higher we go in our spiritual walk, the more alone we seem to march. The road gets narrow, but if we look ahead, far in the distance, we see a man carrying a cross. It is Jesus. We have, indeed, done the three things He asks of us: "Deny thyself, take up thy cross, and follow me" (Matthew 16:24).

The Lord directs my steps and delights in me. He will instruct me in the way I should go.

September 7

When we wear the Helmet of Salvation, not even the devil knows who we are.

Demons get confused when we act like Jesus. They run away in fear when they think we are Jesus. The Helmet of Salvation protects our way of thinking. It is our weapon to counter any mental programming executed on us by government gangstalkers as their ploy to mold us. Case in point: Five years into being gang-stalked, my landlord sent over a janitor to fix a minor plumbing problem. I did not like anyone in my place, unless I was there, so I made the appointment in advance. On the day of the repair, I had turned around for thirty seconds, and when I came back into the room, I found this guy laying stark naked across my bed. I could not believe it! This type of gangstalking behavior is a form of brainwashing and mental programming. It is despicable and unacceptable. Gangstalkers will do things to entertain the rest of the members who are usually watching or listening. The game gets played out the other way, too. A male target incurs female perps that bleed him dry of money and favors. Collectively, they use him up. These games help in brainwashing the target. We think that people are our problem, but they are only the source of evil spirits. The Helmet of Salvation protects our thinking, so we can stand up against all the brainwashing strategies they bring into play.

I know who I am. I understand that spiritual forces of darkness play on my emotions. Therefore, I put on the whole armor of God.

September 8

For the sake of going out dancing, we put on dancing shoes for reasons other than to just tap dance out of a tight spot. Our feet are the foundation for the functionality of our entire body. If we do farm work, we are sure to wear dirt kickers, when jogging—our running shoes. These days, we are in a spiritual battle with gangstalkers, and we must put on our gospel boots (preferably steel-toed).

The *Shoes of Peace* are a vital part of our arsenal for the further destruction of Satan and his demons (Ephesians 6:15). We get to walk in peace, even while we are hated, violated, and exploited. Having our privacy taken away for the sheer entertainment of others makes us feel like we have lost all our civil rights as human beings. The perps instigate us to become livid and "flip out" so we might get arrested. They want us to become our own worst enemy. They get the ball rolling with hopes of sitting back and watching us ruin our lives. No! We are better than that! We must walk in our gospel boots and strive to guard our inner harmony. Jesus says, *Blessed are they who are persecuted (Matthew 5:10).*

Father, help me not to fall before my enemies (2 Chronicles 25:8).

September 9

False intimacy is a cruel form of free entertainment at the expense of the target.

Deprivation of love and affection is a dirty and cruel tactic. Perps profile us and know exactly who to send in to abuse us. They want us to commit suicide after our heart gets broken; or when our money is gone; or if we feel stupid and angry at ourselves. A gay man hears voices in his head that call him a faggot. Other gay men are harassed and exploited through unkind sex. Female targets are often passed around by members looking to get promoted to a higher-rank, or rewarded with an eight-ball of methamphetamine, or to simply get another notch on their belt. Some perps have sex with targets just to entertain their co-workers—those closet voyeurs who work in the background. None of our sexual encounters are ever private. Some targets never realize that the group is using them for free sex and entertainment. Female targets can be relentlessly pursued by a charming perp who is kind, funny, and even brings her expensive gifts (usually stolen items from other targets), all for the finality of having sex. This romancing can take months, but her world will come crashing down when he quickly satisfies himself, quickly gets dressed, and leaves. This is to degrade and totally devastate the target, while the rest of the group partakes in a feeding frenzy from the sidelines—which, unbelievably, includes female perps.

But, once again, God has covered His Elect! Another part of our armor is the *Breastplate of Righteousness* which stands for protection from condemnation. We need this after we are pursued and courted for a long time and then dropped. Our loneliness can get the best of us, and we may have developed feelings for the perp. None of them care about us. They are merely acting onstage while the target is put on public display for group entertainment. Despite this, the

Breastplate of Righteousness goes over our chest to protect our heart. It is part of God's arsenal for a reason. After falling victim to the brutality of false intimacy, we have the incentive to put it on. We neither feel ashamed for falling for what we knew was wrong, nor do we beat ourselves up for thinking it was real. We also do not have to allow it to happen again.

The Breastplate of Righteousness is my ultimate safeguard from this line of assault. Today, I will put it on and hide the important things in my heart.

September 10

The whole foundation for being gang-stalked is based on deception and lies.

The *Belt of Truth* is our weapon against the persecution of deception and confusion. We will never hear the truth from someone we know like a gangstalking neighbor or community member. They will constantly lie to us to mess with our head. They will make it look like they are doing one thing when they are doing something else. They want us to believe that their right hand threw the rock when, in fact, it came from their left. They execute this type of psychological abuse to keep us disarmed and in a state of confusion. We may begin to think wrongly: *God doesn't love me, because if He did, I wouldn't be going through this.* The Belt of Truth brings us back to the correct way of thinking: *God's Word is the truth, and the truth shall set me free (John 8:32).* When we believe that suicide is our only way out, the Belt of Truth reminds us of who we are, due to God's love for us. We must stay alive to fulfill His divine plan for our lives. We are not an accident waiting to happen, but rather a miracle in motion.

Lord, let a cry be heard from their houses when you shall suddenly bring a troop upon them (Jeremiah 18:22).

September 11

Any ship can ride out any storm as long as the water doesn't get in. It is the same with us; we can ride out any attack as long as the attack doesn't get in us.
—John Ramirez, *Unmasking the Devil*

Some of us have been housebound for years. We are afraid to go outside for fear that someone will do something shocking to us. Gangstalking and harassment perps love to say the worst things possible for shock value. Neighbors will introduce themselves while acting warm and hospitable but are much to the contrary. They will invite us over to a dinner party, so the other perps can see who we are. Once we are reeled in and feeling somewhat safe, we will be blindsided with a cheap "below-the-belt" attack—something we never see coming. The perp will trigger us by saying something shocking that only our old neighbors would have known about or mention a town in another state where we just survived a traumatic event; thus, triggering a negative reaction in us. They do this to steal our high vibrational energy and to feed off our trauma. The *Shield of Faith* protects us from these fiery darts: the insults, ideas or thoughts we don't want to take on. We should carry our shield everywhere we go and keep it handy for such attacks made on our psyche.

Today, I will hold up my Shield of Faith to block any cruel words and arrows of hatred that come my way.

September 12

Some images have depicted Jesus with eyes of fire and a sword coming out from His mouth.

The *Sword of the Spirit* is the Word of God and like a double-edged sword (Ephesians 6:17). The sword is widely known as a figurative representation of the power of God's Word when spoken. Once we learn some scripture, we will have acquired the sword that goes along with our shield of faith. We speak scripture when we need to go in for the kill to finish off an opponent. We do not care what the perpetrators think while they spy on us. Let them hear us recite scripture. Who cares? Let them watch and see how powerful our God really is. In addition, if a perp says something hurtful, we can put up our shield and stab with our sword. Now we have the weapons to help us become victors.

Jesus' words are like a safety net; they help to keep me from falling into despair.

September 13

The light shines in the darkness, and the darkness has not overcome it (John 1:5).

We cannot fight darkness with darkness. We can only fight darkness with light and both cannot exist at the same time. When God created the world, He said, "Let there be light," and there was light (Genesis 1:3). He did not say anything to the darkness. He did not tell it to go away or pay it any attention. We can learn from Jesus when we want to keep talking about the negative things that gangstalkers do to us, which gives them more power. We must be careful what we say and try to speak in positive terms of what we want. For example: *Something good is going to happen to me today.* All of us are guilty of negative talk. Our enemies have designed this scheme on purpose, where they lay the negative groundwork, and we help it to grow by constantly talking about it.

Today, I will speak aloud about the things I want in my life, not about the darkness of how things are. I will speak as a commander of power, not as a targeted individual.

September 14

We cry like a baby and then try to give ourselves back to ourselves.

We are as helpless as a baby when we suddenly become strategically disarmed. We flounder around and try to gain knowledge of our deprived situation. We know nothing about this new world, nor are we prepared for it. Most of us have never even caught wind of this underworld crime called gangstalking. Unfortunately, we make the best prospects since we are like newborns: helpless and in awe of everything happening around us. Our lives come crashing down on us while we are left to stand alone and without any comforts. Some targets become professional victims when further controlled by psychiatrists and/or new handlers.[20] We are fortunate to find out about spiritual warfare and how it can help us. We become spiritual babies with a willingness to learn quickly and obediently. We move from "the milk to the meat" of God's Word. We find nourishment in reading the Bible. We grow up spiritually and our reward will last forever.

Like newborn babies crave pure spiritual milk, so that by it you may grow up in your salvation (1 Peter 2:2 [NIV]).

---

[20] Handlers are abusers who closely or intimately control the TI. They are also known as mind-control programmers.

September 15

Happiness comes from the ability to control our own mind and emotions.

It is better to focus on the love God has for us, instead of the hatred we receive from the rest of the world. We are often perplexed with how to make it through another day of torment and deprivation, but we do the best we can. Some people use aluminum blankets or sheets of metal to stay shielded from microwave radiation—those beams directed at us through the windows and walls of our home. We are grateful for any reprieve from these assaults, since God did not create us to be experiments for the government. We cry out for help, but the world does not hear us. Only other targeted individuals truly understand our cry. God is always in the background working things out. He gets flooded with our prayers when we all cry together. He will never fail us, for He promises us:

All who devour you will be devoured; and all your adversaries, every one of them, will go into captivity. All those who prey upon you will I give for a prey. I will restore health to you, and I will heal your wounds, because they have made you an outcast (Jeremiah 30:16-17).

September 16

Our self-centeredness can easily make our loved ones suffer along with us.

We have been on our own for decades, only to wind up living back with our parents. What kind of sense does that make? Harassment groups disarm us from being able to make a living by spreading lies about us, so we go back to our parents' home if we are lucky enough to still have them around. It is stressful for them to see us unhappy and on the verge of committing suicide. Mothers notice our emotions and live our pain as if they are the target themselves. This is unfair on our part. We must change our attitude when we are in their presence. If something must get talked about, we should put a time limit on it. We could say, *Let us talk about this for thirty minutes, and then, we will stop.* Being cheerful, considerate, and loving to the people in our lives will generate good things to come our way. If we go around with a long face, complaining and acting depressed, we take everyone down with us. Plus, we cannot receive God's blessings since we have shut Him out. When we are grateful for the things we have, and we thank God for them, it opens the gateway for more blessings to come our way.

Today, I will smile more and be considerate of the people in my life. I will work on my attitude by being grateful for the things I have.

September 17

We feed and energize our spirit by listening to the preaching of God's Word.

The perpetrators who are doing the gaslighting[21] are like prisoners, themselves. They think that they are running the show, but they are slaves. What they do not realize, when they feel above it all, is that they are leaning toward the tragedy of the group dropping them at some point. They are not aware that they lack the freedom to have their own thoughts by being part of the hive mentality. Every gangstalking secret must be taken to the grave with them. If a member reveals any of the group's secrets, their offspring will be cursed. This is not living a life of abundance, as it may appear to us. Our faith grows as we hear God's Word preached. We become energized when we hear about fighting the enemy, destroying strongholds, and winning our battles. The words are alive and feed our spirit, soul, and body. It is the only thing strong enough to change us from being victims to reigning champions.

Today, I will study the Word of God. I will read Psalm 81 aloud and begin training as a soldier in God's Army, rather than staying a victim.

---

21 Gaslighting: psychological abuse to instill anxiety and confusion in the victim, overwriting their own reality.

September 18

We must venture out from staying stuck indoors and under their silent coercion.

We have become shut-ins because we do not want confrontations. Gangstalkers and community-policing squads will react with hostility whenever we do something nurturing for ourselves. Our perpetrators thrive off our energy by watching us slowly die. Their job is to break us down. So, if we decide to start exercising, we can expect them to counter our efforts with something negative—like a rally of cars or loud motorcycles to zip by us, too closely, while we are walking or jogging. We can learn to live with some flack, in the name of healthy self-care, but we need to be careful, since TIs have been known to get hit by perps in vehicles.

In the name of Jesus, I bind the spirits that would make people find occasion against me even when I am living right.

September 19

We can carry on even with our name on a nationwide hate list.

It is time to stop the nonsense of living an oppressed life just because someone thinks we should. It is not our problem if someone cannot muster up enough self-worth to co-exist on the same planet as us. It is not our cross to bear. It is their problem. Imagine: possessing enough jealousy and hatred for someone that you put a lifetime "hit" on their life—attempting to transfer your misery onto them. Still, these people must live in their own skin, no matter how much juice they have on the streets. They still wake up to themselves in the morning and sit alone on the commode. If we possess an element of "something to be envied", then we surely have what it takes to make our life better. Others do not have our magic. It is ours.

God, help me to step outside of the box today. Help me to allow myself to be who I am intended to be.

September 20

Most people have no idea that there are groups of extremists stalking regular people—adversaries who control people's lives through intimidation.

It is important to step out of the box—away from our basic daily existence of nothingness. We grow sad thinking about not having meaningful conversations anymore. If it means treating our tummy to a bowl of soup at the local deli, we can step out for a while. We do it because it will make us feel good about ourselves. These little hurdles will empower us if we can get through the anxiety of being out in public. A stranger might spark up a ten-cent conversation with us. On the rare occasion that someone does, we will recognize a red flag if the topic, unfortunately, spills over onto sex. Or, if the person appears to be talking loudly and the feel for the conversation is not genuine, our spirit will nudge us. We refuse to feel badly about what was probably a setup. We train our mind to focus on how we have done something positive. Consequently, when we go back to living within, we feel better for stepping out and walking through the fear. We did it!

Today, I will get out and do something different for myself. If I run into a perp, I will not react to their psychological torment, but rather wear the experience like a loose garment.

September 21

Blessed are those who still have peace of mind when everything else is in the toilet.

A great many of us have lost our livelihood and would rather not be living where we are. We might be staying in a parked motor home, our childhood bedroom, or even a tent. No matter how low we have gone, we can still attempt positive changes by doing little things for ourselves. We recall a time, years ago, when the gangstalking started in our workplace. We switched jobs, but the same thing happened; or we decided to quit and are still unable to get rehired anywhere. Conversely, we might have more peace now than when the rug was initially pulled out from under us. Peace of mind is always something we can be thankful for, not only because money cannot always buy it, but because Jesus is the Prince of Peace. His peace comes on us when we follow Him. And that is a promise.

My life gets better when I immediately take care of small issues head-on. Today, I will try to make one thing better in my life.

September 22

There are seeds of greatness in us that intimidate people; they both are the very reasons we are harassed.

There are twelve-step programs, worldwide, that help millions of people with addictions and emotional issues. Newcomers get instructed to quickly find a power greater than themselves, even if it's an inanimate object like an ashtray. It sounds stupid, but it works in the beginning. Hearing about God in the meetings eventually changes that. It is the knowing and understanding about a power greater than us that makes our recovery possible. As targeted individuals, we attain peace by obtaining and maintaining coping skills. In deciding to turn our will and life over to the care of God, as we understand Him, our relationship becomes deeper and more intimate. The inanimate object may only work during the beginning stage of admitting our powerlessness over drugs and alcohol, or sugar and food, or people. Yes, people. We are powerless over people, and we tend to crave a more personal friendship with God through our extreme aloneness. The more we fall in love with Jesus, the more He influences our life. We are on the right road when we make Him our higher power. We get to thrive, despite it all.

I am powerless over gangstalkers. I turn all of them, along with my will and my life, over to the care of God.

September 23

Last week I told my psychiatrist, "I keep thinking about suicide." He told me from now on I have to pay in advance.
—Rodney Dangerfield

When we are isolated and kept away from others, we feel contained and like we have a disease. We are kept in line as a ploy to limit our power. Obviously, someone with authority was extremely threatened by us, or nervous about our talents and potential, to have ordered a nationwide army to take us apart. If we weren't referring to our own life, the topic of gangstalking is every bit as humorous as comedian Rodney Dangerfield's catchphrase: "I don't get no respect!"

But it is about our life, and it isn't funny. Feeling free is a tall order for someone who is surveyed 24/7. On the other hand, there is no job too big for God, since He is not limited by our circumstances. We basically need for Him to breathe in our direction. His favor upon us can change everything in a second. We do not want to remain stuck by our own limited and negative thinking. Our road is not easy, but we are an important part of the big picture. We must have a strong relationship with God, trusting Him to get us through everything: when they are waiting outside for us; when we realize our sibling is one of them; or on our next shopping spree. If we want to be successful, we must know God's Word and let Him breathe on us.

I decree and declare: The people who try to keep me down cannot have me, for I will not stay where I am right now.

September 24

We want to know how the impossible will be made possible.

We tend to disbelieve in the equation when we do not have the formula. Nevertheless, we cannot afford to hold back from the will of God through our own ignorance and pride. The issues we face today are not going away any time soon. We may refuse to commit suicide, but we can go farther than that. We can learn new ways of coping. We can click into God's will for us and exist with a higher level of purpose. God will make a way for us even as we are forced through the dung. We begin to realize: *All things work together for good, for those called according to His purpose* (Romans 8:28). There is much uncertainty these days, and God knows exactly what we are going through. We may not have the recipe, but we know Who does.

Destruction has come to a perpetual end, and the memorials of my enemies perish with them (Psalms 9:6).

September 25

Piece-by-piece, we have lived through the dismantling of our lives.

People are targeted so perpetrators get to live another day. It sounds crazy, but it is true. We play a role in their survival by feeding them our good energy. Embracing this concept will keep us from interacting with them more than is necessary. They have proven themselves to be weak by having a hand in our demise. We must live differently than other people. We see that the world is no longer a big part of our lives. We depend on a divine spirit that has us thinking differently. In the past, it might not have been in our nature to seek God, and maybe we wouldn't have if we were not targeted. Since God has drawn us in, we live more comfortably just knowing the power we have access to, compared to merely being aware of the danger around us. Taking our spirituality seriously will prepare us to be sensitive to the Holy Spirit who dwells in us. He will direct and control us if we let him. We do not need to get tied up with a bunch of people, anyway. One man and one prayer can move mountains to change the world. We must continue to pray for the healing of those targeted individuals who do not have any peace of mind.

God, I thank You for hearing the voice of the enemy against Your anointed.

September 26

Evil has no defense for when we give thanks to God.

We can become worrisome when we disconnect from being grateful, by allowing the enemy to swiftly move in on our lives. Our gratefulness is the force that keeps us connected to God's promises. By being thankful for everything, we automatically refrain from harboring bitterness in our heart. When we are thankful, the doors are open to ask for things we want; this is the best time to take our requests to God. We can use our gratitude as a protective hedge from the enemy.

Do not fret or have any anxiety about anything, but in every circumstance and in everything, by prayer and petition (definite requests), with thanksgiving, continue to make your wants known to God (Philippians 4:6 [AMP]).

September 27

Whatever is going on in our life, faith will work it out.

God has a plan for us and no hound from hell can keep us from it. We are exactly where we are supposed to be at this moment in time. If our faith must create or dominate something, it will do so. Our faith will overcome any evil forces set against our life. The Word of God is for impossible situations such as ours. We are not here by mistake. We put our feelings aside and do things by faith while remaining confident that God has us in the palm of His hand.

Today, I ask for an increase of grace and peace as I gain more knowledge of God's plan for me.

September 28

We live an extraordinarily lonesome life on Earth while there is a battle being waged for our soul in the heavens.

Human beings were created to interact with each other. Smear campaigns have caused most of them to abandon us, and since we have an inner need to connect with people, we often make bad choices. We can easily be pulled into having a conversation with a neighbor, only to be left suffering the consequences of a cheap shot directed at us. We may know our neighbor is part of the harassment group, yet we still incongruously interact in conversation with him. We ridiculously think that if we can get them to like us, they won't hurt us. The fact is: These people do not care about us. Even if they did, it does not matter, because their job is to kill us. Gangstalkers always want to have power over the target; therefore, they creep around our lives. They work on instilling fear in us—sheer terror at times. Even if we are loners, a neighbor may be instructed to pull us into an over-the-fence conversation, simply to drop hints that will trigger us. These hints are custom-made just for us. They are things that only we would understand. If we stay away from people who are involved in destroying us, we will not have to waste energy trying to recover from their cheap shots.

I rebuke all destruction from my gates, in the name of Jesus (Isaiah 60:18).

September 29

Although our life is not how we had imagined it would be, God will always make the crooked places straight.

We can pray for God to take away the gangstalkers. We can ask Him to supernaturally get our name off the hate list. We can bind and rebuke our neighbors and command them to "be thou removed from our lives and cast into the sea." We can even loose God's warrior angels from the heavens to fight our battles for us, but practicing these spiritual principles may not unveil the results we want. The sooner we learn to cooperate with God, the sooner we will learn our lessons, and we can move on to another level of spirituality. Sometimes, God is more interested in changing us than our circumstances. Living life as a target is a tall order, but we can look at how the whole thing is refining us. We have been made perfect in God's eyes for the bigger things. If we stay too busy trying to capture our haters, or build legal cases against them, we miss the point. It could be that God is working on changing our attitude or helping us to master our emotions. Maybe He wants to use us for His Glory.

In the name of Jesus, I am free from those who have tried to put my feet in stocks and mark my path (Job 33:11).

September 30

We finally reach a place where we understand what is going on, and we stop fighting lions because we cannot win.

We reach a level of acceptance when we finally come to grips with where we are. We stop whining and complaining and wondering why life turned out like it did. We see this trial as a never-ending test of our character, endurance, and faith. We are overcomers. Instead of becoming irritable and grouchy, we stand strong and "fight the good fight of faith". When we lean on God, He promotes us; sometimes, not until we've made it through some awful and miserable ordeal like a rape or a robbery. This may not be the promotional opportunity we had signed up for, but God knows what struggles will best develop our strength. Most of us are strong-minded, and we have taken care of ourselves for years. What motivator is better than a mob hit to indirectly route us to Almighty God? Having confidence in the Lord is our default position.

In the name of Jesus, I am not bound by those who have made up their minds against me and count me as an enemy (Job 19:11).

A Bonus Reading

I get overwhelmed thinking of the times God had His hand on me while armies of evildoers baited me.

They had me living on the streets in my Jeep. Fast money sounded good; I could buy a motor home and stand up while I got dressed. Driving a vehicle through the border of Mexico did not seem like a big deal, and when the offer came, I grabbed it. All I had to do was drive through the checkpoint, answer a few questions, and pick up the real driver on the other side of the border. I kept asking him, what would happen if I could not find him? Over and over, he reassured me that he would be there. Well, just as I feared, I could not find him, because he was not there. I frantically drove in and out of parking lots and spinning doughnuts while I madly scanned the area. I could only image what the poor guy was going through—the one who was tucked inside a hidden compartment in the wheel well. When I finally found the driver and we got back to Los Angeles, I collected my money and made plans for the following week.

This time, while going into Mexico, the Border Patrol Inspectors had searched the vehicle and found that I had a loaded pistol in my purse. For some strange reason, I decided to bring it at the last minute. The driver and I were both handcuffed and taken in for questioning. The FBI said the chances of me getting back home that day were zero, as I was probably going to be kidnapped and used as a sex slave, or as he put it "turned out". The Feds had been watching this criminal for years, and on the basis that I carried the gun to protect myself, they let me go. I never saw the pistol again but having it that day had saved my life. The driver and I did not speak all the way back to Los Angeles. I did not get paid, nor did I ever see him again.

Whoever causes the upright to go astray in an evil way, He himself will fall into his own pit (Proverbs 26:27).

October 1

Although we make a conscious effort to live undisturbed, our life seems to be anything but.

To completely lose our grip in a temper tantrum is to be expected. Gangstalkers are thrilled when they cause us to "lose it". We shouldn't beat ourselves up when our composure eludes us. Years of harassment can include being brainwashed, where we begin to treat ourselves the same way our enemies treat us. We must be wary not to allow their attitudes to transfer onto us. Considering what we deal with, most of us do well with controlling our outrages, especially in public. We are up against a ring of people who work collectively to throw curveballs and bait us for one thing or another. The anger inside us is like Mount St. Helens, ready to erupt. Something small ignites us, and we flip right into a rage, completely bypassing anger. We must forgive ourselves and put it behind us. It really is possible for a TI to experience having intervals of peace. We take our defeats in stride and treat ourselves gently. We continue taking care of ourselves while trusting God to tie up any loose ends.

I am not alone in my feelings, actions, or reactions. Today, I do the best I can, accepting myself exactly how I am. I like myself. I am okay.

October 2

We all have character defects we would like to change or do away with.

When we make peace with the parts of us that we do not like, it makes it less of a struggle to change. It seems like our haters mess with whatever it is we need or want. This type of interference causes us frustration because they don't let our desires come to fruition. Some ignorance might be bliss but getting angry at ourselves does not help us in any way. It stunts our emotional growth and causes us to overeat, drink, and abuse ourselves in various ways. The "player-haters" sit back and wait for us to commit suicide. They feed off us, especially, when we burst our seams from harboring negative emotions; whenever we do this, we are helping them in our own destruction. Finding humor in our imperfections is a pleasant and gentle approach to the challenging work we face daily. If we can make some things easier in our life, we may as well go for it!

God, I hand all my troubles over to you. Help me to see the lighter side of things. Help teach me to laugh again.

October 3

Emotional hangovers remind us of how much energy we throw away on situations we have no control over.

Worry robs us of as much energy as having a temper tantrum, but with even less healing benefits. The difference is in how some of us quietly internalize our emotional stuff, while the rest of us process it physically. Temper tantrums not only leave us with emotional hangovers but with physical wounds like cuts, scratches, bruises, and sprains. In addition, we are so emotionally, physically, and mentally drained, it can easily take us two days to recover from such an episode. Concealing shameful feelings about our outrage does not help matters, and guilt is a worthless emotion altogether. Gangstalkers want us to feel badly about ourselves and will rouse us at any chance they get. They will perform a specific act to provoke our reaction, so they can feed. Once we realize they are using us to thrive, we can counter their moves. Certainly, we must avoid complaining aloud. Also, we must discard all negative feelings about who we are. We may as well start enjoying the time we spend with ourselves. We have plenty of it.

In the name of Jesus, I bind and cast out all spirits of frustration, worry, and anger from my life.

October 4

Getting arrested is the dangerous side of publicly displaying our pent-up frustration.

We could commit homicide—or even suicide—in a fit of rage. If the perpetrators know of something that is our weakness, they will use it against us. This is the same technique the devil uses on us, which is proof that we are truly up against pure evil at its best. Our road is not one that is wide, smooth, straight, and full of people. Our road is narrow, rocky, and crooked. It is a lonely road that few people travel. We are anointed (blessed by the Lord) and given the grace to follow Him for whatever reason. We must ask ourselves: *Are we going to follow Jesus or not?* If we decide to stop wavering between having tantrums, planning homicides, and running from the police, then we pick up our cross and move along. We turn our will and life over to the care of God and ground ourselves in the spiritual warfare it takes to survive being gang stalked. Following Jesus means doing what He did. Jesus did not worry himself sick over matters, nor did He ever plan to hurt himself. There is no need for us to waste our energy in ways that feed our enemies.

I may be a target of hate groups, but so was Jesus. I have everything I need to get through today. Right now, my faith will carry me to places I never dreamed possible.

October 5

Living isolated without a friend in the world is a chore.

Some days are too emotionally intense for us to handle alone. We need the Word of God to help us decipher through the trickery and deceit that we are constantly up against. It means that we do not stare at our circumstance or the situation around us. We stand in faith and believe for a promise God has given us. We do not need ten or fifteen promises. We just need to pick one promise and hold onto it, for example: *Though I walk in the midst of trouble, you preserve my life (Psalm 138:7)*. The Bible mentions many lonely people who were called by God. Unlike the carnal path for worlders, the road to heaven is narrow and less travelled.

We were under great pressure...so that we despaired even of life... But this happened that we might not rely on ourselves but on God, who raises the dead (2 Corinthians 1:8-9).

October 6

Problems are a sign of life. The only people who do not have problems are people that live in cemeteries.
—Norman Vincent Peale

Once the perps surround us, we get overloaded with problems that must be solved. Every cloud we are given has a lining of personal loss. We may need to leave behind our apartment, car, job, friends, or even sadly, a beloved pet. We suffer as a loved one mysteriously pulls away from us. These matters are naturally difficult for anyone, but TIs never get a chance to properly grieve losing anything because of the vast amount of losses we sustain. Once it starts, it is like a domino effect, until everyone and everything is gone. While our enemies have plotted to take everything from us, there are some things that remain with us for life. It is as if our haters sow seeds for us to reap. The pressures of loss and lack begin to squeeze the life out of us. We wonder: *Where is God?* He is in the water that we are drowning in. He is in the air we are gasping for. He sees everything and knows who is doing what to His people.

In that day, the burden will be lifted from your shoulders, the yoke from around your neck; and the yoke will be broken (Isaiah 10:27 [NIV]).

October 7

It is how we handle it that matters.

Profilers go to work when the green light gets put on us: investigating our friends; what we like; where we go; why we get mad; how we live; and what makes us happy or sad. They hook their claws into our private lives long before we ever have a clue. Their study is launched way before they engage us in guerrilla warfare and cause our lives to systematically fall apart. They are well organized and clever in gathering vital and personal information on us. After they make us homeless, they can easily take the material items they want and then extort our money. Their entire motive is to break our spirit and take over our soul. By not being deeply rooted in the Babylonian world system, we have a chance at true survival.

Bless the Lord, oh my Soul, and all that is within me (Psalm 103:2).

October 8

God told Apostle Paul that His grace was enough for him and His power was made perfect in weakness.

He carries us and gives us strength when we cannot go on. That is when the glory of God dwells in us and around us. Our relationship with Him helps us to endure those situations we are not happy with. We pull our strength from knowing that He is always with us in the chaos and disaster of life.

Let the weak say, I am strong (Joel 3:10).

October 9

Sometimes, it is best to keep a low profile, even if it means ignoring people.

It is in our best interest to not get windswept into other people's dealings. Our neighbors are the perpetrators who set out to do the most destruction to our soul. It is hard to believe that people in our circle of life are underhandedly paid to harass and torture us. It is apparently all they have going for themselves, and we learn to never second-guess our intuition about any of them. Perpetrators and predators are available for hire in all areas of our life. Yes. They are on the government's payroll to ruin our lives. We may think getting Internet access in our rent is a gift; turns out, our landlord is the administrator and secretly manages our e-mails, while covertly sabotaging whatever he can. If we stay close to God, we will see our landlord punished. If not today, tomorrow, but as God promises, it will come.

You only have to look with your eyes to see the punishment of wicked people (Psalm 91:8 [GW]).

October 10

The world's ways are not for us.

While they are killing, stealing, destroying, and organizing nationwide gangstalking on people, we transform into someone completely different from whom we used to be. We must do this if we want to win. We get a Holy Bible and begin to learn about kingdom principles. We read stories of people who were treated much like we are. We learn that persecution is really a blessing in disguise. We practice having faith and believing in the one thing that has not ever changed: God's Word. We start putting God's Laws to work on our circumstances. As we transform into becoming a good and faithful servant—a soldier with a job to do for humanity, we begin to see our enemies fall by the wayside. We can make it through this life, not without tribulations, but without being conquered. Not all of us will complete our assignment here on Earth. Some will be persuaded to either join the other side or, sadly, commit suicide. We must get victory on our mind. No matter what we are facing, we can cope with it.

If they mean evil against me, my good deeds towards them will heap coals of fire upon their heads, and the Lord shall reward me (Proverbs 25:22).

October 11

This is not a wrestling match against a human opponent. We are wrestling with rulers, authorities, the powers who govern this world of darkness, and spiritual forces that control evil in the heavenly world (Ephesians 6:12 [GW]).

It is world news: Gangs are winning the drug war and drug cartels are becoming untouchable. No one messes with them as the weapons in their arsenal dwarf any border patrol and state police department combined. Sheriff's deputies and police officers are not trained, nor equipped, to even consider battling with them. The success of the gangs is based upon their extreme training and survival skills. The cartels have their own army, and they also hire military specialists. They wear uniforms and combat boots; they drive all-terrain vehicles, climb walls, and know how to survive in the wilderness like Rambo. As young as thirteen years old, a selected few go to a military training camp where they are taught warfare tactics. No stone is left unturned. They even learn how to cope with pain in case they are tortured by the enemy. They are loyal, devoted, and molded into highly trained and specialized soldiers. We must be this dedicated in our training, even though our battle is spiritual. We must devote ourselves to learning about every spiritual weapon available to us. We should practice using them, until it becomes second nature. Our enemies have placed the bull's-eye on us. They know that if they can overpower the way we think, they can break us. We must suit up in the armor of God and stand sober and vigilant to be ready to battle when the enemy attacks. As soldiers in God's army, we shall trample them under our feet: serpents, scorpions, and gangstalking perpetrators.

Today, the Lord is with me like a mighty warrior; so, my persecutors will stumble and not prevail. They will fail and be thoroughly disgraced (Jeremiah 20:11 NIV).

October 12

To thine own self be true.
—Shakespeare

There was a documentary made about psychic kids that Satan was using to communicate with the dead. Some of the kids were only nine years old. For years, they had tried to talk to their parents who would not believe them. By the time the kids were thirteen, they had become introverted because they never had anyone to validate them. They had experiences that were kept a secret for fear of being criticized by non-believers like their parents. These special kids never learned how to live their life because they stayed in isolation. They had no idea that they could walk with Jesus on a higher plane. Unfortunately, most people have the need to be validated to continue living life. We must not be one of them. Some of us were senior citizens when we were introduced to the menacing underworld of gangstalking; targeted for our assets. We cannot fold just because no one justifies us. We endure the task of knocking on spiritual doors, until one of them opens; we seek, until we find what works for us. We continue to run our race, not caring what other people think. We know that God's validation is all that matters.

I will not be afraid to be different from others as I travel on the path that is right for me.

October 13

Not everyone has seen what you have, so some people won't understand.
—Dale Allred, Clarksville, Arizona

A woman was camping in the boonies of Northern Washington when she came face-to-face with a nonhuman creature. She went on to tell the news media about her sighting of what appeared to be Bigfoot. Not everyone believed her. Remarkably, her life mission was not to convince others of what she experienced. She knows what she saw. She believes what she knows. Everyone else's doubts rolled off her like water on a duck. This is how we should live our lives since most people do not have a clue about the underworld of gangstalking. Our friends may not believe us or even try to understand. Sometimes, keeping what we know to ourselves can be empowering.

Today, I will not be consumed by those who were close acquaintances (Psalm 55:13).

October 14

In a fiery trial, we should keep our mouth shut and our hands busy.

We can give away our power to the wrong people simply by verbalizing too much. We know we are being listened to when our landline incessantly beeps each time we use it. We also know when our cell phone is being secretly turned on like a baby monitor whenever a nearby transistor radio emanates heavy static for five seconds. The gangstalkers do not know what we know, so why tell them? They would simply fix the amateur glitch and leave us with no clue as to what they are doing, or when. We can best protect ourselves by keeping valuable information to ourselves. If we know certain things are happening around us, we can simply change our behavior to better achieve some sense of privacy. If we broadcast everything aloud, it gives them more information. It is best for us to do things spontaneously and without broadcasting it. Silence is worth practicing because it can give us more freedom and less hassle.

Lord, help me to keep my power.

October 15

When we do not have someone pointing out what we have done wrong, Satan will use our own mind to do it.

Gangstalkers practice bouts of extreme cruelty, humiliation, shaming, and oppression on the people they are assigned to. Their first goal is to displace us through job loss and homelessness. This also includes obvious disrespect from everyone we are associated with. These evil seeds sown into our lives help our enemies lay the groundwork for our brainwashing. The rest falls into place with little effort by the group, as we begin to exist in total darkness. We must protect our mind from head games that are strategically implemented through degradation and secrecy; this is meant to break us down for a complete takeover of our soul. When we realize the seriousness of the battle, we become motivated to build an arsenal of spiritual weapons to fight back. A vital part of God's Armor is the Helmet of Salvation, which protects our thinking by covering intake channels like our eyes and ears. We should guard these openings from being available to the group. We must be cautious of what we look at, listen to, and ingest. We stand strong in God's strength and do what He prefers us to do.

Lord, help protect me from lower-level tormenting spirits.

October 16

If gangstalkers can keep people in the dark, our own ignorance will destroy us.

We do not have to live in complete squalor just because we are targeted. Poverty thinking is from the kingdom of darkness, where witches and warlocks want us to exist. Ignorance is one of Satan's most powerful weapons that he and his cohorts use on people. Living below our standards, with no friends, is something very real that targeted individuals learn to cope with. Having our possessions stolen by community lowlifes, while no justice is served, can turn a church-going Christian into someone filled with hatred and animosity—someone who has taken on great offense from the community's so-called county workers, church goers, and law officials. Very simply, being gang stalked can turn a holy person into a stone-cold killer. The group's goal is to drive us to suicide, yet homicide seems to be highly applicable. The perps live by a code of silence for this very reason. Evil has keenly manipulated us into becoming our own worst enemy, when our own hatred and anger pushes any good fortune from within our reach. Planting a seed of offense in our heart to keep us from God's blessings is a brilliant form of evil warfare. We must not nurture it. If we do, it will outgrow us by taking us over, until we are destroyed.

Once you lived in the dark, but now the Lord has filled you with light. Have nothing to do with the useless works that darkness produces. Instead, expose them for what they are. Light exposes the true character of everything, because light makes everything easy to see. "Wake up, sleeper! Rise from the dead, and Christ will shine on you" (Ephesians 5:8-14 [GW]).

October 17

It behooves us to discern a gangstalking attack from an everyday problem.

We should not feel inferior to people when we are in public. Many of us live in defeat and darkness (ignorance) due to the lack of God's Word in our lives. We have been deceived by neighbors and family members—those who have swindled valuables from us. We have given plenty of people too many chances. So why not try Jesus? We can enjoy life without exhibiting shame, guilt, condemnation, or a lack of ability. God has given us the power and authority over all evil, including our enemies. Although our haters have power, they do not have any authority over us, unless we give it to them. The only prerequisite to gain spiritual authority over the work of our enemy is to believe that Jesus Christ is the Son of God. (See Salvation Prayer)

I have given you the authority to trample snakes and scorpions and to destroy the enemy's power. Nothing will hurt you (Luke 10:19 [GW]).

October 18

Never again will I be a pencil neck or a spiritual wimp.

Just because we have authority over the power of our enemies does not mean that nothing will come against us. Once we have the tools we need for battle, we are assured to become a conqueror. Many targets learn about their weaponry when they are in the middle of the war. That is like trying to remodel a house while living in it. Though, it is not easy, it is still possible. We can begin to take authority by making these two simple changes:

By speaking the Word of God, rather than speaking about our circumstances.

By speaking the Word of God, rather than speaking about how we think or feel.

We can expect many trials during our on-the-job training. We must grapple for patience and diligence to persevere. What we say and think while we go through any trial will decide how long we stay in it. The key to our success is to keep our mind off what the perps are doing to us and focus on God's bigness, promises, and scriptures.

Lord, have mercy on those who are overwhelmed within and desolate at heart (Psalm 143:4).

October 19

We may not grow leaps and bounds by distracting ourselves from negative emotions, but we can stay out of trouble.

In some self-help programs, becoming healthy and whole means to indulge in *feeling* feelings. It is a big step in recovery for addicts and alcoholics to name feelings while they are having them. This enlightenment occurs in a safe environment with similar people who help us uncover, discover, and discard certain thoughts and emotions. This process transpires as we stay and identify with our feeling, before moving on to the next one. Targeted individuals waver between two feelings: hopelessness and anger. On a good day, we can keep our despair from turning into suicidal thoughts and our anger from acts of homicide. Our emotions can be like a pendulum swinging from one extreme to the other, or it can get stuck between despair and frustration. In our world of being gang stalked, it is better for us to detach from our feelings and focus our attention on something else. Sometimes, a biblical scripture will work. Other times, physical movement or exercise is the answer. Often, a two-hour comedy is what the doctor orders. It is far better than indulging in a bottle of alcohol to numb our emotions, only to fuel us into becoming violent. Having loudmouth confrontations, drunken fights, or throwing rocks through windows will bring us nothing positive.

I have become an outcast and, just for today, I am okay with it.

October 20

If we cannot find a reason to live, let it be to shine the light on those who are in darkness.

Although we are unemployed, we are never at a loss for things to do. It takes a lot of work to resist a take-down by a harassment group. Any feelings we might have of wellbeing, peace, self-esteem, hope, purpose, joy, vitality, and worthiness get chipped away by gangstalkers who have proudly dedicated their lives to this line of work. Most of them function in the background of our life, and we never see them tamper with our text messages, e-mails, US mail, phone calls, appointments, vehicles, plumbing, or anything else they gain access to. Sadly, many TIs go on attributing these mishaps to simply having bad breaks; they live in darkness and never learn about government gangstalking. As children of God, we get to use the Blood of Jesus as a spiritual weapon against evil doers. Imagine how much worse life could be without it. We get to plead the Blood of Jesus over situations and separate ourselves from every curse sent our way.

I plead the blood of Jesus over those whom the enemy has persecuted their souls (Psalm 143:3).

October 21

There are times when our burdens overrule us, and we cannot seem to find peace anywhere.

We must continue with caution when we feel like we could snap at any moment. Sometimes it seems like our frustration is all over us. We carry it in our walk and wear it like a coat. If we allow ourselves to stay on this path, our faith will be replaced by self-reliance without grace, and our hope will turn into desperation. We may balk at the idea of acting happy when we are so miserable, but the Bible says the joy of the Lord is our strength. There is joy in knowing that He is for us. We all have problems, even those mainstream, run-of-the-mill, everyday people. They, too, struggle.

So, do not fear, for I Am with you; do not be dismayed, for I Am your God. I will strengthen you and help you; I will uphold you with my righteous right hand (Isaiah 41:10).

October 22

When I started to lose my hair, I was prepared for it. In fact, after starting chemotherapy, I had my hairdresser cut my hair real short. Then, I went home and had my daughter completely shave my head. I didn't want to lose my hair, so I cut it off myself.
—Cancer survivor

The strategies we use to deal with situations are proven examples of how we cope. Once we are stuck in a system of control and conformity, we hardly know ourselves anymore. Psychologists define coping as the ways in which we interpret and try to change circumstances; how we make them more favorable and less threatening. There are two types of coping: *Problem-focused coping*, where we try to solve the problem and the stress diminishes or goes away. This, of course, does not apply to us. Then there is *Emotion-focused coping*, where we cannot do anything about our problem, but we can try to change the way it makes us feel. Bingo! We address our emotions without addressing the circumstance. In a normal life, a person would find relief in talking to a friend. In our world, we become vulnerable and immobilized from having no form of support; though, we can learn to cope. We can create a life worth living if we are willing to work toward personal goals and trust our Higher Power to guide us. We do not need to become desperate. When life becomes overwhelming, we need to stop struggling and go with the flow. There is a divine plan for our life. We need to relax and let it happen, whether we like it or not.

Staying out of the way of God's plan for my life is my responsibility. God, help me to stay out of my own way today.

October 23

Giving up has more to do with who we are, than the distance between our expectations and our reality.

Frustration can happen when we have an expectation and then reality sets in. A lot of things can go wrong that can cause us disappointment and despair. Some things may take longer than we thought they would, or they cost more than we figured, but we cannot just roll over and give up. There is an outstanding plan that God has set for our lives. Just because our plans may have slowed down or temporarily halted, we cannot live without having any. We become soldiers—people who have a goal and develop the discipline needed to keep fighting.

Lord, help me to adjust, as I realize that certain things are ending, and other things are about to get started.

October 24

Where there is an absence of love, there is an absence of truth.

We are living in perilous times, for darkness reigns now. Some people have knowledge of God's ways, but instead they choose to be haters. Everything becomes distorted and twisted as the organization begins to deceive us. It is like a switch gets flipped and hundreds of people are set in motion. Much to their chagrin, our perpetrators' lives are co-dependent on ours, while most of them are just too ignorant to see it. A creature's prey are those creatures that it hunts and eats to live. Perps will smile at us and act politely while they are merely spiritual forces of wickedness: fakes. They want so badly to see us in degradation that they cloak themselves as angels of light. Having wisdom will help us to avoid becoming caught in their evil plans, but not always. Various street gangs will take part in what they call "gang games". While different gangs get the green light to go after a target, the degree of violation can be brutal, because the target is only a means to win and is not regarded as a person. The nastiest perps are those who smile while they poison their prey, just to gain a few points. It is comparable to two teams playing a heated basketball game while using the TI as their ball.

God, it is because I belong to you that I live under your supernatural shadow of protection.

October 25

In the world of organized harassment, we are programmed to have calculating thoughts of lack and shortage. In God's Kingdom, we have thoughts of abundance.

When we find something in God's Word that sounds good to us, we need to write it down. We meditate on it by thinking about it, chewing on it, and saying it over and over. In time, our insides begin to shift, and we see things that we could not before. When we meditate on scriptures, we notice that God's will for us is opposite from the way we have been thinking. As we work on spiritual change in our health and in acquiring peace, justice, authority, wisdom, or protection, we begin to operate with a higher thought vibration. It feels good to pull ourselves up and out of the gutter.

I quench every fiery dart of deception from attacking my life, in the name of Jesus.

October 26

We look like sitting ducks, while voyeurs encircle us.

We tend to exist where we would rather not be. We notice how the people around us come and go in their lives. Some have jobs. Most have family and friends. They seem to have things to do and places to go. Monitoring our lives is simply incorporated into their daily routine. It is mind-boggling how the neighborhood is orchestrated to keep us in place. It makes us feel like we are living in *The Outer Limits*. How could this have happened to us? How can this crime be so well organized? Having worked our whole lives, we are now unemployed which causes our days to be long and mundane. Watching other people live their lives affects our self-concept and self-esteem. We become oppressed with too much time on our hands. We must not have a lazy attitude during this ideal time to work on our spirituality. We can use this time of aloneness to find our spiritual gifts or to become closer to God and survive life with the peace and acceptance that surpasses all understanding.

I say to the enemy: I am more than this. I am better than this. I am not going to sit in my home and cry. I know where my help comes from—the Lord Almighty! I am going to let you watch God bless me.

October 27

You must find your own happiness.
—Violet Moauro, Shorewood, Illinois

We always end up with the short end of the stick when we judge our insides by other people's outsides. Feeling defeated and condemned will only keep us down in the dumps. Each day, we must find something that flips our switch. We can find a reason to live through our pets—those animals that rely on us for everything. City people discover that walking their dog is a clever way to get outside for exercise. We must find a reason to get up each day. We must handle our own happiness, because no one will do it for us. Once we finish a painting, adopt a pet, or lose those last five pounds, we establish some self-assurance. These small tokens of hard-earned confidence will generate more determination in us. We should create a goal for ourselves and take baby steps toward achieving it.

I have been through a lot and deserve to feel good about myself.

October 28

Victims often become victimizers, like those who perpetrate us.

Most gangstalkers are sociopaths. They are good at making their way into the gangstalking and harassment subculture. They manipulate and bait people into doing self-destructive behavior. They will use whatever we desire as a trap to sabotage us, even if it means causing us to have an accident. They feed off our misery. There is no sense in crying over it, because that just makes their day. We must find our strength in God since our battle is to overcome the world. Instead of asking God to remove our problems, we should ask Him how to handle them. We do not have to be perfect to make progress.

We will be lifted up when the wrath of God comes to the world.

October 29

Sometimes the best place to build from is rock bottom.

A targeted individual has the right to be angry, but it is how we express it—or not—that matters. If we do not express our anger properly, it turns inward and becomes depression with a lid on it. When our mood is low, we tend to look only at what is bad; this is how we swing between depression and that deep, dark, bottomless cavity known as self-pity. We should decide to raise our vibration if we want to have a better outlook on life. For openers, we can change our self-talk by saying only good things about ourselves. Engaging in positive self-talk is something we forgot about since being targeted. Striving to make these slight changes is a productive way to keep our bitterness at arm's length. It begins with our spoken words.

Today, my mouth is enlarged over my enemies (1 Samuel 2:1).

October 30

The powers of evil want to distract us from our destiny.

We focus on Jesus today. We do not look to the left and we do not look to the right. We take our focus off the multitudes encamped around us and any family members who are playing both sides. These offenses are designed to appal us and become a stronghold in our mind. We wake up with them on the forefront of our brain. At lunchtime, we have not thought of anything else. We drift off to sleep with this garbage still living rent-free in our head. Jesus told us, we could have peace if we kept our mind on Him. We can have a peace that is not understandable given the measurement of our circumstances. This one disciplinary act can change our lives: keeping our mind on Jesus. It is the only solution to lowering the volume on this relentless torment.

As I look to Jesus, the restricting chains, bound to my redundant thoughts, fall away and allow me to breathe deeply.

October 31

Do it as quickly and quietly as possible.
—My dad

With blankets tucked around the windows as curtains, the dogs and I were fast asleep in the back of the Jeep. It was around the tail end of the witching hour—the very break of dawn—when we were abruptly woken up by the shrill wail of a siren. Someone had set a car on fire just thirty feet from us. I do not know why such drama no longer fazed me. I quickly slipped into the front of the Jeep and quietly drove off.

That which has been is what will be; that which is done is what will be done: and there is nothing new under the sun (Ecclesiastes 1:9).

November 1

Everyone knew that whoever let the sadness overtake them would sink into the swamp.
—from *The NeverEnding Story*

The manifestations of a Perizzite spirit are through feelings of sorrow, sadness, despair, hopelessness, loneliness, discouragement, and self-pity. When this spirit of heaviness comes upon us, its companion is usually infirmity. Our body can easily get sick when we are sad. Apostle Paul said, we should *think on those things that are lovely and praiseworthy (Philippians 4:8)*. Jesus taught, that we must first bind the strongman before we fight him. We do this by using the name of Jesus, because everything must bow down and obey that name...even Lucifer.

I declare that when a thief is caught, he must give back sevenfold. I bind you—Perizzite spirit—you are a smothering spirit and I rebuke you and command you to leave my life now, in the Almighty Name of Jesus.

November 2

It is time to be humble and admit we are not in control.

We want to do something about our circumstance—anything. We get perplexed and have no idea what to do. We cannot see God working things out while we are in the middle of our mess; we can only see those things in retrospect. That is why we should never forget the times He pulled us through the muck or got us out of something dreadful. It is always better for us to have trust in Him than in ourselves or anyone else. *It will bring health to our body and nourishment to our bones (Proverbs 3:8)*. We let go of trying to figure everything out or having to know all the answers. We let God handle our problems. He has a unique plan for our life—something we can look forward to.

Today, I will trust in the Lord with all my heart and lean not on my own understanding (Proverbs 3:5).

November 3

No matter where we go, organized gangstalking is already set in motion and eagerly awaiting our arrival.

Anxiety rapidly grows when turmoil festers in us. Our mind is unable to rest when we are filled with anxiety. By exuding these lower frequencies of energy, we can bring evil into closer proximity to us. Since gangstalkers are everywhere, all the time, they drain our energy to where we give off these lower vibrations. Being incessantly watched like a lab rat can drive us crazy if we are not linked to an anchor of hope. There is life where there is hope. We will burn out if we stay steadfast on the violations and invasions they execute on us. The same goes for the physical invasion of directed energy weapons—another traceless form of torture. The Holy Spirit lives in us and helps us to hear God, so we can arm ourselves with His mindset. *Let this mind be in you, which was also in Christ Jesus (Philippians 2:5).*

Today, I do not have an anxious mind. I have the mind of Christ. I will not deprive myself of any good thing.

November 4

Gangstalkers have bosses who oversee bosses; everyone must answer to someone.

After the big bang of being methodically swindled out of our savings, we get wrung out and tossed aside like a wet rag. We contemplate suicide, homicide, or just plain drunkenness. The perps know it and stay out of sight, while law enforcement helps to protect and even hide them. Although, we get a moment of reprieve, we are badly beaten up and simply retreat, often too afraid of making another wrong move. We are left shell-shocked and numb as part of being bullied into inactivity. Too tired to even think of gathering up the broken pieces from our beating, we rest in the loving arms of our heavenly Father.

Before acting, I remind myself that I am in the care of my Lord. Together, Jesus and I can do whatever is needed.

November 5

It's everybody, everywhere, all the time.
—Zeph Daniel

You are sitting in a packed waiting room at a doctor's office. The telephone rings. The receptionist slides her counter window to the side and peers out. She takes a moment to scan everyone, until she reaches you. She pauses before responding back into the phone and slides her window shut.

We often see things that no one else does. There is no place to run and hide. It is the dentist, shrink, waitress, cashier, lawn mower repairman—they are all, somehow, coordinated. They are all one. It seems there is no getting away from having our every move tracked. We are pushed aside as being paranoid if we dare to complain. God's plan for us is to be set aside from this world. It is okay to go back home and sit with Jesus. He understands.

Be sober, be vigilant; because your adversary the devil, as a roaring lion, walks about, seeking whom he may devour (1 Peter 5:8).

November 6

Degradation can become a mental stronghold that grips our mind and occupies our entire existence.

It is dreadful to think the only way to quiet our head is to blow it off. These are tactics from the enemy to provoke suicide. It is atrocious when our head keeps playing the images of horrific things being done to us. The thoughts keep rerunning; habitually, they leave our emotions in a state of disorder. This kind of stuff is shame-based and meant to take us out. These abusive thoughts continue to loop like a computer program and naturally become an unshakeable stronghold. Haven't we had enough? We know the only man who has ever beaten Satan is Jesus. We must call on Him when repetitive thoughts become a form of mental torment. These yokes are sent to us from the pit of hell. We can break these tormenting chains by persistently meditating on biblical scripture. The Lord loves us and will rescue us.

Today I will submit my thought life to God. I will draw near to Him, and He will draw near to me (James 4:7-8).

November 7

We listen to what they do not say rather than what comes out their mouth.

I have reunited with a close friend from twenty years ago, and the friendship picks up where it left off. We share pictures of our homes and play catch up. For one year, she eagerly tries to convince me to move from where I live. She does not seem to understand that my little hut is the only thing I have left. It is something my dad gave me. Gangstalkers do not want TIs to have property. If it is the only roof over my head, it cannot be legally taken away, so I am told. Although my dad paid cash for it and put it in my name, I have been through a lot of misery trying to keep it. Initially, law enforcement had unlawfully confiscated my dad's truck, and then lawyers, with help from my sister, set outrageous liens on my property, making me unable to sell it. One day, I let my girlfriend talk while my spirit kept nudging me that something wasn't right. I struggled as my old friend adamantly professed that she wasn't involved in my gangstalking. Still, it is odd that we never seem to talk about the elephant in the room. She grows silent if ever I bring up the topic. Red flag! Silence can often say more than words. At some point, she finds me distraught, complaining about being spied-on in my home over closed-circuit TV (CCTV). I told her that I was being monitored in real time by outside cameras and through my television. She quickly got defensive and claimed that she was under too much stress to hear about it. Really? Two days later, she apologized but never said a word about my issue—nothing! I am devastated that another one bites the dust. Going back to living in silence is bittersweet. It hurts to walk away from another friendship; one that was geared to fish for information and further bait me.

I refuse to be shipwrecked by lies. Love is an action not a feeling. Today, I will bless you before letting you go.

November 8

It seems like we do not have a friend in the world.

We must be terribly lonesome to reconnect with an ex-husband from thirty years ago or to a friend that disappeared when the gangstalking began over fifteen years ago. Whether we reach out to an old colleague from the good old days or try to bond with a former neighbor, we are setting ourselves up for disappointment. Our old life—the one prior to everyone being replaced by perpetrators—seems to seep into the cracks of our mind whenever we sit alone and look at how bare it has become. We scrounge around for a feeling of existence and expect that reaching into our past will somehow fix it. It initially works. We share a few laughs and feel alive again, until headquarters gets involved and these old acquaintances quickly change toward us. It is possible, they do not want to participate in the conspiracy against us, but they are controlled by fear. We must let them go. We do not have to be a burden to those with whom we once shared good times. Our aloneness is a setup to rely solely on God.

Since there is no prosperity without persecution, God will make my haters bless me.

November 9

There is no need to understand anything when we are stuck.

Nowhere in the "Serenity Prayer" does it mention the word "understand". We ask God to grant us the serenity to accept the things we cannot change: people, places, and things. We ask Him for the courage to change those things that we can like our attitude and mindset. Finally, we ask God for the wisdom to know the difference between what we can change and what we cannot. Nothing is mentioned about understanding anything. Maybe, it is because plenty of things cannot be understood, or that it wouldn't change anything anyway. We thank God that it is not our place to have to understand.

God, grant me the serenity

to accept the things I cannot change,

The courage to change the things I can,

And the wisdom to know the difference.

Today, I will keep my energy by letting go of the need to understand and figure things out.

November 10

As long as God's angels hear us, we do not care who else is eavesdropping.

Reading biblical scriptures aloud can change our atmosphere. The legions of angels in the spirit realm give heed to God's Word and go to work on our behalf whenever we speak it. Otherwise, they just hang around and do nothing. In Matthew 26:53, Jesus asks: *Do you think I cannot call on my Father, and he will at once put at my disposal more than twelve legions of angels?* God's angels were made to listen to His spoken Word. We neither pray to these spiritual warriors, nor speak God's Word *at* them. We simply speak scripture aloud and let God's angels go to work. They know what to do more than we could ever figure out. Angelic armies are waiting to hear scripture; it is their cue to pick up their swords and battle for us.

I may have tried many things that have not worked. Today, I will speak God's Word and let angels come to my rescue.

November 11

The more people that come against someone, the more that person grows; that is God's plan.
—Bishop George Bloomer

He was sent in as a plant to extort the inheritance left by my father, while having no boundaries, scruples, or any regard for me and my mother. The sheriff's deputies aided him in stealing my dad's truck; the state crime advocates delighted in being entertained at my expense; the DA's office passed the buck and did even less; and the Criminal Investigation Department laughed whenever I called. All the players were simultaneously orchestrated while hiding behind judicial masks. Their eyes exuded orgasmic satisfaction as they fed off my trauma. Sitting alone in the aftermath of such a community attack is too much for one person. The players think they are big shots by taking orders from higher ups. Their genetic material (DNA) seems to forbid them from recognizing that we are people—not things. The group watches the sexual assaults of drugged targets for sheer entertainment. Neighbors will gather around to watch as a perpetrator vandalizes property. It is like a modern-day version of when people used to gather at the Colosseum in Ancient Rome to see people being fed to hungry lions and watch gruesome fights between animals and gladiators. The battle for our life has somehow made Movie of the Week and is now broadcasted over CCTV. Community perpetrators are ignorant of how our blood cries out for justice and how their involvement in our murder curses their land. We are glad that God sees everything and knows all things. We thank Him that we are not like these creatures that creep on the Earth.

Lord, see how my enemies persecute me! Have mercy and lift me up from the gates of death (Psalm 9:13 [NIV]).

November 12

Gangstalking is too organized and widespread for it to not be demonic.

If Jesus and His Chosen Ones are in this world but not of it, then maybe we are experiencing the separation and regrouping of people. All these player-haters have this incredible knack for acting robotic. They exhibit similar traits that include dead eyes and a queer smirk on their face. Although these features are recognizable as being human, something about them is eerily not right. When they are perpetrating, they are also feeding, so this is when we see them for who and what they truly are. They have an anti-Christ spirit—a one-mindedness, if you will. The Mark of the Beast is not a tattoo on a person's forehead; it is like having a mark on their mind. These souls show a split-personality where they are kind one minute, yet able to torture someone the next. They call what God calls "good" as "evil" and what God calls "evil" as "good", while the dishonorable are honored, and the honorable are dishonored. These are gangstalkers at their best—open vessels for demoniac activity.

These have one mind and shall give their power and strength unto the beast (Revelation 17:13).

November 13

They take us down to zero and hope we kill ourselves.

We do not want to be brainwashed into becoming professional victims by taking on all the blame. Feeling abnormal is not something we want to harbor. Sure, we have become overburdened, love-starved, unemployed, and homeless. We know something about this world that is supposed to be a secret: gangstalkers are all one-minded with a mission to thrive off the slow destruction of someone else's life. It is like we are the sheep on a sheep ranch and the perps are the hired hands. They will lead us to the slaughter, just to preserve their own lives and the lives of their kids. They, too, are slaves. Suicidal thoughts are from the devil, but God is about choosing life. We must cling to what we know is right.

Today, I have nothing to lose by not taking this life too seriously.

November 14

In the beginning, most targets have no idea they are being watched and set up to lose everything.

The first year is the silent phase when the perpetrators study us and plan our annihilation. They are quietly building and paving our road to hell. We do not have a clue that all their planted seeds will sprout at the same time, causing our life to disassemble all at once. It is not until we piece the facts together that we realize we must have made someone jealous or angry. We may have won a lawsuit or witnessed a crime. Perhaps, we dated the wrong person, not being aware of their ex-mate's involvement in Satanism. Nevertheless, God's Word can uproot curses and reroute them back to their senders.

I command, in the name of Jesus, that any curses sent my way are rerouted and sent back to the sender. Let them who love cursing have it unto themselves (Psalm 109:17).

November 15

We can counter evil attacks with scripture—our strongest weapon on earth.

There are counter-spy tools made to find audio bugs, tracking devices. and hidden cameras. There are apps for cell phones that detect fake Wi-Fi cell towers. We can spend hundreds of dollars on one gadget that may or may not register a piece of spy equipment. Some of us have invested in high-tech equipment only to have it malfunction or shut down and never turn back on. When law enforcement is involved, anything is possible: expensive electronics can be fried in an instant; automobiles can be remotely shut off while we are driving them. Our private lives are visually broadcasted around town via closed circuit TV; hidden cameras capture us in real time as we live on our own property. We can entertain the group for years as they covertly watch and listen to us, until we get a clue that a camera might be behind our TV light, or that the audio microphones can be reversed on our television. The microphone on our cordless landline phone can be secretly turned on to listen to our daily activities around the house. This is called "hooked" and occurs when we hear our phone accidently ring a half ring. The call might show up on a separate Caller I.D box connected to the phone line. Also, a fake Wi-Fi tower can be set up near the TI's home to allow the community perps a connection to one another and to listen in on our random encounters. It is all done through their synchronized cell phones with Sim cards and a private Wi-Fi network. It all seems inescapable. We must find some peace of mind, somewhere. We memorize scripture that is relevant to us and recite it throughout the day, especially, *at* the situation. Then the battle is not ours anymore, since it belongs to the Lord. He will dispatch angels and rearrange things on our behalf.

Today, my deliverance is forthcoming.

November 16

It is a trick, not a treat.

We only see the old woman from next door when she comes outside to spy on us, usually when we do our yard work. Not every time, though, since she does not want to give away her involvement. It could simply be her shift or her turn to throw the darts. She wants to talk to us, so she smiles and coaxes us over to the fence. Of course, she has her cell phone in her hand, so the group can tune in. After a dozen times of being set up to listen to her garbage, only to walk away with feelings of fear or dread, we learn to avoid conversation with her altogether. A perpetrator does not have to be mean to infiltrate our space. Plenty of perps play mind games while wearing a friendly smile. They gossip about other neighbors with hopes that we add our two cents worth for the group to overhear. We have been down that neighborly road before. We can ignore her, or simply tell her, we do not want to hear it! We embrace our power and keep it to ourselves by creating personal boundaries.

I will not be tricked by a fake smile or a phony gesture. I can avoid evil people altogether.

November 17

All glory comes from daring to begin.
—Eugene F. Ware

We can get so beaten down that we refuse to go after a dream we have longed to pursue. Living in a constant state of fight or flight tends to beat up our nervous system. Remaining in this state of mind can eventually release toxins to our organs and leave our mind fragile with combat fatigue. We get overwhelmed just thinking about the enormous task it would take to follow our dreams, so we do nothing. The enemy wins when we get bullied into inactivity. We must pursue our dreams by keeping it simple. Thinking of approaching the entire task at once will only make us feel defeated before we ever begin. We do not need to know answers to problems not yet manifested. We can begin to gather information without creating a federal case out of drafting up blueprints. Its development may involve taking risks and actions on our part, but they do not have to be tackled in one day. It is okay to do a little bit and then rest. We can achieve our dreams one step at a time and complete something that was once too enormous to conceive.

Lord, help me to step out of fear and just do it!

November 18

Neighbors are on duty to infiltrate and sabotage our daily activities.

We are loading our vacuum cleaner into the car. Our neighbors already know that we need a small replacement part for it by our numerous phone conversations, personal in-home discussions, and Internet activities. Spying on us is an important part of their job, because with no information collected, no harassment is possible. They will call ahead to the repair shop and, without us knowing, the technician will be expecting us. They do this just to further play with our mind. When we get there, we stand in the shop for ten minutes, totally ignored like we are invisible. We watch the technician walk past us several times without saying a word. He goes back to his desk as if we are not there. He is following a script. This is how the systemic mind game of minimizing and discounting a person gets played out. If we do not know any better, we think the entire world is in on it. However, we do the best we can with the best possible attitude. It works every time. Remember, the group wants us to get upset, to kick and scream, and have an altercation so police officers are called out. With the right attitude, we can view the counter clerk's behavior as outrageous. It is like watching a clip from the old TV show *Candid Camera*. The way we win is to get the man's attention, buy the part, and bring the vacuum cleaner back home with us. We focus on the fact: We will have done something positive for ourselves, despite the negativity we must face. It takes effort to train our mind this way. We are smart to not just drop it off, for something could be planted in it or further broken on it, or God forbid, it gets lost in the shuffle. We took care of ourselves by witnessing the repair and then leaving with it. Phew!

Today, I will be careful to take care of my business. I will pray before I try to connect with anyone. I will dress nicely, speak politely, and manage my emotions to the best of my ability.

November 19

The gangstalking and harassment groups work diligently to put us away—if not six feet under, in a mental facility or locked up in the prison system.

When we stay connected to the Holy Spirit, we have knowledge of things we would not otherwise know. We begin to see, instinctively, when people are lying to us. Reading the Word of God keeps our slant on life in proper perspective, so our thoughts do not get blown out of proportion. Some of our fears can be diffused by merely gaining knowledge and putting our grandiosity in check. It can also help us to hear stories of other TIs, who give us the willpower to live another day. We begin to relate to others after being severely isolated for years. It is almost like getting a reward for staying strong, when there weren't other targets to connect with (before 2015), and we were in this thing alone. Our physical health slowly returns, and our mental state is gradually renewed. We regain strength and endurance as a byproduct of our newly acquired knowledge.

Ignorance is not bliss. It is expensive and can be deadly.

November 20

See what happens when you poison other people's minds with ideas?
—from *The Gift*

Some of us suffer from the curses and spells put on us by Satan-worshipping gangstalkers. We also suffer from the repercussions of neighborhood fake news: lies. This energy can make us feel like we are covered in sludge or stuck in quicksand; it pulls us down and drains us of our good energy. The goal of a lie is to trap people into believing something that is not true. All of it is trickery. We can change our environment by reciting Bible scripture. We can also plead the Blood of Jesus over our mind and body since nothing can permeate the Blood of Jesus. We go to work the minute this draining energy rears its ugly head. Even if there are eighteen hooded goons chanting around a bonfire in our backyard, wicked spirits cannot withstand the name of Jesus and will quickly reroute. We have some tools: the Bible, the Blood, and the Name of Jesus. Like most tools, they do nothing until we use them.

(Suggested scripture reading: Psalm 18.)

In the name of Jesus, I stand in the gap for those who the enemy has smitten their life down to the ground (Ezekiel 22:30).

November 21

Only in Jesus Christ do we have the authority to keep demons under our feet.

Fear will negate God's ability to deliver us. Deliver us from what? Deliver us from anything: Gangstalking, Organized Electronic Harassment, Remote Neural Monitoring, and Voice-to-Skull (V2K) Mind Control. We must not be afraid! The Bible tells us to *Fear Not*—365 times; that is one time for each day of the year. But how do we fight against such an army of evil doers when their tactics of persecution have inundated our lives? We are protected in a permanent way when we dwell in the light, while always searching for more of it. When we dwell in the secret place (Psalm 91:1), we safely stay under God's covering. Our world is safer when we stay within the guidelines of practicing kingdom principles. When we get out of the will of God, we revert into dangerous thinking and allow the grip of fear to return.

Father, I declare that I will not rejoice when my enemies fall, and my heart will not be glad when they stumble (Proverbs 24:17).

November 22

In the movie, Platoon, a US soldier runs to a helicopter that has swooped down to lift soldiers out of a combat region. As he keeps running toward the aircraft, we watch in horror as his body gets bullet-ridden and blown to pieces. He just wants to go home, but soon, his lifeless body falls to the ground. He was only human.

Our struggles give us strength. Without them, we would not have reason to grow. Our human tendency is to want things the easier, softer way. Some retired athletes and military trained individuals perform best while under pressure. We have the ingredient that drives us to go the distance and beyond the ordinary. Yes, we make our death sentence an extended road for gangstalkers. Though it may take a long time to kill us, it is no skin off their knuckles, since we are used for entertainment in the interim. Determination is what pushes us. However, we too can break since we are only human. Our faith is what gets us through those nights when evil comes knocking in the midnight hour. We can be nothing more than entertainment for our enemies, but anything can happen with God on our side. Moreover, our adversaries know this because they watch us. They see how God helps us make it through the unacceptable.

Today, I have a promise of life and a life that is to come (1Timothy 4:8).

November 23

For it is only by grace that we can withstand some things.

Everything else takes a back seat when we become privy to changes around our environment. We cannot live with our head in the sand, but we must accept that there is little we can do about certain things. We try to stay current on our education of gangstalking techniques, so we can protect ourselves. We must also keep an eye on the wellbeing of our furry friends. If electronic weaponry is being used, our pets will be affected, too. Their symptoms can show up as skin redness or irritation. Any changes in their mood or behavior can be an immediate clue. We can go on YouTube to watch videos on psychotronic mind control, posted by other targets. We can leave an encouraging word for someone in the comment section. This interacting gets us out of our shell. We begin to feel a part of a social network, instead of staying isolated in our head. We must always stay connected to our Higher Power as we eat properly, spend quality time with our pets, read, or watch a comedy—these are all things we should do for ourselves. We must keep living, even while our life is falling apart.

Today, I will not allow my troubles to keep me isolated in anger and bitterness.

November 24

Sometimes, our emotions can go from feeling slightly irritated to a full-blown rage in three seconds.

We should always try to keep our composure. Forgiving ourselves for feeding our enemies, by giving away our power, is good practice. We can expect to have a temper tantrum, every now and then, from all the negativity thrown our way. In all honesty, we do feel better since tearing the bathroom door off its frame and throwing it out the front door! This may not be the appropriate way to let off steam, but targets don't have average options. The fact is: We let off some steam. What the heck, we didn't shoot anybody. This is a good thing. The sooner we can laugh at ourselves, the quicker we can get back on board to better health. Once our open wounds begin to heal, our emotions are no longer like exposed nerve endings. Believe it or not: We *can* be somewhat productive in this controlled life of ours.

Today, I will try to be grateful for my troubles, so they do not have the ability to weigh me down.

November 25

So, I think I'll keep walking
with my head held high,
I'll keep moving on,
and only God knows why.
—Kid Rock

It was Thanksgiving Day 2005, and having had enough nonsense, I was ready to move on. My sixth vehicle in two years had been tampered with to the degree I could not fix it. The Bronco sat in a corner parking lot in Wilmington, California, with a burnt-out clutch, along with my travel trailer hooked up behind it. I had been there for two weeks and LAPD was starting to turn up the heat. I had been pushing my vehicles in and out of the lot, from one side of the street to the other. I was hungry, thirsty, dirty, and tired. My storage units of personal belongings and bodybuilding memorabilia, as well as any gym equipment, were long gone. I was willing to let go of the little bit that I had left, which was junk anyway, if it meant getting out of there alive. I sat down and told God that I would leave the West Coast where, obviously, nobody wanted me. I had been against this decision from day one, but I had lost both the battle and the war, and it was time I came to grips with my defeat. I would walk away from everything I had been familiar with for the last twenty-five years if I could get a vehicle to take both Mama and Prettygirl with me. There was no way I would leave without them. Later that day, I would not have seen the opportunity had I blinked twice. Seven hours later, we were in Arizona. I figured my request must have been aligned with God's will since the opportunity never arose until I asked Him for it. I guess I needed to be willing to let go of everything. Not knowing my next move, I pressed on in faith.

Today, I have faith that God knows what He is doing. I am in God's timing at all times.

November 26

Other gods from other religions are usually found in some far-off place and people spend a lifetime searching for them. Not Jesus! He is in us. Although, it is the last place we look.

Organized gangstalkers will try to stress us out, zap our energy, spend our time, and remove anything that brings us joy. If we have animals in our life, we must be careful that they are not drugged or poisoned. We stay one step ahead of the game by taking precautions to protect ourselves and those important to us. We must never leave our animals, or their bowls of food and water, unattended; not ever. We cannot trust anyone, let alone those who watch us all day and want us dead. We take care of business to make sure our pets have up-to-date shots and tags. We need to keep them legal. There could be a time when we go to court to show proof of current shots because our dog bit a gangstalker. These perps would like nothing more than to crush us by having our animals taken away. It will not matter if the dogs were on duty in their own yard or that there were numerous signs posting: *Beware of Dogs* and *No Trespassing*. We will still have to take the case full circle. Keeping us busy with fixing things is part of the gangstalking and harassment agenda. We *fear not* for the Lord has His angels encamped around us. We may still go through the fire, but we will not burn.

Lord, show me where I need to protect myself in case perpetrators are planning to hurt me.

November 27

Our brain can think up to 1500 words per minute. We must change our thinking to something more powerful than the thoughts we are set up to think.

The energy we put into catching our perpetrators is overwhelming. Searching for a hearing device can make us want to pull our hair out, especially, since spying is now carried out through air waves. We can change bank accounts, buy new cell phones, look for different places to live, and even file police reports—all to gain some sort of privacy and obtain some level of justice. By the end of the day, we have managed to spend hours focusing on our enemies. If we were magically plucked out of our situation, there would be a huge void; leaving those of us who have been spinning for years at a complete loss of what to do with our time. This happens to targets who have something of value that the organization wants such as guns, jewelry, or vehicles. After the burglary is over, everything stops. The phony people that smiled at us the most turn out to give us the cold shoulder. The job is over, and they have no more use for us. If we are on the streets, this is when the police officers begin to ticket us to make us leave. After years of being gang stalked where the "extreme theme" is the norm and our lives are constantly in flux—we can become addicted to chaos without realizing it. Now we have something else to work on. When we focus on Jesus, we can break the negative addictions and mental strongholds created by our enemies.

Lord, help me to undo what the devil has done.

November 28

*Stop the world
and let me off,
I'm tired of going
round and round.*
—Waylon Jennings

We are always being watched and listened to, so the gangstalkers can control our moves and watch us spin our wheels. We each have our own energies, vibrations, frequencies, and extraordinary gifts that attract hungry perpetrators wanting to feed off our power. We all go through an initial phase of gathering incriminating information, only to be disappointed by gangstalking-affiliated lawyers and judges. Our misdirected energy exhausts us, leaving us to exist on low emotions like resentment and sorrow. Our enemies want us to function at these lower frequencies to hinder our influence of any free thinking. We must not get wrapped up in ourselves and forget about helping the newcomer. We can share a wealth of knowledge with others via the Internet. Perhaps somebody took apart their car engine, looking for a tracking device, and now they want to commit murder. If we can step out of our box, we might be able to help another target refrain from suicide.

By refocusing my energy, I can turn any situation that most people would see as a tragedy into a blessing.

November 29

If we have the will, we can find a way and that is no lie.

Police-organized vigilante groups is the old term for what we now refer to as gangstalking. They have infiltrated all over the USA and are among our allies in Canada and overseas. If we are investigated and nothing incriminating can be found, even our siblings will help to create something against us. Fear-based pressure from external sources must be causing our siblings to act this way. They can set us up to say something in the presence of witnesses or while being recorded. This is a lifetime investigation that will not take *No Result* for an answer. If the vigilante haters cannot get something on us, they will make up a false report. This gets the ball rolling for us to become involved with cops and law enforcement. Even our Internet browsing habits will be used against us. We have a great need to protect ourselves, not only from our own immoral behavior, but from those who want to continually torture us. We must always keep our property insured, our pets legally supported, and any legal status like our personal state I.D. current. In the Book of Job, we learn that man is made to sin; it is sin that causes us to fall and allow more demons in our life. We are not perfect, and we do the best we can. We must be cautious as nothing is private anymore, while all eyes seem to be on us.

Today, I will keep a low profile, speak the Word of God, and mind my own business.

November 30

Contentment is a powerful state of mind.

Contentment is the opposite of being anxious, but we should not confuse it with complacency. Gangstalkers continually try to cheat us out of enjoying our existence. We are quickly and systematically barred from anything that seems to bring us pleasure. One targeted individual found joy in feeding the squirrels while she sat in the park. Once the group caught wind of this, they would drive by with loud engines to disrupt the serene environment. Contentment is a state of mind and is not based on where we are physically.

Today, I will not be thankful for my circumstances, but rather that God is with me in them.

A Bonus Reading

When I get that hole in my gut, I know it is God-shaped and nothing else can fill it.

Before my husband died, I took a paralegal job in a high-rise office building on Ventura Boulevard in Woodland Hills. I sat at a desk across from the lawyer's office. As I keyboarded data into my computer, he proceeded to pile legal folders on my desk. This would become the "to do" pile. I never saw any clients during the few weeks I was there, nor did the pile of folders ever go down—only up as fast as I could type. I never lifted my head from the keyboard and never made a dent in the pile. I was drowning. I would leave at night feeling like I never accomplished anything.

Fast forward to a couple years later, after my husband's death: The police gangstalking and harassment had begun, and I wound up living in Long Beach—over an hour away from Studio City and North Hollywood, where I had lived for 22 years. I sat at a coffee shop with a phony friend one day. A big player in the South Bay gangstalking agenda, he was also the son of a retired District Attorney. A goofy-looking man approached us and began to talk about Milwaukee, Wisconsin, where I was born. He was talking to me about my life like it was his. I was not hip to the way gangstalkers played games; in retrospect, this is what he was doing. He wore big false teeth with a wig and sunglasses under a hat, and had risers in his shoes, so I did not recognize him. Today, I know it was a setup and my so-called friend knew him all along. I think he was another undercover cop that did gangstalking on the side. We sat and watched people park their cars and walk into the coffee shop for hours. One man looked familiar to me, which was odd, because I did not know anybody in Long Beach; I had been cruelly displaced. After a few minutes, I realized that he was the crazy lawyer from

Woodland Hills; the guy who stacked folders up to the ceiling. I remembered it like it was a skit from the TV show *Laugh In*. To this day, seeing him at that coffee shop still bewilders me, because the timing of the gangstalking started two years after I worked for him. Or did it? Could an investigation have shown that I worked for him and he was called to take part in my demise? After all, lawyers are heavily involved in gangstalking and God knows what else. Or had he been involved all along because the gangstalking started much earlier than I thought? It is all so odd, so multi-dimensional, and so crazy-making.

Lord, help me to stay focused on You today; to not think on those things the enemy would have me wonder about.

December 1

To overcome the anguish of being constantly watched and listened to, we must have a conscious contact with God.

The enemy wants our mind and will go to any length to cause us a mental and emotional breakdown. Naturally, with all sorts of head games played on us, we become accustomed to living in our head where we meditate on the evil things being done to us. This is not good since we tend to bring into our life those things that we focus on most. The meddling forces and constant surveillance by our creepy neighbors border on the practice of voyeurism. Their ability to watch us through a closed-circuit system allows the community to view us in real time. Living our everyday life while knowing that people are violating our privacy is enough to push us over the edge. The Lord knew these days would come—the perilous end times. He not only warns us in the Bible, but He gives us the tools we need for survival. Satanists will always try to destroy us, so we cannot fulfill our assignment. The secret place of the Most

High is our refuge. We find shelter under His wings because we are His special warriors.

Lord, here am I—build me as Thou wilt. Release me of the bondage of self, so that I may better do thy will.

December 2

In the pit of hell, there is a blueprint for the destruction of our perpetrators.

Since chucking the TV, neighbors are walking up and down the country road, trying to figure out if I am home or not. I have spotted two electrical workers in a white truck doing something next door, yet nobody has lived there in over a year. Synchronized events tip me off that my every move is being captured by hidden cameras outside my property line. This, of course, informs the perps when I come and go, as well as what I am doing in my yard. The violation is infuriating. After confronting the plumber working for me, he suddenly quit with no good reason. When one of the members reveals something they shouldn't, they are fired from the group and ordered to have no further contact with the target. Although I have been left empty-handed, I must engage in confrontation whenever I feel it necessary to do so. In the story of David and Goliath, David spoke scripture as he attacked the giant. We must be like him and run toward our enemies, not away from them. The Bible tells us that we are more than conquerors. The Word of God is the double-edged sword that we read about in the Book of Ephesians. Like David, we must verbally fight our battles. The perpetrators involved in our destruction are controlled by demons sent by Satan. Their duty is to stop us from moving ahead and cause us frustration and despair. Their job is to drive us nuts. We must remind the devil that our mind is not up for grabs because we do not belong to him or our circumstances.

Today, I will take authority over Satan and the people influenced by him.

December 3

Those who follow Jesus must take up their cross.

In the Book of Acts, Chapter 27, Apostle Paul is caught in a storm while on a ship. When the situation gets so overpowering that there is no hope left, God sends an angel to tell Paul that everything will be all right; they would escape safely and without harm. The next day, the ship was scattered in pieces, but the crew was safe and on dry land. Things will get worse as we get closer to the time of the Mark of the Beast. There will be more people on Earth following Satan than Christ Jesus. We are seeing it now with ancient political secrets beginning to openly unravel into government chaos. Jesus came to give us the faith and hope we will need to survive. The evil doers will have eternal life in hell, as everyone's day is destined to come. Although, we live in a world filled with hatred and deception, we must not worry, for we are always under God's supernatural protection.

In the name of Jesus, let every yoke of bondage in my life be destroyed, right now, in this very moment (Galatians 5:1).

December 4

No one engaged in warfare entangles himself with the affairs of this life, that he may please Him who enlisted him as a soldier (2 Timothy 2:4).

We have been prepared our whole life for what we are up against right now. We are persecuted and oppressed in a similar way to the people in the Bible. In David's Psalms, he tells us how his enemies camped around him to constantly watch him. They wanted him dead. He was up against loneliness and confusion as he wondered just how they would try to trick him into their net. He was tired of being hunted—very much the way we feel. In the life of Job, as soon as one messenger came and went, another one showed up with even worse news. Each problem that Job faced was more complex and devastating than the one before. All the while, God was silently preparing him for an increase. It was like God was saying, *Job is doing well, but he is nowhere near what I have in store for him. I am going to increase his blessings and bless his life. When I finish, he will be twice as blessed.* At some point, we will have a breakthrough too. The greater our suffering; the greater our blessing. We are warriors for the Lord.

Ask, and it shall be given to you; seek, and you shall find; knock, and it shall be opened unto you (Matthew 7:7).

December 5

We do not want our loved ones to feel guilty for not being able to stop our suffering.

Constant anger and ugly talk about gangstalking and harassment can take its toll on our loved ones. Our elderly parents may feel helpless in taking away our pain. Most of them have never heard of gangstalking or harassment groups. It is hard for them to understand harassment tactics like *wrong number calls*[22] and *telephone redirects.*[23] We must continue in our affairs with love and understanding that not everyone is going to comprehend our difficulties or want to play catch-up to our level of knowledge. If we are blessed to have a loved one in our life, let our time with them distract us from the negativity. As targeted individuals, we seldom get a chance to do anything normal with someone special. Most of us are absurdly isolated. Being with a loved one can be a part of our healing. It is good for us to refrain from talking about our gangstalking. It is healthy for us to abstain from being despondent about it. Engaging in this type of freedom for one hour a day can energize and stabilize our emotions, as well as those of our loved ones. We owe it to them and ourselves: a daily reprieve from the insanity of gangstalking.

Today, I will use my time with a loved one to laugh and take part in life as if I were not a target.

---

[22] Wrong Number Calls: when perps want to annoy a target and keep in constant contact with them.

[23] Telephone Redirects: when a call is intercepted by gangstalkers pretending to be from the company a target is trying to call.

December 6

Boredom steals our joy and makes our life listless and lifeless.

Our enemies love it when we sit and do nothing but breathe and barely survive. We are watched in an era of computer-controlled surveillance. All the while, our lives have been squashed into mere existence. Their gangstalking hooks get embedded in us, and we find ourselves too entangled to get free. We still cannot allow them to rob us of our good energy or we will end up having lowlife emotions like hatred, depression, and hopelessness. These feelings are a part of the mind manipulation and psychological warfare that is executed on us daily. We can take back our energy and use it to pray. Sometimes our prayers take a little longer to get answered because we are sowing seeds when we pray. If we went outside today and planted tomato seeds, there would not be any fully grown tomatoes tomorrow. It takes time for seeds to grow. The Bible tells us: the blade comes first, then the ear, then the full ear of corn. Fighting the good fight of faith builds us up to overcome this world. We cannot become a victim of our circumstance. We must be fighters. We fight to keep our sanity if for nothing else.

Lord, I live in a deeply fallen world where my adversaries are too strong for me. Help!

December 7

Our day-to-day choices may seem insignificant, but each one is part of God's plan for us.

A *Hittite* spirit is a demonic spirit of fear. The word demon literally means sons of terror. We must not allow fear into our life, even if it is manufactured through satellite technology. This dark spirit will induce us to doubt ourselves with double-minded thinking. It will keep us vacillating between whether we are wrong or have simply gone crazy. God is aware of how technology has advanced in this world. Back in the day, before technology, the gospel was preached on foot. The apostles were divinely protected but had to dig deep for faith at times. Even though we too have been handpicked by Jesus, we still fear when we might be killed, run off our property, or made to encounter any number of dreadful gangstalking scenarios. We must dig deep for our faith at times, too. We need to rely on those things that do not change. Jesus Christ is the same yesterday and today and forever (Hebrews 13:8).

Spirit of fear, I bind you and your powers from running rampant in my life. I command you to loosen me from the emotions of fear and double mindedness. I decree and declare with absolute faith that I am also free from the grips of any electronically induced negative emotions, in Jesus' almighty name.

December 8

Funny how falling
feels like flying,
even for a little while.
—Jeff Bridges, *Crazy Heart*

Many of us have never had a run-in with the law. Since we have been targeted, we run around looking for refuge as though we are criminals. We are homeless with nowhere to hang our hat while constantly looking over our shoulder to dodge police officers. It is preposterous. There are hundreds of gangstalkers against one target. We cannot go to the justice system since it is infiltrated by perps who are placed in high and lawful places. We were once outgoing people with vast ideas of creativity. We were among the movers and shakers of the world. Now the quality of our life is nothing more than weather-beaten. This does not make us any less important in God's eyes. He sees everything. Even though we are not *of* this world, it is not a time for us to fold. We must *bind spiritual wickedness in high places (Ephesians 6:12)*. We may look as though we are alone, but God is with us. His angels begin to move around us as we speak scripture aloud. He has us covered.

Today, I will call upon Jesus for help while the world tries to erase me.

December 9

We must not let them catch us in their net.

Gangstalkers will occasionally drop a hint about watching us but will omit giving any details. We are made to think we cannot do anything about it. We sometimes think too technical and miss the simplicity of how our TV could be a monitor in our home. This comes from the subtle brainwashing technique of learned helplessness. By simply unplugging the TV from the electrical wall socket, we cut off all power to the hidden camera behind the red light. They will also do something as trivial and childish as to remove a stick out of our window, just to let us know they were there when we weren't. We pick up the stick and put it back, shaking off the incident. They might leave a handprint on the outside of our picture window to give off the impression of a peeping Tom. These things can psychically drain us of our vibrant energy. The enemy wants us to wonder: who, what, where, how, and why? We can fervently focus on it all night, letting it get to us, until it takes over. We must continue to stand on God's Word and thank Him for His divine protection, blessings, and the many gifts with our name on them.

Lord, I thank you for delivering me from the reproach of men considered to be my friends [and family] (Psalm 55:12-13).

December 10

We are being trained through psychological terrorism to become our own worst enemy.

It does not take much for our thinking to get messed-up in the snap of a finger. It is part of the brainwashing we encounter through our many negative experiences. It could be something that someone says to us or something we overhear. It could be the sound of a helicopter overhead, the sight of a car with a missing hubcap, a disgusting odor, or the annoying sound of someone constantly clearing their throat. Without a strong spiritual foundation, we can dwell on something small until it takes over our entire day. This is how they steal our energy and power. This psychological warfare tactic called *sensitization*[24] will continue to work on a TI when there are no perpetrators around. Until we desensitize from whatever we are sensitized to, we fall prey to an endless slew of mind-controlling games. A sensitized target can be convinced that something is going on when it isn't. It is like a combat soldier having flashbacks of time spent in the military when war scenes are shown on television. Gangstalking sensitization techniques are highly effective in causing suicides. When we catch ourselves dwindling down this spiral of emotions, we must stop the ride and get off at once. Even if we fall to the bottom and stay there for days, we can still crawl out. It does not matter if we have no one to support us; God shall supply all our needs. It is our faith that takes us to that crucial moment when He suddenly comes through for us. This is how we overcome the world by faith.

Lord, let not my mind dwell on thoughts of sorrow today, but on thoughts of peace.

---

24 Sensitization: getting a target sensitive to specific stimuli to trigger negative emotions.

December 11

When we are in a deeply threatening situation, we can roll the burden of our heart unto the Lord.

Fabricated devices can send silent sound frequencies that not only convey suggestions but can transmit cloned emotions. These are silent and efficient methods of controlling the human brain. Our spirit is the last link in the chain keeping us anchored. Thoughts of suicide are never ours to embrace because they are *of* the devil and *by* the devil. It is his cheap shot to win souls, designed out of sheer desperation. Gangstalkers will put these sound systems around our home with the intentions of robbing our life energy. These perps are often envious of us. They are too weak or underdeveloped to create their own life energy, so they sap ours. Lots of targeted individuals refer to them as "sappers" or "psychic fleas".[25] Whenever we start to think of gruesome or unpleasant thoughts, we must put on our Helmet of Salvation (Ephesians 6:17) to protect our mind from these psychological attacks and to keep our thoughts on those things from above, instead of on our earthly situation.

As a man thinketh in his heart, so is he (Proverbs 23:7).

---

25 Sappers: gangstalking perpetrators who are weak and underdeveloped people looking for an energy transfer from a being that has already assimilated it into a useable form. This is no different than sticking a needle in someone's arm and stealing their blood.

December 12

Just as God assigns us a guardian angel when we are born, Satan assigns us a personal demon to deal with.

Having a sound mind comes with the very presence of God. An emotional and mental breakdown is a sign that we are under a satanic curse. Since most of us are alone, we must get delivered through self-deliverance. We can speak to our situation and break the curse by using Jesus' name. It might sound strange because this war is not from the earthly realm where there is logic and reasoning. This is spiritual warfare at its finest.

Our struggle is not against flesh and blood but against the rulers...and spiritual forces of evil in the heavenly realms (Ephesians 6:12).

December 13

Sometimes we only have two choices: one crappy and the other crappier.
—John F. Elliott, MFT, North Hollywood, California

Sometimes, we do not want to learn the truth about a situation to make a decision, since emotional hurts can often cut the deepest. One day we can find ourselves happy after landing a job in a Christian home. We finally feel like we are in a safe place. We even become a part of the family functions. In time, a family member does something that we know is a gangstalking maneuver: he leaves the cordless house phone in our workroom. It belongs upstairs and is never in our work area. We know it can be used like a baby monitor to listen to our moves. Our internal signal goes off, and we take note. Later, we pick up another signal from a different family member. Again, we take note. Finally, the day comes when we know, without a doubt, that the family has either been bribed, bought out, or threatened into becoming a part of the conspiracy. It breaks our heart. Jesus knows all about betrayal, backstabbing, and heartache. It was one of Jesus' beloved disciples, Judas, who sold Him out for thirty silver coins. As a covert identification clue for the soldiers, He walked up to Jesus and, of all things, kissed him. Jesus would then be whipped, tortured, and hung on a cross. Judas was so overwhelmed with shame and remorse that he could not forgive himself and committed suicide. Jesus knew all along that the devil would enter Judas since he was a necessary part of God's divine plan. Our experiences help us to grow and fulfill our destiny. Although, we have been targeted for a treacherous ride, we are not in this boat alone or by mistake.

Lord, let those who seek to hurt me be clothed with shame (Psalm 35:26).

December 14

We learn to spiritually discern what is going on around us.

It never fails to be a onetime shot when we finally find a decent mechanic. The second time we need a repair, we are treated as if we have the plague. The more spiritual we become and the closer we cling to God, the better we can spot subtle moves—even those of a frightened mechanic. All we want is to get an oil leak repaired, but the owner is trying his best to turn us away. We can see him running on fear and acting as though he is taking orders from someone. His phone rings. He quickly answers it and walks away. We are left standing alone in the garage for over ten minutes. Maybe, he is hoping we will leave. *Won't someone help me with my oil leak?* In the Book of James (1:5), we learn that if we want wisdom, we must ask the Father for it; however, some knowledge could be a bummer. Yet, it is always better to know the truth, especially, if someone is in the background of our life, messing with the controls. In this case, we must have been tracked to the garage through the GPS on our car or phone. Through it all, we still need the oil leak fixed.

Be not thou envious against evil men, neither desire to be with them (Proverbs 24:1).

December 15

It is in our brokenness we find a blessing.

I was horror-stricken to realize the community was watching me over my television when I thought I was in the privacy of my own home. This went on for five years until someone told me to cover the red light on the front of my TV. Strange activities would soon start up with neighbors walking up and down the country road, wanting to see if I was home or not. In my despondency, I happened to come across a video on YouTube. It was by a young man who worked heavy manual labor by day and battled psychotronic mind control and electronic harassment at night. *Remote Neural Monitoring* is about as invasive as it gets with targeted individuals having their thoughts manipulated. They mess with him while he sleeps, causing him to have incestuous dreams and wake up in a wet bed, feeling shameful and disgusted about himself. By staying grounded in the Word of God and humbly sharing his story on the Internet, he struggles through life, one day at a time. There is always a targeted individual, somewhere, who has it worse. For them, we must pray.

God, guide me with your eye (Psalm 32:8).

December 16

What we do with our life is our gift back to God.

As our life slowly diminishes, our enemies wait for our self-hatred to build. They want us to feel every bit like the misfit we appear to be in this Babylonian World System. Soft kill targeting gets carried out by first causing us to become destitute. We then buy into the belief system: We are unloved and unnecessary. Most of mankind's misery stems from feeling unloved. In our case, we are treated like we are repulsive. Perps are planted around us for this very reason. These emotional attacks are so influential, they not only tear down our good looks but can cause physical damage to our brain organ. The enemy works on our mind through the power of suggestive thinking. If our mind and psyche are unprotected, they will brainwash us into hating ourselves. This is when they come in for the kill. They turn up the heat with more setbacks and heartaches to instigate us to commit murder. We must not be baited by the power of this deception. Just because our ideas for our life were shattered, it does not mean we do not have a higher calling. Our life is a gift from God. He is still running the show. We cannot be set on higher ground for all to see God's Glory if we do ourselves in. We must stick around for the big event.

I have a purpose on this planet; watch and see.

December 17

At the point of turmoil and utter confusion, we had better get a Holy Bible.

It is a tough and perpetual fight to refrain from becoming discouraged or paralyzed by apathy. Gangstalking Satanists work out of a big bag of tricks, and our job is to slay each dragon as they raise their ugly head. It may take us weeks or even years to slay one, only to be faced with another peering over our fence. They never stop, and we mustn't either. We are disciples, learning ways of handling schemes sent to us by the devil and his workers. We learn to pray about our problems and maintain our grateful attitude to obtain some peace of mind. We pray in tongues when we slay dragons, and we recite scriptures aloud until our condition changes around us.

Father, hide me from the secret plots of the wicked (Psalm 64:2).

December 18

Life with the Lord, to whom we turn to when in deep trouble, may confront us with new challenges.

We may not look at our misfortunes as a way of life—a way of life where our challenges are necessary for keeping us relying solely on God. Indeed, we have our doubts when He does not yank us out of our misery, but if our life was problem-free, we would probably slack on our relationship with Him. We would then face everyday tasks alone. To meet the many trials of being a targeted individual, we need to have a relationship with the Father, Son, and Holy Spirit.

Today, I jump back on the bandwagon of spiritual growth to guard and guide me through life.

December 19

If we do not offend the Holy Spirit, He is always at work in our life.

We must get off the gerbil wheel and occasionally take a breather. Constant drama and chaos is not good for us and our enemies know it. When our adrenaline is pumping, and our mind is racing, any number of things can accidentally happen. Some of those things can bring about legal problems. We are wise to set aside time for refreshing our mind through rest and meditation. No matter how tough of a warrior we have become, we need to stop and recharge our battery. Even Jesus had to withdraw from the crowds to rejuvenate.

Today, I will retreat and rest my mind from the rat race of the world, even for a little while.

December 20

We are not our enemy's keeper.

When we get tagged by an organization, we are marked for death. Our loved ones will turn on us, so they, too, are not tagged. It breaks our heart to realize a friendship was compromised, or a family member went to the other side and left us holding the bag, if you will. We feel marginalized and out-casted because we are. We are alone with no support or enjoyment of any kind. It is not a healthy place to be. Jesus' disciples lived the closest to this type of hell, but they had each other to fall back on. It is our faith—something not tangible—that will overcome this world. It is our ticket to survival. It is all we have. Jesus taught: We only need to have faith the size of a mustard seed for His grace to be enough for us. His power is made perfect in our weakness.

I do not have to learn through bitter experience that trying to change the mind of an enemy is fruitless.

December 21

We must break our silence.

> We are troubled on every side, yet not distressed;
> We are perplexed, but not in despair;
> Persecuted, but not forsaken;
> Cast down, but not destroyed.
> (2 Corinthians 4:8-9)

At this point, I know I can make it.

December 22

God did not design the human body for constant stress.

Statistics show that about 80 percent of diseases are stress-related, and 92 percent of our worries never come to fruition. Being worried and anxious is a waste of our time and energy. Living from one crisis to another, while tolerating episodes of getting upset, can cause us to prematurely age. It is acceptable to get upset, but it will surely affect our health if we allow it to continue month after month. Worry can ruin our body by releasing enough acid in our gut to burn holes in it. Imagine that! God did not design us to bear the kind of anxiety gangstalking causes us. There is a difference between letting the nonsense of life fester in us and wearing it like a loose garment. It is like walking through a garbage dump to get to the other side or stopping to eat it along the way. God intended us to have peace and joy by focusing on Him.

Today, God frees me from having my heart be troubled or worried.

December 23

The Word of God is designed to do the impossible in life.
—Dr. Bill Winston

The Bible tells us to guard our heart. Oh, how bitterness can destroy us worse than anything, because it is a major blessing blocker. We need all the blessings we can get and holding onto bitterness will stop us from receiving any. Targets hardly ever begin the process of emotional healing because our harassment never ends. These ongoing knockdowns will destroy us from the inside out. When family members and lifelong friends become perpetrators, it is with the intent to plant a seed of bitterness in our heart. It is easier for a family member to break us down than a stranger—someone we would not allow in our life in the first place. The organization carefully selects people like a friend or sibling to come in for the kill. They are rewarded in various personal ways like finding an apartment or they are given drugs for their next fix. They are offered whatever it takes to bribe them to come onboard. We must not blame our friends or family members. Fear can be very powerful. F.E.A.R. is false-evidence-appearing-real. They, too, have been deceived.

Today, I will hide something special in my heart; I will not tell anyone.

December 24

The game is tailored specifically to each participant. Think of it as a great vacation, except you don't go to it, it comes to you.
—from *The Game*

Life is sometimes like being out to sea in uncharted waters without any knowledge of sailing. We can look for direction through psychotherapy, medication, or various group meetings, but without Jesus, nothing is going to give us the peace we long for. Why go to a hardware store to buy a loaf of bread? If we want peace we may as well go straight to Jesus, the Prince of Peace. Having unrealistic expectations on how people should treat us can send us into an abyss of depression, faster than anything. We must take accountability for our thoughts and actions while managing our coping skills. This means that self-care is on the top of the list. Our enemies are serious in their efforts to beat our soul into submission. They do not give up until the job is done. We cannot give up, either.

It is my responsibility to find a new way of life. I can do it by following a spiritual warfare strategy taught by Jesus. With faith, I can climb out of any hole the hounds of hell have dug for me.

December 25

A perpetrator will eventually become a victim of his own behavior.

Satan is busy these days. He builds his own laws and tries to get Godly people to bow down to them. He uses gangstalkers to destroy souls. Perhaps they get paid off with money, drugs or favors; maybe some agree to participate out of sheer fear of being harassed, too. Most people probably take part in gangstalking to be a part of something bigger than them, collectively. There are also those perps who are downright voyeurs, pedophiles, and sadists who eagerly jump at any opportunity to feed off new prey. It is always amazing when a person from church decides to become a gangstalking perpetrator. The devil wants them as badly as he wants us. The closer any of us are to God, the more of a threat we become to the kingdom of hell. Few of us could ever do something as heartless as to deliberately push someone over the edge of life. The Lord will deal with those serpents. If a reborn Christian decides to become a perpetrator, he is doing it while knowing God. We have pity for these people, for they will come up against the wrath of God. We can be thankful for not being one of them: those who attend church services while going against one of God's Sheep.

(Suggested scripture reading: 2 Peter 2:20-21.)

Vengeance belongs to me, and I will recompense, says The Lord (Hebrews 10:30).

December 26

Great opposition equals great victories.

Our aloneness has a perfect friendship with God who lives in a quiet chamber within us. It is another example of how He takes something meant for evil and uses it for good (Romans 8:28). How frustrating that must be for the wicked ones who come against us. God dwells in our inner space where we have a knowingness that nothing shall, by any means, harm us. It is an honor and privilege to be one of the few who enter life through the narrow gate. It becomes clear why most people opt for the easier, softer way—the path of reduced discipline and less reliance on God. The narrow road is lonely, and few travel it. However, we have the divine protection of the Great One when we surrender our life to Him; though it should never be assumed that we cannot veer off that divine path. More times than not, we end up right back on it all battered and bruised. It is in these humbling times, we realize that we are becoming heroes. God will accelerate us in our appointed time and make people wonder.

I am secure, and I feel confident, because there is hope; yes, I look around and take my rest in safety. I lie down, and none make me afraid (Job 11:18).

December 27

No decision can be rightly made, nor any battle won, without the Holy Spirit.

Water baptism gives us the gift of the Holy Spirit who then guides us through life. Baptism-by-immersion is a life-changer. It can empower us for when our mind is attacked with head games, setups, psychotronic weaponry, or when we must rely solely on our spirit for sheer survival. Every one of us needs a divine safety measure for the many fiery darts sent to us by our haters. Jesus refers to the Holy Spirit as "our comforter". He promises to give us the gift of the Holy Spirit when we get baptized in His name.

Holy Spirit, you are welcome here. I have prayed the Prayer of Salvation, and I invite you into my life. Lead me and guide me. Be my direct line to heaven.

December 28

The devil is still God's devil.

We each travel a lonely road while uncovering our personal strengths. Jesus could not go into the city after he performed miracles on the Sabbath, so He stayed in secluded places and the people came to Him. Loneliness is necessary sometimes. It is okay to find ourselves in lonely places on our journey. The Lord knows our heart and always sees what we are going through. He knows in what manner the life of a targeted individual is a lonely life of isolation. We are never alone once we establish a relationship with the Holy Spirit, who will always tell us what God wants us to know.

Today, I will not let my heart be troubled or afraid.

December 29

Making a homicide look like an accident is not a stretch.

It would be nothing out of the ordinary for government gang-stalkers to deceive our family about the cause of our death. There are group members who are good for nothing except to loosen every nut and screw on a vehicle, so a homicide looks like an accident. Other perps are cleaners—those who tie up loose ends and attend to specific details. We will never meet most of our perpetrators. They stay hidden to successfully play a vital role in murdering people.

I will not let myself become deceived that evil spirits have boundaries.

December 30

The brave do not live forever, but the cautious do not live at all.

We can live beyond the everyday hatred of being gang stalked. We can rise above the military methods of pursuit, destruction, mind control, bullying, and the everyday tireless casting of burdens. Deprivation from genuine human contact can easily promote us a slow death; it is like ten thousand paper cuts. Human beings were not created to live under such intense conditions of isolation and hatred, such as we endure. We can blossom, even while being restricted from receiving nourishment by anyone. If we are end-time warriors, then perhaps these methods of torture are to push us into living on a higher level of consciousness. For us to survive, we must be *in* this world but not *of* it. We must create an environment where we can safely flourish until our time with the Lord arrives. When we begin to do the things we can, then God will do those things for us that we cannot.

Today, I will allow wisdom to enter my heart; this knowledge will be pleasant for my soul.

December 31

Beware of false prophets which come to you in sheep's clothing, but inwardly they are ravening wolves (Matthew 7:15).

It was after midnight and I was rummaging through the infamous "purse dumpster"—some well-known spot, where local merchants collected designer handbags for Third World countries. Go figure.

A car rolled up and a guy yelled out his window, "You still here?" He said it like we were friends or something. I had been there an hour already, and it wasn't like I didn't sense a thousand eyes on me. I ignored him, but watched closely as he got out of his car. He walked to the back of it and opened the trunk. "When was the last time someone gave you something?" he hollered.

Oh-oh. My heart started to race, as I intently watched him fumble around in his trunk. He managed to pull out a weird looking instrument that, I would later learn, was an engraver. Then he held up a delicate, long-stemmed wineglass, and with a big smile on his face, he proceeded to engrave these words on it: *Tina, I love you and will always be with you. Love, God.* I would rather have had my name engraved on a Maglite flashlight. Being down at the yards for two years with no electricity or running water, what was I going to do with a wineglass? Then he asked me to sit with him in his car, but I didn't. I crouched down on the passenger side with the door opened, and he sat behind the steering wheel. After he took a big snort, he offered me some white powder that was piled high on a piece of paper. I told him that I did not do crack, which was true.

"I was on my way home to get some sleep, when I got the call," he stated, cheerfully.

I just quietly watched him, while my dogs laid behind me. I knew that people were sent to me for a reason. Oddly, he nodded off for ten seconds. When he came to, he abruptly shouted, "There's no getting out of this, no matter what you do!"

Bingo! That was it: the message, he was supposed to deliver. Oh, but I shouldn't worry because my name was "written in the book". I guess that meant, The Lamb's Book of Life, which I knew nothing about then, so, of course, I worried. *What book was my name written in? A book for what? Hits?* The guy had more Christian knowledge than I did, at the time. He kept nodding off and, at that point, it never crossed my mind that the powder might have been heroin—something that could have done me in. Finally, after a few minutes, he came to.

"You will go to Heaven," he mumbled. "Not like me—I have to stay here." He then plummeted into a deep state of sobbing, which seemed to last an eternity. And that did it for me. The light bulb went on. Locals had been referring to the area as "hell's gateway", and because Satanists have a knack for saying things backwards, it didn't dawn on me that I had been stationed, literally, at the gates of hell. I was finally convinced that I had been sent to a place that had an opening—a porthole—into another dimension, for demons to come and go.

Before he nodded off again, I had an urge to blurt out, "So, when am I going to heaven?" I really needed to know when they were planning to kill me.

"Oh," he moaned. "You are going to live a long life." He passed out again.

I quickly and quietly grabbed my dumpster purses, along with the engraved glass, and we made our getaway. Five minutes later, I would be down the road, parked for the night, where Mama and Prettygirl would curl up next to me.

Jesus, please let next year be better than this one.

Prayer Section

Prayer for Salvation

A prayer to get born again & spirit-filled
(*Read aloud*)

    Heavenly Father, I come to You in the Name of your Son, Jesus Christ. You said in Your Word that whosoever shall call on the Name of The Lord shall be saved. Father, I believe You sent Your only begotten Son to die on the cross for my sins. You raised Him from the dead on the third day, and He is alive right now. I repent of my sins and surrender myself completely to you. Lord Jesus, I am asking you to come into my heart. Live Your Life through me. Guide my life and help me to do Your will. Use me for your higher good. Father, by faith I now confess Jesus Christ as my Lord and my savior. I pray this in the name of Jesus. Amen.

A Special Prayer for TIs
(*Read aloud*)

Father, I ask in your son Jesus' powerful name that you Bind, Incapacitate, Divert, Confuse, Thwart, and Destroy the forces arrayed against me and my life. Erect a hedge of protection around me, so my enemies will no longer have any right to attack me, by the Blood of Jesus. Bring me on a peaceful walk with You. Give me victory over my difficulties that I would bear witness to those I could help of your Power, Love, and Way of Life. In Jesus' name, I pray. Amen.

A Deliverance Prayer
For Gangstalking, Bullying & Harassment
(*Read Aloud*)

My Lord, my God, Maker of Heaven, and Earth; You are my Creator, my Sustainer, and my Protector. You are the Just God of all things, sitting on Your throne of Judgment, the High Court of Heaven. Lord, you execute righteousness and justice for all who are oppressed. You are Lord of the angelic armies, releasing angels to fight my battles for me. Lord, God, you know all things and see everything I am going through. I ask You, Lord, to release Your angels to destroy the dark forces put up around me by people, organizations, governments, educational and economic systems, and even high technology—structures designed by man.

Father, I know you had solutions for my problems way before I ever got here. The Bible is full of stories of persecution, stalking, bullying, harassment, and oppression. There is nothing too big for

You, God. You have designed me to believe with my heart, and not my head, that *all things are possible with You.* Even when no one is on my side, I know that You, Lord, understand what I am going through. You see that I am outnumbered, and my enemies have formed themselves around me; watching and listening, while giving me no privacy, consideration, or compassion. In fact, these people who slander my name to recruit other haters do not even know me. Yet, my friends and family join them as a tag team, relentless in their efforts to break me, hoping that I will commit suicide.

Lord, do not let them gain access to my soul. I can see no way out, for I am worn-out, beaten into isolation and despair. Help me, Lord. The Bible tells me: My *Shield of Faith* will block the angry arrows of lies and insults aimed at me; the *Helmet of Salvation* will keep me of sound mind when they slaughter my good thinking. Lord, keep me under Your wings in the secret place, so that I may see the day when You destroy them. Keep my loins girded up with the *Belt of Truth* for when they gather together to trick my emotions and then shame me. Let me wear the *Breastplate of Righteousness* to protect my heart when they break it and laugh at me, wanting to plant bitterness in it, as though my existence is merely for their pleasure. Lord, let them fall into the net that they have secretly laid out for my destruction. Keep me calm as I walk by them, wearing my *Shoes of Peace*, and as I follow Jesus, the Prince of Peace. Thank You, Father; I believe I receive these things in Jesus' almighty name, Amen.

Resources

The Holy Bible: KJV, NKJV, NIV, AMP, GW.

Courage to Change: One Day at a Time in Al-Anon II

Rich, Mark M. (2008), *The Hidden Evil*

Eckhardt, John (2008), *Prayers that Rout Demons*

Ramirez, John (2015), *Out of the Devil's Cauldron, Unmasking the Devil*

Ti, June (2016), *No Ordinary Stalking*

Erol (1999), Veracity Vs Adversity

Electronic Resources

Daniel, Zeph (2018), *The Zeph Report.* http://www.spreaker.com/user/zephdaniel

Dizdar, Russ (2018), *Shatter the Darkness.* http://www.shatterthedarkness.com

McBride, Erol (2018), http://youtube.com/ChristlikeBe

Recommended Podcasts & Videos & DVDs

Blake, Robert (2012), *All Heart & No Pants*

McTernan, John (2014), *Healing the Broken Heart*

Ewing, Kevin (2017, March 26), *The Mystery of Knowledge.* Kevin L.A. Ewing Ministry

Recommended Movies

Cold in July

The Shack

Code 46

A Beautiful Mind

The Good Lie

The NeverEnding Story
A Monster Calls
John Wick: Chapter 2
Flight of the Phoenix
If you're not in the Obit, Eat Breakfast (Carl Reiner, HBO Documentary)
Solitary: Inside Red Onion State Prison (Kristi Jacobson, HBO Documentary)

Photos

Tina Plakinger with Don Rickles

Tina Plakinger with Don Rickles

Tina Plakinger with Dr. Franco Columbu

BODY & POWER

THE ART & SPORT OF WOMEN'S BODYBUILDING

UK 115P
FDC 63-404

MAY 1983
$ 2.00
£1:15

Gain Muscle & Gain Confidence

Be Supremely Fit!

Bodybuilding's **SUPERBOWL II**

TINA PLAKINGER
Milwaukee, WI

Tina Plakinger and Geoffrey Lewis, training the No Nonsense way!

Tina Plakinger with Geoffrey Lewis

My NO-NONSENSE THIGH ROUTINE

By Tina Plakinger
Photography by John Balik

I chuckle when I think back on my early bodybuilding days and recall Johnny, the local gym hero, who would often train until he threw up and then return to complete his program.

I believed that his awesome physique was the direct result of his training style, which had me emulating Johnny for a long time afterward. I actually drove myself to nausea while doing squats, a clear indication to me that I'd had a great workout. I must have been crazy!

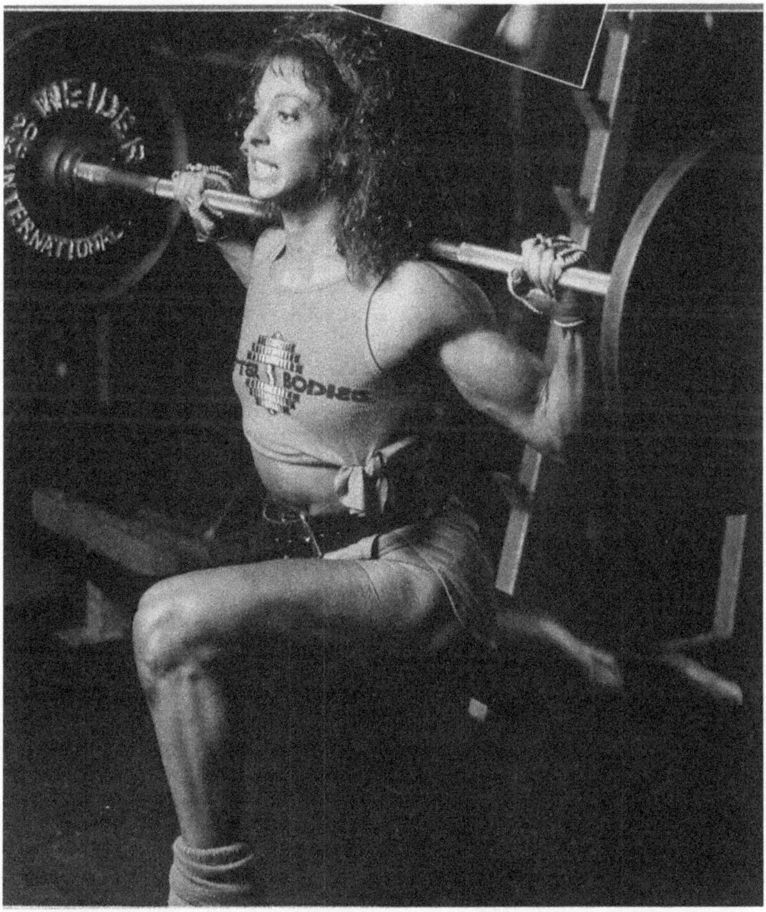

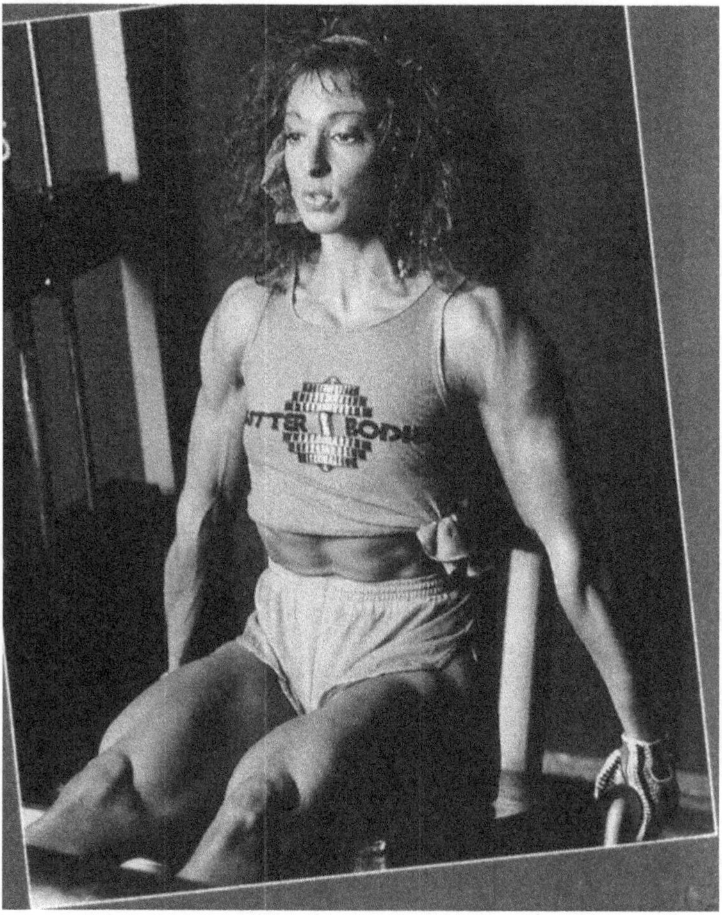

Tina Plakinger Competition Photo

Tina Plakinger Competition Photo

Author

Tina Plakinger is an author and former World Champion bodybuilder. In the 1980s, she was celebrated as an entertainer and trendsetter, having received awards for both "Best" and "Most Unique Poser" in the professional ranks of women's bodybuilding. In addition to competing and guest posing, she privately trained Warren Beatty during the filming of *Dick Tracey* and worked as a spokesperson at U.S. military bases for Joe Weider's Muscle & Fitness products. Tina's work extended into television and film, as she starred in *Pumping Iron II: The Women;* played a recurring role in *General Hospital;* and had a supporting and stunt role in *Armed & Dangerous* (1986). As an avid and experienced writer, Tina freelanced for multiple publications, including *Muscle & Fitness Magazine* and *Muscular Development Magazine*. She also co-authored a monthly column with Dr. Franco Columbu in *Flex Magazine*. Tina featured the current whereabouts and lives of former champion bodybuilders for *Iron Man Magazine* in her monthly column *Whatever Happened to...*. She also received screenwriter credit for scenes in the motion picture, *Liberty & Bash*, starring Lou Ferrigno.

But that all changed in 2002, when Tina became a targeted individual within a nationwide underworld of gangstalking networks. She was coerced from her North Hollywood home to the South Bay area, where she lived in community-enforced isolation. She eventually managed to escape in a stolen car with only her two dogs. She is a survivor of smear campaigns, legal corruption, oppression, thievery rings, and satanic worshiping. *Treading on Serpents* is her first book, aimed at supporting other targeted individuals. The sequel is forthcoming. Tina Plakinger can be contacted at www.tinaplakinger.com

THE END

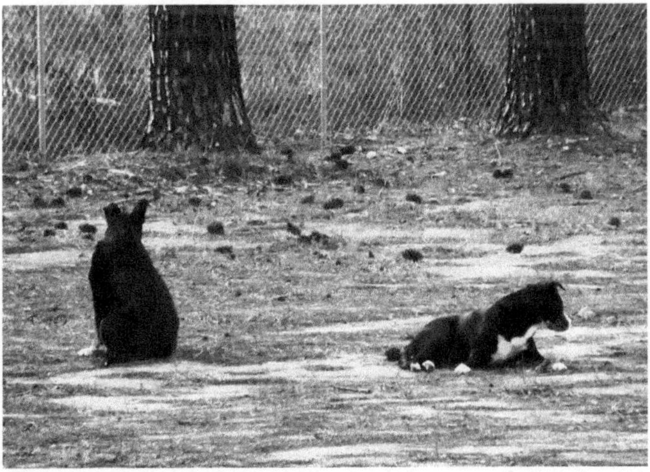

CPSIA information can be obtained
at www.ICGtesting.com
Printed in the USA
LVHW03s2126060718
582980LV00001B/42/P